# Charles Taylor

Charles Taylor is beyond question one of the most distinctive figures in the landscape of contemporary philosophy. In a time of increasing specialization, Taylor's ability to contribute to philosophical conversations across a wide spectrum of ideas is distinctive and impressive. These areas include moral theory, theories of subjectivity, political theory, epistemology, hermeneutics, philosophy of mind, philosophy of language, and aesthetics. His most recent writings have seen him branching into the study of religion. His attack on the narrowness and rigidity of much modern moral theory, his critique of the atomism and proceduralism of rights theory, his delineation of the new moral possibilities that have emerged with modernity, his analysis of the politics of recognition, and his insistence on the need for the social sciences to take self-interpretations into account in the explanation of behavior have placed him in direct engagement with current debates and lend his writings an immediacy and vitality.

Written by a team of international authorities, this collection will be read primarily by students and professionals in philosophy, political science, and religious studies, but will appeal to a broad swathe of professionals across the humanities and social sciences.

Ruth Abbey is Senior Lecturer in the Department of Politics and International Relations at the University of Kent.

# Contemporary Philosophy in Focus

**Contemporary Philosophy in Focus** offers a series of introductory volumes to many of the dominant philosophical thinkers of the current age. Each volume consists of newly commissioned essays that cover major contributions of a preeminent philosopher in a systematic and accessible manner. Comparable in scope and rationale to the highly successful series **Cambridge Companions to Philosophy**, the volumes do not presuppose that readers are already intimately familiar with the details of each philosopher's work. They thus combine exposition and critical analysis in a manner that will appeal to students of philosophy and to professionals as well as to students across the humanities and social sciences.

FORTHCOMING VOLUMES:

*Paul Churchland* edited by Brian Keeley
*Ronald Dworkin* edited by Arthur Ripstein
*Jerry Fodor* edited by Tim Crane
*Saul Kripke* edited by Alan Berger
*David Lewis* edited by Theodore Sider and Dean Zimmermann
*Hilary Putnam* edited by Yemima Ben-Menahem
*Bernard Williams* edited by Alan Thomas

PUBLISHED VOLUMES:

*Stanley Cavell* edited by Richard Eldridge
*Donald Davidson* edited by Kirk Ludwig
*Daniel Dennett* edited by Andrew Brook and Don Ross
*Thomas Kuhn* edited by Thomas Nickles
*Alasdair MacIntyre* edited by Mark Murphy
*Richard Rorty* edited by Charles Guignon and David Hiley
*John Searle* edited by Barry Smith

# Charles Taylor

Edited by

**RUTH ABBEY**
*University of Kent*

CAMBRIDGE
UNIVERSITY PRESS

PUBLISHED BY THE PRESS SYNDICATE OF THE UNIVERSITY OF CAMBRIDGE
The Pitt Building, Trumpington Street, Cambridge, United Kingdom

CAMBRIDGE UNIVERSITY PRESS
The Edinburgh Building, Cambridge CB2 2RU, UK
40 West 20th Street, New York, NY 10011-4211, USA
477 Williamstown Road, Port Melbourne, VIC 3207, Australia
Ruiz de Alarcón 13, 28014 Madrid, Spain
Dock House, The Waterfront, Cape Town 8001, South Africa

http://www.cambridge.org

First published 2004

Printed in the United States of America

*Typefaces* Janson Text Roman 10/13 pt. *and* ITC Officina Sans      *System* LaTeX $2_\varepsilon$   [TB]

*A catalog record for this book is available from the British Library.*

*Library of Congress Cataloging in Publication Data*

Charles Taylor / edited by Ruth Abbey.
p.   cm. – (Contemporary philosophy in focus)
Includes bibliographical references (p. ) and index.
ISBN 0-521-80136-2 – ISBN 0-521-80522-8 (pb.)
1. Taylor, Charles, 1931–   I. Abbey, Ruth, 1961–   II. Series.
B995.T34C47   2004
191–dc21          2003055311

ISBN 0 521 80136 2 hardback
ISBN 0 521 80522 8 paperback

# Contents

# Contributors

RUTH ABBEY is a Senior Lecturer in Political Theory at the University of Kent. She is the author of *Philosophy Now: Charles Taylor* (2000) and *Nietzsche's Middle Period* (2000).

WILLIAM E. CONNOLLY is Professor and Chair in the Department of Political Science at the Johns Hopkins University. His book *The Terms of Political Discourse* was awarded the Benjamin Lippincott Award in 1999 for a "work of exceptional quality still considered significant after a time span of at least 15 years." His most recent publications include *The Ethos of Pluralization* (1995), *Why I Am Not a Secularist* (1999), and *Neuropolitics: Thinking, Culture, Speed* (2002).

HUBERT L. DREYFUS is a member of the Department of Philosophy at the University of California, Berkeley. His major research interests are phenomenology, existentialism, philosophy of psychology, philosophy of literature, and the philosophical implications of artificial intelligence. As well as more than a hundred journal articles, he has authored *What Computers (Still) Can't Do: A Critique of Artificial Reason* (2nd edition 1992), *Michel Foucault: Beyond Structuralism and Hermeneutics* (with Paul Rabinow, 1983), *Mind Over Machine* (with Stuart Dreyfus, 1988), *Being-in-the-World* (1991), and *On the Internet* (2001).

JEAN BETHKE ELSHTAIN is the Laura Spelman Rockefeller Professor of Social and Political Ethics at the University of Chicago. A Fellow of the American Academy of Arts and Sciences, Elshtain is the author of many books, most recently of *Jane Addams and the Dream of American Democracy*.

FERGUS KERR is the Regent of Blackfriars Hall, Oxford University. He is the author of *Theology after Wittgenstein* (1986), *Immortal Longings: Versions of Transcending Humanity* (1997), and *After Aquinas: Versions of Thomism* (2002). He is also the editor of the journal *New Blackfriars*.

STEPHEN MULHALL is a Fellow of New College and a member of the Philosophy Faculty at Oxford University. His works include *Stanley Cavell: Philosophy's Recounting of the Ordinary* (1999), *Inheritance and Originality – Wittgenstein, Heidegger, Kierkegaard* (2001), and *On Film* (2002). With Adam Swift he is the co-author of *Liberals and Communitarians*.

MELISSA A. ORLIE is an Associate Professor in the Department of Political Science at the University of Illinois, Urbana-Champaign. She is the author of *Living Ethically, Acting Politically* (1997). She is currently completing a book on new moral sources in the work of Nietzsche, Emerson, and Freud and is continuing work on another book on citizenship, consumption, and global economic justice.

TERRY PINKARD is a Professor in the Department of Philosophy at Northwestern University. His interests include German philosophy from Kant to the present, particularly the period covering the development from Kant to Hegel. He has also published in the philosophy of law, political philosophy, and bioethics. His books include *Hegel's Phenomenology: The Sociality of Reason* (1994) and *Hegel: A Biography* (2000). His latest book is *German Philosophy 1760–1860: The Legacy of Idealism* (2002).

NICHOLAS H. SMITH is a Senior Lecturer in Philosophy at Macquarie University, Sydney. He is the author of *Strong Hermeneutics: Contingency and Moral Identity* (1997) and *Charles Taylor* (2002). He is the editor of *Reading McDowell: On Mind and World* (2002).

# Acknowledgments

Of all the debts one can incur, that of gratitude is perhaps the most pleasant. Repaying it is also a pleasure, even though the debt can never be fully discharged. My primary debt of gratitude in the making of this volume is to James Tully. I also wish to thank the eight contributors, both for their willingness to participate and for their fine essays. Encouragement from Gary Gutting in the volume's early stages meant a lot. Terence Moore has been supportive throughout. Those who have helped along the way include Clifford Ando, Deane-Peter Baker, Alison Chapman, and Jeremy Moon. Finally, thanks are due to Charles Taylor for continuing to inspire his readers.

# Introduction

## Timely Meditations in an Untimely Mode - The Thought of Charles Taylor

*RUTH ABBEY*

Several things mark Charles Taylor as a distinctive figure in the landscape of contemporary philosophy. Taylor has been publishing consistently and prolifically for over four decades and despite his retirement from McGill University some years ago, his intellectual energies continue unabated. He carries on writing, teaching, and addressing audiences across the world. As his magnum opus, *Sources of the Self*, indicates, Taylor draws on a wide range of western thinkers – both canonical and lesser known – in adducing his own approach to philosophical questions. He writes and speaks as easily in French or German as in English. Perhaps the most remarkable thing about Taylor's work is its range of concerns. Even his critics would have to concede that Taylor has made significant contributions to debates across a wide spectrum of philosophical areas: moral theory, theories of subjectivity, political theory, epistemology, hermeneutics, philosophy of mind, philosophy of language, and aesthetics. His more recent writings see him branching into the study of religion.

In a time of increasing academic specialisation, in the era of the *Fachidiot* as Nietzsche put it, Taylor's ability to contribute to philosophical conversations in all these areas distinguishes him as an untimely thinker. This feature of his thought can be characterised as untimely because the wide and widening span of his work means that he resembles the canonical thinkers of the western philosophical tradition more than he does most contemporary philosophers. Whatever the charges that can be levelled at them of sexism, racism, and/or ethnocentrism, figures like Plato, Aristotle, Augustine, Hobbes, Locke, Rousseau, Kant, Hegel, John Stuart Mill, and Nietzsche – the list is not intended to be exhaustive – all had something important to contribute to several departments of philosophical inquiry. Taylor, too, philosophises in this now untimely mode.[1]

At the same time, there is something very timely about many of Taylor's contributions to philosophical debates: his interventions often seem to be sparked by dissatisfaction with the ideas that are dominant at the time, or at least with the ways in which problems are formulated. Taylor's attack on the narrowness and rigidity of much modern moral theory, his critique of the atomism and proceduralism of rights thinking, his delineation of the new moral possibilities that have emerged with modernity, his analysis of the politics of recognition, and his insistence on the need for the social sciences to take self-interpretations into account in the explanation of behaviour, all appear in response to what he takes to be lacunae or distortions in the way these issues have been conceptualised.[2] Such direct engagement with the formulations of particular problems at particular times explains the sense one often has of Taylor's thinking beginning almost in media res: When we read his work we so often find ourselves plunged into the midst of a current debate. This lends his writing an immediacy and vitality that sets it apart from the more formal and detached tone of many other contemporary philosophers.

This blend of timely thinking and untimely mode raises the question of system in Taylor's thought. On the one hand, a thinker with something to say on a diverse range of philosophical questions might be expected to display a rigid, and possibly even predictable, consistency in response to different issues. On the other hand, one who so directly engages the debates of the day might understandably be more sporadic and targeted in his or her contributions. In Taylor's case we find neither tendency: instead he displays a consistency across philosophical areas that is not rigidly systematic. There is, as many of the chapters in this volume illustrate, considerable consonance among his various interventions in the different areas of philosophy. Yet he is flexible and responsive enough not to cleave to the dictates of any philosophical system in approaching specific issues.

## TAYLOR AND THE HERMENEUTIC TRADITION

Taking a wide view of Taylor's thinking, Nicholas Smith situates it within the hermeneutical tradition of philosophy. In so doing, Smith introduces several of the themes and concerns taken up by the following contributors in more specific contexts. Smith's chapter traverses such a wide terrain because it is his contention that the importance of the human capacity to make meaning is a thread running through many elements of Taylor's thought.

Smith begins by outlining several meanings of the term hermeneutics but goes on to show the term's specificity when applied to Taylor's work. Taylor's interest in hermeneutics derives primarily from his philosophical anthropology: He can be classed as a hermeneutical thinker because of his conviction that human beings are self-interpreting creatures. He thus follows Heidegger's lead in linking hermeneutics to ontology. Further examination of Taylor's philosophical anthropology shows hermeneutics to be central to his epistemology, too. This is because he views human knowledge as the product of engaged, embodied agency. Along with the influence of Heidegger, in this we see the powerful legacy of another twentieth-century continental thinker – Merleau-Ponty – for the development of Taylor's thought. (Merleau-Ponty's legacy for Taylor also comes through in the chapters by Dreyfus and Kerr.)

Taylor insists that knowledge is, in the first instance, the outcome of embodied existence and experience. The way we encounter the world cognitively is shaped and constrained by the fact that we are bodies. This gives us an initial perceptual orientation to the world that reflects the relative position of our sense organs both in our bodies and vis-à-vis the world. In the first instance, for example, we can only see things from certain angles but can change the angle from which we see something by moving our bodies or the object and so on. Of course the creation of ever more sophisticated tools has, over the centuries, enabled us to know things in ways that transcend these bodily limitations, but here Taylor is concerned with the fundaments of knowledge, with knowledge in its most ontologically primitive condition. He argues, moreover, that these more sophisticated ways of knowing made possible through technology and/or scientific theory, are themselves embedded within and ultimately dependent on, this ontologically primitive mode of knowing. With the aid of her microscope, for example, the scientist might be able to see things unimaginable to the unaided eye, but in doing so she is still using this tool with her body, placing her eye just so, and so forth.

Such embodied knowers are also engaged agents who learn about their environment initially through practical experience rather than detached contemplation. The surrounding world appears as a meaningful context in which individuals act, interact, and pursue their purposes. Smith issues the important reminder that depicting knowledge as hermeneutic does not mean that it is necessarily conscious or articulate; interpretations can be tacit and prereflective. As such they typically form part of the taken-for-granted background of knowledge, there to be joined by what we might call postreflective knowledge – information and ideas that have been questioned or actively reflected on but which then become familiar and lapse into the taken for granted. This tacit background provides the backdrop against which items of knowledge or anomalies and puzzles can become objects of conscious interrogation. But as Taylor repeatedly emphasises, in this narrow sense is not directed at a purely historical conception of knowledge, for Taylor contends that some contemporary theorists are still imprisoned in this epistemological model, even when they claim to have overcome it.

Drefyus discusses some of the salient questions arising from Taylor's views about knowledge by outlining where Taylor stands, considering some possible challenges to his position, and then deciding how fatal or otherwise these challenges are. The first such challenge Dreyfus engages is the "brain in a vat" argument. As Taylor sees it, one of the weaknesses of the mediational approach to knowledge is that it understands knowledge in an excessively intellectualist or mentalist fashion. Because of the mind/world separation that underpins it, it construes knowledge in terms of propositions in the mind that reflect the contents of the world more or less correctly. For Taylor, by contrast, the more primordial source of knowledge is, as we have seen, our active, involved coping with the world. Dreyfus wonders whether Taylor's stance here commits him to a sort of metaphysical realism, to a claim that the world outside the self exists independently of the knower. He explores this question by reference to the Cartesian-inspired "brain in a vat" scenario. Dreyfus asks whether Taylor's engaged, embodied agents of knowledge can be sure that they really are coping with an actually existing world or whether they could just be having an experience of coping. (Another shorthand Dreyfus adopts for this possibility is "*The Matrix* world" because in the film of this name experiences were generated and organised by an intelligent computer and supplied to brains which were in vats.) Is there room in Taylor's outlook for the possibility that the mind isn't really embodied or engaged with an external world but is just an entity located somewhere which receives the impression that it is so embodied and engaged? No matter how unlikely this scenario might be, the challenge is an important one because if Taylor can accommodate the mere possibility that the perceptions humans have of being engaged, embodied agents are false, he would have to concede that our experience of the world could be indirect and thus mediated. With such a concession, the distance he tries to establish between his position and the mediationalist approach would be reduced.

Dreyfus concludes that this does not pose such a challenge for Taylor after all. To support his view of knowledge generation, Taylor does not need to insist that embodied agents actually are coping with a real world. What matters most is their perception that they are. Yet with even the perception of embodied agency, any strong mind/world division is hard to sustain, because coping must be experienced as an unmediated interaction with his conviction that human beings are self-interpreting creatures. He thus follows Heidegger's lead in linking hermeneutics to ontology. Further examination of Taylor's philosophical anthropology shows hermeneutics to be central to his epistemology, too. This is because he views human knowledge as the product of engaged, embodied agency. Along with the influence of Heidegger, in this we see the powerful legacy of another twentieth-century continental thinker – Merleau-Ponty – for the development of Taylor's thought. (Merleau-Ponty's legacy for Taylor also comes through in the chapters by Dreyfus and Kerr.)

Taylor insists that knowledge is, in the first instance, the outcome of embodied existence and experience. The way we encounter the world cognitively is shaped and constrained by the fact that we are bodies. This gives us an initial perceptual orientation to the world that reflects the relative position of our sense organs both in our bodies and vis-à-vis the world. In the first instance, for example, we can only see things from certain angles but can change the angle from which we see something by moving our bodies or the object and so on. Of course the creation of ever more sophisticated tools has, over the centuries, enabled us to know things in ways that transcend these bodily limitations, but here Taylor is concerned with the fundaments of knowledge, with knowledge in its most ontologically primitive condition. He argues, moreover, that these more sophisticated ways of knowing made possible through technology and/or scientific theory, are themselves embedded within and ultimately dependent on, this ontologically primitive mode of knowing. With the aid of her microscope, for example, the scientist might be able to see things unimaginable to the unaided eye, but in doing so she is still using this tool with her body, placing her eye just so, and so forth.

Such embodied knowers are also engaged agents who learn about their environment initially through practical experience rather than detached contemplation. The surrounding world appears as a meaningful context in which individuals act, interact, and pursue their purposes. Smith issues the important reminder that depicting knowledge as hermeneutic does not mean that it is necessarily conscious or articulate; interpretations can be tacit and prereflective. As such they typically form part of the taken-for-granted background of knowledge, there to be joined by what we might call postreflective knowledge – information and ideas that have been questioned or actively reflected on but which then become familiar and lapse into the taken for granted. This tacit background provides the backdrop against which items of knowledge or anomalies and puzzles can become objects of conscious interrogation. But as Taylor repeatedly emphasises, the background itself cannot be turned into an object of reflection in this way. The existence of an unexamined background is the precondition for reflective knowing: In order for some things to be studied and examined, others must remain in place.

Taylor's view of humans as self-interpreting animals accords great importance to the place of language in human life. Just as his approach to epistemology makes embodied agency fundamental, so his account of language makes the human capacity for expression primary.[3] Other more instrumental uses of language – for the purposes of effective communication, for example – abstract from, and are parasitic on, this foundational expressive capacity. In this connection, Smith explores Taylor's claim that the existence of the linguistic or semantic dimension highlights something unique in humans' relationship to language. The phrase "the semantic dimension" refers to the idea that there is a way of expressing things correctly that can be evaluated only by standards internal to expression itself. To express something rightly means more than simply transmitting information correctly. For example, the quest to find the apposite word or phrase to characterise emotions, experiences, or situations, places one within the semantic dimension of language. Several different expressions might suffice to relay information about what is being recounted but one will be more expressively correct than the others. And because language is partly constitutive of identity for Taylor, "getting it right" in these instances can affect and alter the way we interpret ourselves and others. Striving for a correct articulation in this way is, moreover, an ongoing process: Success in getting something right semantically is always provisional and the best characterisation can potentially be superseded by a yet better description of things.

Smith goes on to examine what ramifications Taylor's view of humans as self-interpreting animals has for ethics. For Taylor, strong evaluations are a necessary component of self-understandings: He believes that normally functioning adults hold some ethical values or ideals to be worthier and more important or more fundamental than others. Thus there is an inherently ethical component to hermeneutics when, as in Taylor's case, the hermeneutical inquiry focuses mainly on how we interpret ourselves. However, here again hermeneutics should not be conflated with conscious articulation; we can have understandings of ourselves that are subconscious or implicit or taken for granted. Yet because language is such an important component of human identity, we often strive to articulate our self-understandings. This is especially so when those understandings are challenged by others or when some turn of events prompts us to reexamine what had formerly been accepted without question.

Our self-interpretations are therefore structured on a vertical plane by strong evaluation, in the sense that these evaluations reflect a sense of what is of higher and lower ethical significance. Our self-interpretations are also structured on a horizontal plane, across time. Here again the presence of Heidegger can be felt, for Taylor adopts his *leitmotif* of humans as beings in time. According to Taylor, when we interpret ourselves, we see ourselves as beings with a past that can be remembered, reconstructed, and re-interpreted just as we imaginatively project ourselves and our purposes into the future.[4] Taylor contends that as beings in time we naturally create a narrative interpretation of our lives. We see our lives as stories that unfold, and in which we move closer to or further away from different strongly valued goods and goals. Whether this characteristic deserves a place in an ontology of the human is, however, questionable in Smith's view.

## TAYLOR'S (ANTI-) EPISTEMOLOGY

Some of the key elements of Taylor's epistemology that Smith notes are explored in more detail by Hubert Dreyfus. Dreyfus's article surveys some of Taylor's long-standing ideas about epistemology but brings them up to date by drawing on recent unpublished correspondence with Taylor on these questions. Taylor's belief that human knowledge is the product of engaged, embodied agency provides the starting point for Dreyfus's critical analysis of what he calls Taylor's anti-epistemology. This label makes sense if we take epistemology not in the wide sense, as referring to that subdiscipline of philosophy concerned with questions of knowledge, truth, and certainty, but in the more narrow sense of an approach to knowledge pioneered by Descartes. According to this narrower definition, epistemology treats questions of knowledge in a way that presupposes a series of mutually reinforcing dualisms such as subject/object, knower/known, mind/world and inside/outside. When the generation of knowledge is considered from within this framework, the key question becomes how the two sides of each pair are linked. What Taylor calls mediational epistemology provides an answer to this. As Drefyus characterises it, "The radical gap between what is inside the mind and what is outside in the world must be mediated in order for a subject to have knowledge of the world, and epistemology is the study of this mediation" (see Chapter 2). When Taylor speaks of overcoming epistemology, he means going beyond, or perhaps beneath, this mediational view of knowledge to an understanding of knowledge as produced by engaged, embodied agents. However, his critique of epistemology in this narrow sense is not directed at a purely historical conception of knowledge, for Taylor contends that some contemporary theorists are still imprisoned in this epistemological model, even when they claim to have overcome it.

Drefyus discusses some of the salient questions arising from Taylor's views about knowledge by outlining where Taylor stands, considering some possible challenges to his position, and then deciding how fatal or otherwise these challenges are. The first such challenge Dreyfus engages is the "brain in a vat" argument. As Taylor sees it, one of the weaknesses of the mediational approach to knowledge is that it understands knowledge in an excessively intellectualist or mentalist fashion. Because of the mind/world separation that underpins it, it construes knowledge in terms of propositions in the mind that reflect the contents of the world more or less correctly. For Taylor, by contrast, the more primordial source of knowledge is, as we have seen, our active, involved coping with the world. Dreyfus wonders whether Taylor's stance here commits him to a sort of metaphysical realism, to a claim that the world outside the self exists independently of the knower. He explores this question by reference to the Cartesian-inspired "brain in a vat" scenario. Dreyfus asks whether Taylor's engaged, embodied agents of knowledge can be sure that they really are coping with an actually existing world or whether they could just be having an experience of coping. (Another shorthand Dreyfus adopts for this possibility is "*The Matrix* world" because in the film of this name experiences were generated and organised by an intelligent computer and supplied to brains which were in vats.) Is there room in Taylor's outlook for the possibility that the mind isn't really embodied or engaged with an external world but is just an entity located somewhere which receives the impression that it is so embodied and engaged? No matter how unlikely this scenario might be, the challenge is an important one because if Taylor can accommodate the mere possibility that the perceptions humans have of being engaged, embodied agents are false, he would have to concede that our experience of the world could be indirect and thus mediated. With such a concession, the distance he tries to establish between his position and the mediationalist approach would be reduced.

Dreyfus concludes that this does not pose such a challenge for Taylor after all. To support his view of knowledge generation, Taylor does not need to insist that embodied agents actually are coping with a real world. What matters most is their perception that they are. Yet with even the perception of embodied agency, any strong mind/world division is hard to sustain, because coping must be experienced as an unmediated interaction with things. This is also a nonintellectualist approach to knowledge compared with the mediational view because the perception of actively coping with a world remains more fundamental to knowledge than do beliefs about that world.

Taylor advances a sort of realism when it comes to scientific knowledge, believing that science can lead us towards a true understanding of the way the natural world really is. This provides the basis for the second challenge Dreyfus entertains. This challenge emanates mainly from Richard Rorty who charges Taylor with being ensnared in the modern epistemological model because he continues to uphold a distinction between the world as it is for us and the world as it is in itself. From Rorty's perspective, this approach to knowledge is itself trapped within a false inner/outer dichotomy. Because of his Nietzschean conclusion that there is no knowledge of the world in itself, but only ever of the world for us, Rorty has been able to transcend this dichotomy. Can Taylor's claim that Rorty has not overcome epistemology be volleyed immediately back at Taylor by Rorty?

The belief that there is a difference between the world as it is and the world as it is for us seems particularly problematic for Taylor given his whole phenomenological insistence that we know the world through involved coping. This seems to privilege, if not claim exclusivity for, knowledge about the world as it is for us. Dreyfus gives the name of "deflationary realism" to the position that accepts that all we can know is the world as it is for us. Taylor, however, subscribes to a more robust and traditional realism, believing that it is possible to know the world as it is in itself, or at least to get closer to this sort of knowledge. Modern science is the vehicle that makes this increasing proximity possible. Its mechanisms make it possible for us to strive for a view from nowhere that allows us to see an independent reality in a disengaged way.

Yet rather than driving a wedge between Taylor's emphasis on the knowledge that comes from engaged coping on the one hand and his belief that some understandings of the world are truer than others on the other hand, the fundamental fact of coping provides a starting point for their reconciliation. Taylor suggests that when coping with the world, we develop a sense that there is a deeper reality that does not depend solely on the meanings we accord to it. This deeper reality sets limits or boundary conditions on the ways in which we can cope with it: When it comes to coping with the world, it is not a case that anything goes or thinking makes it so. There are structural realities to which we accommodate ourselves, not vice versa. And the more responsive to these realities we are, the better able are we to cope with the universe.

In the conclusion to his essay, Dreyfus wrestles with the question of whether Taylor's arguments on this topic can be squared with his cultural pluralism. Doesn't his belief that true scientific assertions isolate the essential properties of things as they are in themselves necessarily consign other cultures' ways of looking at these same things to falsehoods? One of the unique qualities of modern science is precisely its aspiration to give an account of the universe as it is in itself. Insofar as other cultures do not claim to be describing the essential properties of things, their depictions cannot be immediately weighed against those of modern science and found wanting. Such approaches do not fit neatly into the robust or deflationary realist dyad. Insofar as there is no direct contradiction between the essential properties as revealed by science and those attributed by another culture to the same entity, a pluralist would allow that both approaches can bring to light real aspects of that entity. Science may thus provide a true, but not therefore comprehensive or exhaustive, account of entities in the natural world. As Dreyfus says, Taylor can accept on the one hand that there is no single correct language for describing the universe, while holding on the other that there could be several true descriptions that correspond to various aspects of nature. Hence his depiction of Taylor's anti-epistemology as pluralistic robust realism.

## THE SELF AND THE GOOD: CHARLES TAYLOR'S MORAL ONTOLOGY

An overview of some of the key moments in Taylor's thinking about ethics is provided by Fergus Kerr. The guiding concern of this overview is Taylor's attempt to transcend subjectivism or anthropocentrism in ethical thinking by adumbrating a moral ontology that makes room for sources of moral motivation and allegiance that are non- or extrahuman. In valuing certain things, people often feel that they are responding to the call of something bigger or higher than they. Kerr emphasises that in attempting this account of moral experience, Taylor is continuing the work of Iris Murdoch and her arguments about the sovereignty of good, for he paints a picture of the moral world in which individuals do not necessarily experience themselves and their choices as sovereign. (The question of Murdoch's legacy for Taylor's thought is also addressed in Melissa Orlie's chapter.) As Kerr points out, for Taylor a moral theory that transcends subjectivism in this way is more valuable than most modern moral theories which have gone to great lengths to deny or suppress this dimension of moral experience.

But as Kerr suggests, modern moral philosophies are not the only approaches to obscure and conceal what Taylor takes to be the realities of human experience. Returning to Taylor's first book, *The Explanation of Behaviour*, Kerr shows that even then Taylor strove to attack theories that departed too much from individuals' understandings of their ordinary experience. Although this early work was more obviously interested in questions of psychology and methodology, Kerr contends that issues about moral experience were never far from Taylor's mind. He reads Taylor as attempting to defend a sort of Aristotelean inspired philosophical anthropology against a naturalistic explanation of human behaviour which was modelled on the natural sciences.

Kerr points out that *The Explanation of Behaviour* contained the germs of one of Taylor's next important contributions to philosophical anthropology – his critique of atomism. Here Taylor takes aim at another distinctively modern doctrine. Just as any idea that the goods we value must be exclusively human creations would have been incomprehensible to the ancients, so the image of individuals as potentially self-sufficient entities for whom society fulfills primarily instrumental purposes is a creation of modern thought. In this case, too, Taylor draws inspiration from the ideas of Aristotle to argue for the importance of an obligation to restore and sustain the society and culture that make available the goods we affirm.[5]

With *Sources of the Self*, Taylor's views on the moral life and theories thereof receive their most obvious and sustained articulation. Kerr observes that in this work Taylor's method of defending a nonsubjectivist account of morality involves not so much detailed engagements with and critiques of subjectivist approaches as the construction of an historical narrative about how they came to dominate our thinking about ethics.[6] Part of Taylor's purpose in recounting this narrative is to suggest that such a story cannot have a happy ending: Accounts of the moral life that occlude all references to and acknowledgements of the experience of transsubjective sources of the good are doomed to be unsatisfactory and incomplete.

Yet alongside this cultural-historical delineation of the goods that have developed in western modernity, there are certain values that Taylor sees as being common to all human beings. In discussing this aspect of Taylor's thought, Kerr shows us that here again there is a fusion of ethics and philosophical anthropology. "Certain moral reactions . . . display something fundamental about the nature and status of human being. Certain of our reactions turn out, as Taylor puts it, to be practical affirmations of an 'ontology of the human'" (Chapter 3). One of the central aspects of human ethics drawn out of Taylor's work by Kerr is the desire to avoid unnecessary suffering in other human beings.

However, although the details about what is genuinely natural or intrinsic to humans can, as Kerr acknowledges, be contested, what cannot be gainsaid is the sheer unsuitability of approaches to ethics that are based on or inspired by the natural sciences. For Taylor it is inappropriate, and even destructive, to try to think about ethics in these disengaged or neutral ways – in ways that require us to prescind from our ordinary experience of the world. He has, perforce, to reach back to older approaches to the good that were not infected by the modern elevation of natural science as the paradigmatic form of knowledge. In order to understand moral life more fully we must, rather than attempting to bracket or negate our ordinary reactions and responses, engage more directly with them. This often involves trying to illuminate elements of our understanding that have fallen into the taken-for-granted background of our awareness. In this portion of his chapter, Kerr shows how the idea of the background plays a role in Taylor's ethics, just as Smith did in his discussion of epistemology. One of the things to be revealed by this process of disinterring elements of the background so as to make better sense of our experiences of ethical life is, to use the shorthand suggested by Kerr in his chapter, the profound sense humans have of the sovereignty of the good.

Although a conception of God is an obvious, and for Taylor important, instance of a nonanthropocentric source of the good, Kerr explores an alternative source based on Taylor's discussion of deep ecology. In this Taylor again takes some of his inspiration from Heidegger. We sense that some things, such as the natural environment and nonhuman animals, can make claims on us by virtue of their intrinsic worth. Conceding that Taylor's thoughts on this topic are tentative and exploratory, Kerr suggests that there is a possible paradox in finding inspiration in Heidegger for conceptions of human flourishing. A similar scepticism pervades the chapter's conclusion as Kerr problematises from a number of angles the priority Taylor accords to theism as a moral source.

## TAYLOR'S POLITICAL PHILOSOPHY

Drawing on his expertise in contemporary political theory, Stephen Mulhall provides an account of some of Taylor's most important interventions in political philosophy. Mulhall recommends that these be seen as part of Taylor's larger attempt to promote articulation of the moral horizons of modernity.

In his critique of atomism, his reflections on negative freedom, and his analysis of the politics of recognition, Taylor draws attention to the ways in which certain interpretations of liberalism shape and distort our thinking about what is normal, necessary, or possible in politics. What he typically offers in these individual essays and his political thought as a whole is not a frontal assault on liberalism per se but an attempt to correct false understandings of politics or to supplement partial, limited ones. Although he might resist this way of describing his method, it is also characteristic of Taylor to deconstruct what seem to others to be binary oppositions in political analysis. Thus he shows that the distinction between positive and negative freedom is not as rigid as has been suggested and that the antagonism between liberalism and communitarianism is not as insurmountable as it has been portrayed by some. In challenging us to re-examine and re-configure the dominant terms of political discourse in these ways, Taylor also puts his own work beyond the reach of easy categories. As John Dunn has said, "Taylor is such a fascinating political theorist [because] in the face of distressing choices he is apt to cling tenaciously to both horns of the dilemma, refusing, for what are often humanly excellent motives, to let either of them go."[7]

Mulhall's chapter also illuminates some of the connections between Taylor's moral theory and his political philosophy. Much of Taylor's criticism of strict versions of negative freedom, for example, derives from a belief in what he calls strong evaluation – the idea, referred to above, that we experience some goods to be higher, worthier, or more important than others. Crude versions of negative freedom are unable to recognise or accommodate this sort of qualitative discrimination and thus are inferior to those versions which prize negative freedom for the space it creates for the development of significant human qualities or capacities. The cardinal importance of qualitative distinctions also informs Taylor's approach to rights, both in his early critique of atomist liberalism and in his more recent account of the politics of recognition. In these cases Taylor implies that the language of rights provides politics with a sort of normative shorthand: To call something, such as freedom of speech, a right is to confer great normative and political significance on it. For Taylor this signifies that this right protects, preserves, and fosters a highly valued human capacity. But using the language of rights to signal normative gravity creates the obvious temptation of calling something a right in the hope that this will endow it with such gravity. Thus, just because something is called or claimed as a right does not mean that it must be respected as such. As Taylor's discussion of the politics of recognition indicates, he does not believe that there is an inviolable right to freedom of commercial signage. This good simply does not enjoy the same fundamental status as the right to free assembly or habeas corpus, for example. In a liberal society, genuine rights claims – those underpinned by strong evaluations – must be respected, whereas other goods can legitimately trump the claims of those capacities or freedoms which, on fuller articulation, do not express or protect some fundamental good. Taylor's arguments encourage us to look always for the strong evaluation behind the imputation of any right.

Taylor's critique of ethical subjectivism also plays a role in his analysis of rights and informs his more general critique of atomist liberalism. As we have seen, he contends that when something is the object of strong evaluation, the individual experiences this good as valuable for reasons that go beyond the mere fact of it being affirmed as good by the individual. When it comes to rights, Taylor claims that if a right protects a strongly valued capacity or good, those who claim and enjoy such rights should also see it as incumbent on them to make this good accessible to others who might value it in the same way. The good a right expresses and protects is not just good for those who claim it – this would be the political equivalent of ethical subjectivism. Rather, people experience that good as being of value in itself and thus it should be made available to others in the society and/or to future generations. This is one of the ways in which, from the enjoyment of individual rights, Taylor infers an obligation to contribute to and reproduce the society that makes such rights possible. Thus rights are seen not just as individual desiderata but as having some independent value. Individuals claim and respect rights because of this independent value rather than rights having value because individuals claim them. To find some support for Taylor's analysis one only has to consider the proliferation of bills and charters of rights at all levels of society which attempt to entrench and institutionalise them.

The links across the different departments of Taylor's thought also emerge in Mulhall's reflections on Taylor's practice as a political theorist. Mulhall suggests that Taylor's characteristic style is best captured by Taylor's own model of practical reason. Mulhall observes that Taylor's contributions to political theory are typically specific, contextual, and indeed ad hominem in the sense of being directed at the position of a particular other. Taylor operates largely within the parameters of debate set out by the approach to which he is responding and he proceeds by showing internal flaws and inconsistencies in that approach. A more correct interpretation of the existing approach is offered, even if this can yield conclusions opposite to those reached within the existing position. Thus for Taylor political theory is a sort of reasoning in transitions – a view of rights or of freedom shows its value by demonstrating how it can be arrived at through a series of moves that reduce or eliminate the errors in existing positions. Seeing Taylor's method in this light underscores Mulhall's general point about Taylor's examination of the liberal horizons of modern western politics, for much of his political theory can be seen as continuing a dialogue within the liberal tradition. Drawing on insights from such figures in the liberal tradition as John Stuart Mill and Alexis de Tocqueville, Taylor has encouraged us to question how credible the self-interpretations of contemporary liberalism are and has urged its proponents on to fuller, more adequate explanations of liberal values and practices.

## TOLERATION, PROSELYTIZING, AND THE POLITICS OF RECOGNITION

Mulhall's depiction of Taylor as a thinker who critically interrogates the given terms and categories of theoretical debates about politics is echoed in Jean Bethke Elsthain's contribution to this volume. Elshtain fuses elements of Taylor's view of the self with his analysis of the politics of recognition in order to consider some contentious questions regarding the public expression of religious belief. She observes that since the seventeenth century, the dominant response to religious diversity in liberal-democratic societies has been to advocate toleration. Toleration requires that individuals and groups learn to live peacefully with those who hold different, sometimes antagonistic, and possibly offensive, beliefs and values. Elshtain suggests that since Locke, the ethos of toleration has required the privatisation and subjectivisation of religious belief. Religious beliefs should not be brought into the public arena: They are seen as freely chosen and voluntarily acted on, and are acceptable so long as they are not imposed on others. Proselytization, which occurs when a person or group aims to change another's mind about a matter basic to his identity, is out of place in a climate dominated by this ethos of toleration.

Elshtain suggests that some of Taylor's arguments can be used to pose a challenge to the ethos of toleration as sketched in this way. Taylor situates the self against a framework or horizon of moral values. It is from this background that people make sense of themselves, others, and the world around them. And as we have already seen, for Taylor selves are also strong evaluators. But as Elshtain points out, there is a problem for the modern ethos of toleration if these strong evaluations become too strong and prevent some individuals from accepting that others do, and are at liberty to, value other goods strongly. The climate of toleration would be threatened if some groups or individuals were so firmly enframed by their particular moral values that they could not see this as one possible framework among other legitimate possibilities. The politics of recognition also seems to run counter to the idea of toleration, for it suggests that aspects of identity that had traditionally been classified as private and thus irrelevant to politics should be allowed to be expressed in the public domain.

Another questionable feature of the modern ethos of toleration identified by Elshtain is the tendency to require all social organisations, including religiously based ones, to operate by the same rules and to respect the same rights for all.[8] She sees this as confusing equality with uniformity. This procrustean conception of equality militates against robust pluralism by generating a normalising, homogenising pressure on all groups and associations to operate in the same way. In making this argument, Elshtain is effectively applying at a more micro-level the point Taylor makes about asymmetrical federalism in the context of Quebec's place in Canada. For him, taking the deep diversity of Canadian society seriously means entertaining the possibility that different provinces and different peoples can be part of Canada in different ways.[9]

With the aid of some of Taylor's ideas, Elshtain tries to transcend the toleration/proselytization dyad to consider an alternative way of approaching the expression and exchange of religious views in society. For her, a more genuinely pluralist treatment of religious diversity would allow individuals to express their strongly held views without seeing this as the thin edge of the Inquisition wedge. Committed believers would be able to present their views and values to their fellow citizens with the possibility that some of the latter would be genuinely persuaded by the positions thereby explored. This freer, fuller, and more open discussion of religious commitments would leave some feeling uncomfortable, but for Elshtain that is a price worth paying. She rejects the idea that people should forebear from expressing their beliefs because it might make others feel awkward, threatened, or unaffirmed. In arguing thus, Elshtain adduces a notion, which she attributes to Taylor, of deep toleration.

The model of deep toleration is based on the Taylorean depiction of the self as constitutively dialogical. Selves define themselves and others through exchange with others, and there is nothing to prevent this exchange from including deeply held religious convictions that might be unusual or even repellent to some. This dialogue always harbours, moreover, the possibility of proselytization, which means that some will be persuaded by the positions of others and on this basis change their views and adopt new values.

As this indicates, Elshtain unearths the divergent conceptions of the self that underpin this whole debate about religion, toleration, and recognition. She suggests that much identity politics is informed by either an essentialist or a deconstructionist approach to the self. Despite their differences, both the essentialist and the deconstructionist approach to the self are ultimately monological: Neither can accommodate, albeit for different reasons, the possibility that selves can be moved by, and reconstituted through, their exchanges with others. As both these options are flawed, Elshtain turns to Taylor for a third, more satisfactory, understanding of selfhood, one that is neither as rigid as essentialism nor as protean as deconstructionism. Taylor's view of the self as constitutively dialogical avoids the obduracy of essentialism, for people can change their deeply held beliefs. Yet, although holding out the possibility of identity transformation, this approach is free from the hyperflexibility of some postmodernism, for it allows that individuals do have deeply held views which they take to be true and formative for their identities. This approach encourages a detailed and analytical interrogation of different positions on the grounds that some might be more legitimately persuasive than others.

Like Elshtain, Anna Galeotti has recently been engaged in rethinking the liberal conception of toleration in a way that accords pride of place to the notion of recognition. In *Toleration as Recognition*, Galeotti tries to reconfigure the notion of toleration as a commitment to recognising a plurality of identities in the public realm. Like Elshtain, Galeotti rejects the traditional liberal idea that people should be free to express their supposedly particular identities only in the private realm: She too wants toleration to become a positive attitude of accepting difference rather than the more traditionally negative stance of noninterference.[10] Galeotti's interests lie, however, not just in religious toleration but in the full inclusion of all members of society, whatever the features that serve to marginalise them. Although Galeotti credits Taylor with underlining "the central role of recognition in contemporary politics,"[11] her analysis owes little to his work. Indeed, she interprets Taylor as advocating what she calls strong recognition, according to which the recognition of difference requires the acknowledgement, and perhaps even the affirmation, of the intrinsic value of the difference in question. In contrast to this concept of strong recognition, she promotes a less exacting notion. According to this weaker conception of recognition, what those recognising the claims to recognition of others respect are not the differences themselves but the value they have for the groups which press them, and whose identities they express.[12]

Yet in presenting Taylor's conception of recognition as a foil to her own, Galeotti refers only to his essay on the politics of recognition in general and not to any specific passage that illustrates her interpretation of his position. This failure to provide such specific support for her reading is disappointing because it is arguable that what Taylor adduces in this essay is an idea much closer to her own – that insofar as differences should be recognised, this is because their acknowledgement would affirm the dignity of their bearers. It is unclear that Taylor's essay supports the idea that recognition requires any endorsement of the intrinsic value of the differences being recognised. It seems to me that in interpreting Taylor as saying this, Galeotti is mistaking an argument he makes in the last section of the *Politics of Recognition* for his position as a whole. In Section V of the essay, Taylor makes it clear that he is shifting the debate about recognition to another level. As he says

> Recognition of equal value was not what was at stake – at least in a strong sense – in the preceding section. There it was a question of whether cultural survival will be acknowledged as a legitimate goal, whether collective ends will be allowed as legitimate considerations in judicial review, or for other purposes of major social policy. The demand there was that we let cultures defend themselves, within reasonable bounds. But the further demand we are looking at here is that we all *recognize* the equal value of different cultures; that we not only let them survive, but acknowledge their *worth*.[13]

As I interpret this passage, Taylor's position on recognition in most of the essay is consonant with Galleoti's: The reason for respecting claims to recognition, insofar as we do, seems to be based on the fact that certain things are valued by those making the claims, rather than by the inherent worth of the goods. Arguments about inherent worth come into play with the idea that we should recognise the equal value of cultures, but Taylor goes on to argue that as an a priori demand, this makes no sense. Judgements about the worth of any culture can only come about after close engagement with its particular features and achievements. As he explains, although it may be reasonable to start with the presumption that any culture has value that makes it equal to others, this cannot reasonably be required as a conclusion.[14] Yet as this brief reply to Galeotti suggests, and as the following chapter bears out, there is still room for debate about what Taylor is arguing in his influential essay on the politics of recognition. The argument was contentious from the beginning. Taylor's analysis of the politics of recognition was originally presented as the inaugural address at the Princeton University Center for Human Values. It was then the subject of formal responses from Michael Walzer, Susan Wolf, and Steven C. Rockefeller and was published along with their replies. It has since been republished with additional responses from Jürgen Habermas and K. Anthony Appiah. From its inception, then, this has been a controversial essay and it continues to be debated and disputed.[15]

## TAYLOR AND FEMINISM

Feminist thought has played a minor role in the development of Taylor's thinking, and issues relating to gender do not appear to be central to his philosophical concerns. Conversely, feminists en masse have not responded to or developed Taylor's ideas, despite some obvious points of intersection. Taylor's insistence, for example, on the primacy of embodied knowing could be conducive to some feminists. His critique of the reification of the scientific model of knowledge, with its objectification of what is known and its disengagement of the knowing subject, is also compatible with some strands of feminist epistemology. Taylor's attack on the atomised individual subject of much liberal political theory is also consonant with some feminist objections to liberalism. Taylor's approach to moral theory could also strike chords with some feminist ethicists.[16] Yet, despite these, and no doubt other areas for fruitful exchange, the terms feminism and Taylor are rarely mentioned in the same breath.

Stepping into this breach, Melissa Orlie considers the relationship between Taylor's thought and feminism, asking whether some of the major aspects of his ethical and political thinking are compatible with or antagonistic to feminist concerns. Orlie contends that Taylor's analysis of the politics of recognition touches on something that is both important and troubling in contemporary politics and culture. She recommends that political struggles, and particularly feminist struggles, go beyond a preoccupation with the recognition of identity or identities to a concern with the good, and she finds resources elsewhere in Taylor's work to foster this movement. In light of the importance Taylor attributes to articulating the goods to which individuals and groups cleave, Orlie suggests that a politics of the good would urge actors to articulate the good as they see it.

Of course the close connection Taylor posits between selfhood and ethics means that a politics of the good must have implications for identity. But the most important aspect of identity from this perspective is the good or goods advocated and these cannot be predetermined by or inferred from one's socio-cultural location. Orlie fears, moreover, that there is something static and closed in the politics of recognition with its focus on who

I am or we are. A politics of the good has, by contrast, the potential to be more open-ended and dynamic. This is because articulating the good is always a challenge and articulations of the good are, as a consequence, always corrigible. A related reason for this approach being more dynamic and open-ended is that the good is not something that can be possessed once and for all but is, rather, that which we can only move towards (or away from).

Here Orlie is, by her own admission, interpreting Taylor's conception of the good in a particular way. To justify her interpretation, she identifies two divergent conceptions of the good in his thought. The first, which she favours, is characterised as sceptical whereas the second is substantialising. The sceptical approach is much more tentative and cautious in its identification of the good than the substantialising approach which believes that the good can be turned into a thing to be clearly seen, reliably known, and confidently articulated. For the sceptical approach, the good is a problem in the sense that on the one hand, we cannot do without some conception of it and must believe that the good is attainable but, on the other, we can never be convinced that we have it in our grip. The grasp always eludes the reach, but reach we must. Orlie detects the more sceptical approach in those parts of Taylor's work that seem to have been influenced by Iris Murdoch's thought while speculating that the substantialising tendency could be part of Hegel's legacy. These competing approaches to the good are, in turn, mapped by Orlie onto the distinction between a politics of the good and the politics of recognition. A politics of the good is characterised by a sceptical approach to the good whereas the politics of recognition substantialises the good, embedding it within particular communities or groups.

Although Orlie's observations are not directed at feminists alone, she suggests that feminism in particular would be reinvigorated by an approach to politics that was powerfully concerned with advancing visions of the good. Feminist thought has offered ever more astute and incisive analyses of power, but this has been to the detriment of inspiring visions of the good. Yet without such visions, feminism's ability to project ideas and images of more desirable futures is depleted and this, in turn, limits its capacity to inspire action. Orlie acknowledges that many feminists might resist her urging them towards a politics of the good on the grounds that ideals of the good have typically promised liberation but are also freighted with impulses of power and domination. She hopes that the more tentative, searching attitude to the good she finds in Taylor will go some way to assuaging this legitimate concern. Ultimately, then, what Orlie proposes is a dialogue between Taylor and feminist theory, whereby feminist theory can be enriched by an encounter with some of Taylor's ideas and Taylor's work can, in turn, be enhanced by some feminist ideas and insights.

## CATHOLICISM AND PHILOSOPHY

Although he is a self-identified post-Nietzschean, William E. Connolly finds much that provokes admiration and inspiration in Taylor's work. Like Kerr, Mulhall, and Elshtain, Connolly draws attention to Taylor's refusal to accept as given the dominant terms of discourse in the major philosophical debates and his capacity to draw connections across seemingly discrete areas of inquiry. Although he adheres to a different moral source than that provided by Taylor's theism, Connolly agrees with Taylor's general view that the separation between faith and philosophy is not, nor ever can be, as tight as some philosophers would have it. Connolly is impressed by Taylor's identification of the distance that can exist between ethical values and their deeper moral sources and of the difficulties involved in, and rewards consequent on, attempts to bridge that gap through articulation. He nominates two reasons why Taylor sees moral sources as unsusceptible to full articulation. The first is because "that which subsists below articulation is moved and altered as it is drawn into an historically specific world of dense contrasts, similarities, identities, and negations" (Chapter 7). The second is that for Taylor, the master source, or perhaps the Ur-source, is the Christian God, who eludes human powers of expression. To this pair of reasons why the articulation of moral sources can never be complete, I would add a third. Taylor reasons about morality in a manner analogous to his approach to language. Inspired by the later Wittgenstein, he contends that we can never fully understand or objectify the language we speak. Some elements of the wider system have to remain in place or unquestioned in order for others to be questioned or even just reflected on: Some things have to remain in the obscure background for others to come to light. So a live moral source, just like a living language, can never be fully transparent to those who live within it. Articulation is itself a form of mastery, and we can never fully master the moral sources that help to constitute us.[17]

These attractive features of Taylor's thought have inspired in Connolly a stance which he terms "indebted engagement." Yet there are also important differences between them, and Connolly responds to these with an attitude of "agonistic respect." One of the major questions posed in Connolly's chapter is whether Taylor reciprocates this respectful attitude toward difference. The way one responds to, and represents, ethical sources that differ markedly from one's own is for Connolly a hallmark of agonistic respect. Although conceding that Taylor prizes diversity within and among religious traditions, Connolly is sceptical about how consistent and robust Taylor's pluralism is in the face of nontheistic moral sources. He fears that Taylor can be dismissive, disrespectful, and ungenerous towards nontheistic moral sources that emanate from within the western tradition. In arguing thus, Connolly questions not only the depth and extent of Taylor's pluralism but also effectively his self-interpretation, for Taylor depicts himself as a religious believer who "also find[s] spiritual greatness in the views of unbelievers."[18] Mark Redhead makes a point complementary to Connolly's, arguing that

> Taylor takes his faith to be driven by a message that is inclusive and receptive to different theistic perspectives. Yet Taylor accords this theistic vision a privileged position in his moral thought, making it synonymous with the most prized of what Taylor takes to be the diverse yet well-defined set of moral goods that modern subjects cannot fail but to embrace in their daily lives.[19]

In Connolly's case, such concerns about Taylor's stance towards nontheistic sources are assuaged somewhat by the idea, and experience, of Taylor's laughter, for Connolly finds that its "infectious quality . . . [rolls across] an entrenched line of difference" (Chapter 7). Such laughter can transcend the fault lines of intellectual positions, bearing with it the promise of agonistic respect. Connolly's ideal of agonistic respect offers, moreover, more than the enrichment of philosophical exchange: It provides a model for peaceful and respectful interaction in increasingly diverse societies. Given the improbability and, for Connolly, undesirability, that all members of a society will ever share constitutive moral sources, the ability to engage respectfully with difference is a crucial ethical and political capacity.

At the time of submitting his essay, Connolly had not, as he notes, examined Taylor's latest work on religion, *Varieties of Religion Today*, so it is worth considering whether this work perpetuates the weakness Connolly identifies – the absence of agonistic respect – in Taylor's treatment of nontheistic sources of the good. Although in this book Taylor is writing more about different standpoints along a spiritual continuum than about sources of the good as such, it seems that the outline he sketches of contemporary religious experience is in a general sense less vulnerable to Connolly's critique. Informing Taylor's analysis in *Varieties* is a deep sense of the diversity of contemporary spiritual, rather than just theistic, positions and experiences. When looking at contemporary western societies, Taylor sees not simply the theistic/nontheistic or believing/nonbelieving alternative but rather a proliferation of spiritual views. To complicate this mosaic yet further, he suggests that those who occupy one particular spiritual stance do not feel themselves confined within or by this, for they do not find themselves immune to the attractions of the other spiritual possibilities around them. Rather, many individuals feel cross-pressured – they inhabit one particular spiritual stance but can imagine themselves migrating to another or at least can see why some of the others might be attractive. Obviously this picture of the pluralised and mobile contemporary spiritual condition reflects some positions and sensibilities better than others. Fundamentalists of any denomination, including fundamentalist atheists, are less likely to imagine themselves occupying other spiritual standpoints. So what Taylor is really characterising is a wide and variegated middle ground of spiritual life with individuals occupying quite different positions but nonetheless feeling themselves able to recognise the locations of others as not only viable, but as conceivably desirable.[20]

It could be argued that Taylor is here simply attempting to describe the character of spirituality in contemporary societies rather than rendering any favourable judgement on it. At one level this is correct, but one gets the sense that Taylor approves of this variety. His approval can be inferred from three strands of evidence. First, Taylor at least expects this spiritual pluralism to be irreversible, and when pointing this out, he reminds those who might long for the halcyon days of greater religious certainty and conformity that this mode of religious life had its attendant disadvantages. He enumerates "the spiritual costs of various kinds of forced conformity: hypocrisy, spiritual stultification, inner revolt against the Gospel, the confusion of faith and power, and even worse."[21] He concludes that, on balance, the contemporary condition and its problems, are not just inevitable but also preferable.

Second, what Taylor is effectively doing in this discussion is showing how the ethic of authenticity has penetrated spiritual life. According to this ethic, which has been hugely influential in modern culture, there is an ethical imperative to be true to one's own self. Each person is seen as having his or her own mode of being human and is encouraged to realize this rather than conform to a pre-existing model or a pattern imposed from outside. Each has to discover an original way of being, has to recognise it as a true or faithful expression of who she is and has to adopt and take responsibility for it. As Taylor says, under this new dispensation "The religious life or practice that I become part of not only must be my choice, but must speak to me; it must make sense in terms of my spiritual development as I understand this."[22] When this ethic is extended to spiritual life, we see the proliferation of, and possibility for movement between, positions described above. In *The Malaise of Modernity*, Taylor sets out to show that there is a normative core to the quest for authenticity. In response to those who see only selfishness, self-indulgence, and the loss of a moral sense in the modern accent on self-expression and individual fulfillment, Taylor argues that there is a moral ideal underlying this. He would presumably identify the same ethical impulse in contemporary spirituality.

Taylor cautions, however, that just because individuals seek what I am calling an authentic form of spiritual experience and expression it should not be inferred that this will take a wholly individualistic form. For some, and he thinks many, individuals, an authentic spiritual life will involve joining with others. As he says, "The new framework has a strongly individualistic component, but this will not necessarily mean that the content will be individuating. Many people will find themselves joining extremely powerful religious communities, because that's where many people's sense of the spiritual will lead them."[23] There are parallels between this claim and his analysis of post-Romantic art in *Sources*. In characterising that new understanding of art, Taylor distinguishes between a subjectivisation of manner and of matter. The manner of expression is subjective in that the artist gives a powerfully personal expression of his or her vision. But the matter is not wholly subjective; the artist is connecting his or her audience with a wider reality, with a moral source.[24] In the contemporary spiritual context, individuals are therefore drawn to particular positions because they feel a powerful personal resonance, but this does not doom them to sole occupancy. This highly personal resonance can be shared by others.

Further evidence that Taylor accepts, and probably approves of, this plural and porous spiritual condition appears in his nomination of William James as a thinker who provided a prescient account of this condition. Taylor identifies an awareness of this cross-pressure, of this fragilisation of belief as he calls it,[25] in James's work and admires greatly this aspect of James's analysis of religion. As Taylor says,

> James . . . tells us more than anyone else what it's like to stand in that open space and feel the winds pulling you now here, now there. He describes a crucial site of modernity and articulates the decisive drama enacted there. It took very exceptional qualities to do this. . . . It also needed someone of wide sympathy, and extraordinary powers of phenomenological description; further it needed someone who could feel and articulate the continuing ambivalence in himself.[26]

Yet just at the point where Taylor comes closest to manifesting something like the attitude Connolly calls agonistic respect, right at the point where religious unbelief is not the other to be externalised, objectified, or abjected but rather embraced as an enrichment of the self, Taylor pulls away. He goes on to speculate that in order to provide this wonderfully rich and prophetic depiction of spiritual ambivalence, James had to be someone who ultimately situated himself on the side of faith. Taylor concedes that this conjecture might be dismissed as "a bit of believer's chauvinism"[27] and here seems to vindicate some of Connolly's critical remarks.

## HISTORY, AGENCY, AND THE HISTORY OF PHILOSOPHY

The final chapter of this volume is a richly discursive essay in which Terry Pinkard reflects on some of the historical aspects of Taylor's thinking. Pinkard proposes, for example, that a guiding theme in Taylor's work from *The Explanation of Behaviour* to *Sources of the Self* (and no doubt beyond) is the need to consider agency historically. Taylor's work also contains an argument about how history itself is to be approached and interpreted. Although this argument is most evident in *Sources*, in *The Ethics of Authenticity* Taylor challenges both the view of history as an optimistic story of progress and that which sees it as loss. Part of Taylor's purpose is to show that each of these narratives of modernity is incomplete.

In *Sources* Taylor charts the changing western conceptions of the self from ancient to modern times, but in so doing is not offering a causal historical explanation. He does not aspire to provide a complete answer to the question of what brought about these changes in conceptions of the self, for, as he acknowledges, this sort of historical explanation would require reference to socio-economic forces rather than just philosophical, literary, and ethical sources. But he does argue that these new conceptions of the self had a drawing power that has to be recognised as part of the reason for their taking hold. One way of expressing Pinkard's interpretation of Taylor is to say that just as agency needs to be understood historically, so history needs to be understood "agentically," that is, by reference to the ways in which those undergoing historical transitions interpret their experiences.

In emphasising the need to understand why such conceptions of the self were attractive to people, Taylor is reworking a long-standing theme of his *oeuvre* – that agency must be understood from the inside. In trying to understand or explain human behaviour, we need to know what goods and values mattered, and in what ways they mattered, to the individuals under discussion. As Pinkard puts it, understanding agency is a normative, rather than a simply factual, endeavour. Other contributors to this volume have pointed to the ways in which Taylor's thinking about the significance of meaning and mattering has been influenced by Heidegger, Wittgenstein, and Merleau-Ponty, but Pinkard identifies another strand in the history of philosophy that contributes to this. This is the Kantian insistence on the need for the "I think" to accompany all representations. Pinkard's point is borne out in this passage from one of Taylor's more recent writings:

> Kant is a crucial figure in the overcoming of the I/O [the Inside/Outside conception in epistemology]...nothing could be a percept without a surrounding sense of myself as perceiving agent, moving in some surroundings...If we try to think all this orientation away, then we get something which is close to unthinkable as an experience, "less than even a dream" as Kant puts it.[28]

Pinkard goes on to discuss the important role that strong evaluations play in structuring agency and self-interpretations for Taylor. In doing so, he advances a subtle interpretation of the individual's relationship to the good. On the one hand, Taylor describes the central role that goods play in constituting identity and the way in which the goods we recognise move, draw, or call upon us. As we have seen, in Taylor's depiction the appeal of these goods does not derive from subjective choice alone: In affirming them we feel that we are responding to something other than or extra to our own desires. On the other hand, the goods we value are made available to us through language and culture, and these same resources allow us to take some distance from the goods. Because humans are self-interpreting animals, it is always possible to achieve some reflective distance from these goods and thus be able to offer reasons as to why we cleave to them. Language both orients us toward goods at the same time as it separates us from them and gives us the potential to articulate their power and appeal for us. Although the goods that claim our allegiances should not be thought of as merely objects of choice, we should never be so immersed in or overwhelmed by these goods that we cannot achieve some distance from them.

This point about our capacity to reflect on the goods to which we cleave leads Pinkard into a discussion of Taylor's conception of practical reason. Practical reason, or reasoning in transitions, is the most suitable way of thinking about and attempting to justify goods, whether to ourselves or to others. As Pinkard rightly points out, through the process of practical reasoning, self-interpretations may be amended and improved. Just because Taylor insists on the importance of self-interpretation to agency, there is nothing in his work to suggest that self-interpretations are incorrigible.

Pinkard goes on to observe that the idea of reasoning practically about historical change – that is, seeing it as a series of transitions to better or fuller self-understandings – has distinctly Hegelian undertones. However, as he helpfully points out, some changes in self-interpretation are fostered or thrust on us by forces exogenous to the self. For example, my sense of myself as a coal miner and the value I attach to this life-style might be rudely interrupted by the closing of the pit. In cases like this, there is no necessary reason to assume that the change will be interpreted as a gain.[29] In such cases, a rational account of the change can be given, even though it is not interpreted as an improvement in one's situation.

For Taylor a threshold change in western self-understanding was ushered in by the Scientific Revolution of the seventeenth century. Pinkard identifies some of the challenges posed for understanding the self's relationship to the good that this posed. A second influential strand in the modern self-understanding is the inward turn and Pinkard brings out once again the Kantian contribution to this development. However, Kant's attempt to forge out a space for moral freedom in a disenchanted world generated a paradox. If the will were to be free, it could not be lawless. But if constrained by laws, how could the will be free? Pinkard captures the paradox thus: "Kantian autonomy . . . seemed to admit only self-imposed norms and nonetheless to require non-self-imposed norms" (Chapter 8). As he explains, neither Kant nor his successors among the early Romantics were oblivious to this conundrum. In the final part of his essay, Pinkard outlines some of those early reactions and presents them as part of the background to both Taylor's discussion of Hegel and his own attempt to resolve this dilemma.

As they explore some area of Taylor's thinking, each of the contributions to this volume combines exegesis, critical evaluation, and development of his ideas. Although all the contributors admire Taylor's work, they convey varying degrees of sympathy with it. Yet even the more critical contributors argue with Taylor in an ad hominem, Taylor contra Taylor style: They criticise his work by identifying areas where he fails to develop or fulfill the logic of his own ideas. This tendency toward immanent critique will disappoint those in search of radical critiques of Taylor's thought, but it has the significant advantage of yielding well informed and well targeted criticisms. This is advantageous because although Taylor's work has inspired a voluminous secondary literature, he is not always well served by his critics. Some of the criticisms levelled at his work are ill-conceived and based on an incomplete appreciation of his wider position. This is, no doubt, partly a consequence of the unusual combination of features of his work described above: his contribution to debates in many fields and the mutually reinforcing, or at least mutually illuminating, stances he takes on these different issues.

### Notes

1. One area of inquiry to which Taylor now rarely contributes is economics. It is a moot point whether economics can be considered an area of philosophical inquiry but many of the canonical thinkers listed above did advance ideas about the proper organisation of material life. Taylor, moreover, was once more willing to argue about economics than he now is, as is well illustrated in the first part of Chapter 7 of Nicholas Smith's book *Charles Taylor: Meaning, Morals and Modernity*, Cambridge: Polity, 2002; and Chapter 2 of Mark Redhead's book, *Charles Taylor: Thinking and Living Deep Diversity*, Lanham, MD: Rowman and Littlefield, 2002. Since the mid-1970s, Taylor has had less to say about the organisation of economic life. There seem to be several reasons for this shift. One is his reaction against a crude version of Marxism that focuses on economics to the detriment of culture and values as important facets of human life. Another is the general trend within mainstream Anglo-American political theory towards normative theorising, largely to the neglect of economic questions. Third, Taylor fears that he lacks the specialised technical knowledge necessary to comment on economics. For a fuller discussion of this, see Ruth Abbey, "The Articulated Life: An Interview with Charles Taylor," *Reason in Practice*, 1: 3, 2001, pp. 3–9. But this is not to say that Taylor is mute on economic questions: When asked about growing economic inequalities in western societies, he advocates a sort of maximin strategy which improves the position of those at the bottom rather than trying to reduce the income of high earners. He also favours universal provision of health care services, but more for the impact this would have on ideas of equal citizenship than for any economic consequences. "On Identity, Alienation and the Consequences of September 11th: Interview with Hartmut Rosa and Arto Laitinen," A. Laitinen and N. H. Smith (eds.), *Perspectives on the Philosophy of Charles Taylor*, Acta Philosophica Fennica. Helsinki: The Philosophical Society of Finland, Vol. 71, 2002, p. 173.
2. Thanks to Jean Bethke Elshtain for impressing this point on me.
3. As Sartre, who was also influenced by Merleau-Ponty, wrote "We are within language as within our body," *What Is Literature?* London: Routledge, 2001, p. 12.
4. As some of Taylor's recent reflections on the rise of a secular society suggest, however, the very homogeneous conception of time implicit in my suggestion that it be imagined along a horizontal plane betrays a distinctly secular outlook. Traditionally time was seen as also having what I am calling a vertical dimension: Time was seen as amenable to qualitative distinctions. There was ordinary time in the way we typically think of it now, but this could be punctured by divine events, interventions, and memorialisations that occurred outside and beyond ordinary time. See Taylor's "Modes of Secularism" in *Secularism and its Critics*, Rajeev Bhargava (ed.), Delhi: Oxford University Press, 1998, pp. 31–2.

5. I have suggested that Hegel is also an important influence on this line of argument. Ruth Abbey, *Charles Taylor*. Teddington/Princeton: Acumen Press/Princeton University Press, 2000, p. 106.

6. One exception to this trend noted by Kerr is Taylor's engagement with the work of J. L. Mackie. For a fuller discussion of this, see Deane-Peter Baker, "Mackie's ethical theory: Is there space for a Taylor-made conception of the good?" *South African Journal of Philosophy*, 20 (2), 2001, pp 145–58.

7. "Elusive Community: The Political Theory of Charles Taylor," *Interpreting Political Responsibility: Essays 1981–1989*, Polity Press, London, 1990, p. 186.

8. Jeff Spinner-Halev also makes this observation in *Surviving Diversity: Religion and Democratic Citizenship*, Baltimore: Johns Hopkins University Press, 2000.

9. "Deep Diversity – Shared and Divergent Values," in *Reconciling the Solitudes*, p. 183.

10. Anna Galeotti, *Toleration as Recognition*, Cambridge, U.K.: Cambridge University Press, 2002, pp. 10, 12, 100, and 105.

11. Ibid., p. 6.

12. Ibid., pp. 14–15, 103–4.

13. Charles Taylor, "The Politics of Recognition" in *Multiculturalism: Examining the Politics of Recognition*, Amy Gutmann (ed.), Princeton: Princeton University Press, 1994, pp. 63–4. Emphasis in the original.

14. Ibid., pp. 66–73. Stephen Mulhall takes up this point in his chapter, too.

15. For a fuller discussion of some of the issues on this topic, see Ruth Abbey, 2003. "Recognising Taylor Rightly." *Ethnicities*. 3 (1), pp. 115–31. Taylor's book, *A Catholic Modernity? Charles Taylor's Marianist Award Lecture*, was also born in contention.

16. To take just one example, Margaret Urban Walker's approach to morality resembles Taylor's in several important ways. In *Moral Understandings: A Feminist Study in Ethics* (London: Routledge, 1998), she advances an expressive-collaborative model of morality and both these terms dovetail with Taylor's analysis. Like Taylor she recommends an approach to moral theory that takes as its subject matter the way ordinary people live their lives rather than the ideas philosophers have about what morality is. For her, as for Taylor, morality consists primarily of practices, not theories. Neither thinks that the sphere of morality can be neatly demarcated from social life more generally. Yet although Urban Walker acknowledges that she has learnt much from thinkers like Taylor and Alasdair MacIntyre (1998, 19), her discussions of Taylor's work are primarily critical.

17. This applies only to live moral sources. I see no reason why a defunct one could not, in principle, be fully articulated because it no longer plays a constitutive role in identity. See Charles Taylor. *Sources of the Self: The Making of the Modern Identity*, Cambridge, MA: Harvard University Press, 1989, p. 34, for Taylor's explanation as to why articulation can never be complete.

18. Charles Taylor, "Comments and Replies," *Inquiry* 34 (1991): 241.

19. Mark Redhead, *Charles Taylor: Thinking and Living Deep Diversity*, Lanham, MD: Rowman and Littlefield, 2002, p. 3. See also pp. 16, 176, 197, 213, and 216.

20. Charles Taylor, *Varieties of Religion Today: William James Revisited*, Cambridge, MA: Harvard University Press, 2002, p. 57.

21. Ibid., p. 114.

22. Ibid., p. 94.

23. Ibid., p. 113.

24. Charles Taylor. *Sources of the Self: The Making of the Modern Identity*. Cambridge, MA: Harvard University Press, 1989, p. 425.

25. Charles Taylor. *Varieties of Religion Today: William James Revisited*. Cambridge, MA: Harvard University Press, 2002, p. 57.

26. Ibid., p. 59.

27. Ibid., pp. 59–60.

28. Charles Taylor, "Foundationalism and the Inner-Outer Distinction" in *Reading McDowell*, Nicholas H. Smith (ed.), London, Routledge, 2002, p. 112. Taylor is citing Kant's *Critique of Pure Reason*, A112.

29. Compare Quentin Skinner's point that a knowledge of history can inculcate a sense of loss, given the ways of life that have been obliterated on the path to modernity. "Modernity and disenchantment: some historical reflections," J. Tully and D. Weinstock (eds.), 1994, *Philosophy in an Age of Pluralism: The Philosophy of Charles Taylor in Question*, Cambridge, U.K.: Cambridge University Press, p. 43.

# 1 | Taylor and the Hermeneutic Tradition

### NICHOLAS H. SMITH

There are various ways of defining hermeneutics.[1] The word derives from the Greek *hermeneuein* – to interpret – and according to the standard definition, hermeneutics is the theory or art of interpreting texts. Hermeneutics, so understood, evolved as a distinct field of enquiry in response to specific interpretative disputes. The question of how to interpret the Bible correctly gave rise to a tradition of biblical hermeneutics; traditions of legal hermeneutics arose to provide guidance in the interpretation of written law; and literary hermeneutics is concerned with the interpretation of works of "literature" in general, however that is defined. It would not be too far off the mark to say that within these contexts – in theological, legal, and literary studies – the term hermeneutics is associated with the theory and practice of sound exegesis.

The term has a quite different signification in contemporary Anglo-Saxon philosophy. Sometimes it is used to signify a cluster of epistemological problems relating to the validity or objectivity of textual interpretation and translation. Hermeneutics, in this sense, is a region of philosophical inquiry, a more or less self-contained source of philosophical puzzlement. Confusingly, hermeneutics is also a label used to designate a particular stance on these issues, one that rejects the idea that interpretations admit of objectivity, or at least objectivity in its fully blown form, at all. The term hermeneutics is also commonly employed in discussions of methodology in the social sciences. A social science is said to be hermeneutic if it follows the "interpretative method," if it proceeds by way of "interpretations," and hermeneutic philosophy of social science demarcates the social sciences from the natural sciences because of their interpretative procedure. Since it disclaims the kind of objectivity attained in the natural sciences, hermeneutics is routinely associated with relativism in the social sciences.[2]

Although it is true that Charles Taylor has done important work clarifying and defending the role of interpretation in social science,[3] his core interests and intellectual commitments barely touch on hermeneutics in any of the senses just mentioned. He has very little to say about the principles of sound textual exegesis, he is only marginally concerned with issues of "poetics" or "literary hermeneutics," and he has never shown much enthusiasm for elaborating a technically detailed hermeneutic or interpretative "methodology." To get to the sense in which Taylor does propound a hermeneutic philosophy, we need to think of hermeneutics differently: We need to ask, in the first instance, what interpretations are interpretations of; and second, with an answer to this question in mind, we need to reflect on what interpretation tells us about human existence.

## MEANING AND BEING

The answer to the question "what are interpretations of?" is meanings: things that are in some manner, in some degree, meaningful. Only meaningful things, or things that have prima facie or potential meaning, need to be interpreted, and the aim of the interpretation is to bring out that meaning or make it more vivid. But what really falls under the category of things that contain or express a meaning? Modern science challenges the idea that physical systems or entities do. It makes the existence of some physical object, or the happening of some physical event, intelligible as the outcome of a causal, mechanical process rather than as a signifier of anything. Perhaps, then, it is mental objects or events – that is, thoughts – that are the true bearers of meaning. But to the extent that mental phenomena are also ultimately answerable to the mechanistic laws discovered by science, the mind seems to fare no better. And if meaning belongs to neither mind nor matter, the suspicion can easily arise that there is something ontologically or metaphysically "queer" about it, that there is no room for meaning in our best accounts of existence and reality.[4] Modern naturalism embraces this thought and seeks to explain all phenomena, irrespective of the meaning they appear to contain, as if they fell under the kinds of categories employed in the modern sciences of nature.

Naturalism has been challenged by several strands of nineteenth- and twentieth-century philosophy. A common theme in these antinaturalistic movements has been an insistence on the irreducible normativity of thought and action. The basic idea here is that thoughts and actions are subject to norms, rules, or reasons, and therefore have a different kind of intelligibility from the causally determined happenings of nature. Unlike phenomena that are "natural" because they are intelligible in the latter way – that is, as objects of natural science – thoughts and actions can be correct or incorrect, valid or invalid, true or false, right or wrong, and so forth. Many different accounts have been offered about what gives rise to this normativity, or as it is sometimes put, what the "sources of normativity" are.[5] But most modern antinaturalisms share the conviction – first formulated by Kant – that the source is intrinsically connected to structures of human subjectivity or intersubjectivity rather than some human-independent, transcendent, or "supernatural" order of Ideas. Amongst the philosophers who have taken this path, some (though by no means all)[6] have argued that normativity has its roots in what it is like to be a subject. They have argued that thought and action owe their distinctive form of intelligibility to the mode of existence they give expression to.

By far the most important philosopher to have argued along these lines is Heidegger. For Heidegger, the normativity of thought and action has its basis in our "being-in-the-world."[7] He tries to show that even the most abstract norm-guided practices, such as doing epistemology, are in a philosophically very important sense grounded in the concrete concerns of mundane existence. Furthermore, as these concerns have to be interpreted, we must regard the capacity for interpretation as an irreducible existential structure. What it is to be human depends on how this capacity is exercised: In the course of interpreting its fundamental concerns, a human existence (*Dasein*) becomes what it distinctively is. In other words, human existence is constituted by the meanings things have for it, meanings determined more or less explicitly by self-interpretations. Who I am, as a subject or person, depends on what is meaningful or what is an issue for me; and even before I know it, my identity is shaped by the way those concerns and issues are interpreted. With this move, hermeneutics took its so-called ontological turn: Interpretation is conceived fundamentally as a natural human capacity which at once makes human existence a set of possibilities and circumscribes those possibilities within a horizon of finitude. Only now are we talking about hermeneutics in a sense that touches decisively on Taylor's core philosophical concerns.

When Taylor expresses his affinity with and indebtedness to the tradition of "post-Heideggerian hermeneutics,"[8] he is aligning himself with what he takes to be its central thesis: that human beings are "self-interpreting animals."[9] In fact, the thesis that human beings are self-interpreting animals presupposes a more fundamental one: that human existence is expressive of and constituted by meanings shaped by self-interpretations. It is worth noting that the more fundamental thesis belongs not just to the post-Heideggerian hermeneutics of Gadamer, Ricoeur, and Taylor, but also to the post-Heideggerian existential phenomenology exemplified by the likes of Merleau-Ponty and Sartre. Merleau-Ponty is a key influence on

Taylor – certainly more important than Dilthey and probably more so than Gadamer (the names most often associated with hermeneutics) – and it is important, when locating Taylor in the hermeneutic tradition, to bear this in mind. For an unfortunate consequence of defining hermeneutics exclusively in terms of interpretation is that it can keep from view the crucial dimension of pre-interpreted, prereflexive meaning explored by Merleau-Ponty and other existential phenomenologists.[10] It is meaning, not the reflective act of interpretation, and meaning in relation to human existence rather than to literary texts, that is first in the order of Taylor's concerns, and it must be our point of departure for thinking about Taylor as a hermeneutic philosopher.

In the remainder of this essay I try to show how the theme of meaning-constitution in relation to human subjectivity runs like a red thread through Taylor's work on epistemology, philosophy of language, and ethics. Just as epistemology is of concern to Taylor because of what it has to say, if often only implicitly, about what it is like to be a subject or agent who knows, so Taylor's philosophy of language is directed at the issue of what it is to be a linguistic being. The same holds for ethics, and indeed politics, which Taylor treats first and foremost as a dimension of human subjectivity, that is, in terms of self-defining human capacities, developed in plural and contingent ways across history and between cultures, that need to be examined as such through a kind of hermeneutic reflection. Although my task here is primarily expository, I shall also draw attention to issues that are commonly regarded as weak points for the hermeneutic tradition Taylor identifies with, and I shall consider whether Taylor is any more successful when dealing with these issues himself.

## THE KNOWING SUBJECT

As I mentioned above, the idea that there is something ontologically or metaphysically "queer" about meaning comes naturally to a mode of thought that divides the world into an "outer realm" of physical facts and an "inner realm" of mental ones. An important feature of the hermeneutic attempt to rehabilitate meaning as an indispensable category for understanding what it is to be human is to identify and dismantle the motivations for carving up the world this way. Along with other hermeneutic philosophers, Taylor maintains that one of the most potent motivations is epistemological: The inner–outer sorting is driven in no small measure by a certain conception of what it is to know.[11] He then argues that this is a

faulty conception and that, understood aright, the knowing subject inhabits a realm of meaning – is part of a meaningful world – that is in no way
mysterious, "queer," or spooky.

Let us first briefly consider perceptual knowledge. Taylor follows
Merleau-Ponty in taking perception to be our primary access to the world.
We perceive before we reflect, theorise, or judge. And if we are to understand what it is to be a perceiving subject, we must first be able to describe
how things appear to the subject prior to reflection and judgement. If we do
that, as Merleau-Ponty does in an exemplary manner in his phenomenology
of perception,[12] we are reminded of a world in which particular things are
always only partially disclosed, which invariably point beyond themselves
to other things, and which serve as points of orientation for the subject's
activity. The particulars of this perceptual, pre-objective world "announce
more than they contain" – they signify – and they signify informatively in
a way that relates to the desires and purposes of the perceiver. Perceptual
knowledge is thus a form of "agent's knowledge."[13] Perception is inseparable from a dealing, coping, or engagement with things. As such, the
content of perception is noncontingently related to the world in which the
perceiving, knowing subject is embodied. And since perception is our primary mode of access to the world, the predicament of knowing subjects is
never entirely free of its agent structure.

This way of thinking about perception stands in stark contrast to the
classical Cartesian and Lockean doctrines of the mind, which Taylor is
convinced are paradigmatic not just for a whole range of positions in contemporary philosophy of mind but also for modern "common sense" understandings. According to the classical doctrines, the mind is furnished by
"ideas" that form the building blocks of knowledge. For Lockean empiricism, ideas derive from perceptual "impressions," or as more recent empiricism puts it, "sensory data," that can be picked out and thematised by
sober, disengaged philosophical-scientific reflection. Although Descartes
had a different, more intellectualist view of the source of these ideas, he
too thought of mental contents as neutral, self-contained units of information which, when suitably processed, could yield objective knowledge of
the world. Knowledge thus seemed to have its basis in discrete, separably
identifiable "mental" items or representations, which are self-contained in
the sense that they are only contingently connected to the world disclosed
to an engaged point of view.

Along with Merleau-Ponty and others, Taylor points out that as a phenomenology of mind this account is totally inadequate. "Ideas," "impressions," and "sensory data" are static, reified entities that bear very little

resemblance to lived experience. But Taylor also owes an account of how the classical theorists could go so wrong in their phenomenology. His answer is that the classical picture transposes aspects of the high-level, reflective procedures for generating objective knowledge onto the very nature of the perceiving subject. The method of analysing a complex phenomenon into simple components, treating them as neutral bits of information, and rationally reprocessing them, is written into "the mind" itself. This "ontologizing of rational procedure"[14] explains how something as phenomenologically implausible as the classical accounts of perception could ever hold sway. A picture of what it is to know obscures our understanding of what it is like to be a perceiver.

Furthermore, the picture is a dangerously incomplete model of knowledge itself, and not just because it rests on an impoverished phenomenology of perceptual experience. The reason, according to Taylor, is that it fails to acknowledge the conditions of possibility of objective knowledge, that is, its transcendental conditions. It is undeniable, Taylor thinks, that human beings do have a capacity for generating objective representations of the world. We possess knowledge that takes this objective form. But this mode of knowing can only arise against a "background" of concerns that cannot itself be the object of such knowledge. The fundamental mistake of the classical doctrine – which persists in contemporary "naturalistic" approaches to knowledge – is to suppose that the background is merely a causal antecedent of our cognitions. If that were the case, then the background would itself be as amenable to cognitive representation as any object within it. The problem with this construction, however, is that it confuses a transcendental condition of knowledge with a causal-empirical one; or rather, it fails to acknowledge that there is an issue about transcendental conditions for epistemology to address as well as an issue about the mechanisms of representation. The background is a transcendental condition of knowledge in the sense that it is required for the intelligibility of the knowledge claims we make. It cannot be completely objectified (or represented), since any objective knowledge claimed of it, to be intelligible at all, must itself have a "background" presupposition – precisely what complete objectification would annul. This transcendental level of reflection, therefore, exposes limits to the objectifiable, representable world. This is how Taylor interprets the epistemological significance of Heidegger's (and Gadamer's) reclamation of human finitude. For Taylor, as for other thinkers in the hermeneutic tradition, finitude is an inescapable structure of human knowledge, a point we need reminding of in view of widely held presumptions about the in-principle limitlessness of objective enquiry, which in turn reflect a blindness to the transcendental issue of intelligibility.

The claim so far has been that our knowledge of the objective world is only intelligible when set against a background of practically oriented perceptual awareness. Our primary sense of reality is bound up with our being in the world, and without this sense representational cognitions of nature would be impossible. Essentially the same point holds, according to Taylor, for our knowledge of the human world. That is to say, for Taylor the human sciences as much as the natural sciences are grounded in a prereflective, practically structured grasp of reality. But whereas the natural sciences refine the pre-objective sense of reality by depicting nature from a subject-neutral point of view, this strategy is unsuitable for deepening our knowledge or understanding of the human world. For meaning-content and subject-relatedness are integral to the very notion of human activity. Human activity is by its very nature directed by desires and purposes – without them, we wouldn't have actions to understand or explain – and interpreting these desires and purposes is an essential part of reaching an understanding or explanation of the activity. For the most part, we understand the meaning of actions in a prereflective, pretheoretical manner. The distinctive aim of the human sciences, according to Taylor, is to improve on these shared pretheoretical interpretations that arise spontaneously within a lifeworld, without ever completely cancelling them out, and without abandoning their interpretative form. The task of a science like anthropology, for instance, is to advance the prevailing understandings of the purposes expressed in a particular culture. Taylor draws heavily on Gadamer's notion of a "fusion of horizons" to explicate this learning process.[15] And in doing so, he contributes to the clarification of the hermeneutic claim that the social sciences have an "interpretative logic" that departs in key ways from the logic of the natural sciences.

Let us now briefly consider some of the main criticisms that are commonly made of the hermeneutic approach to knowledge. Perhaps the most widespread objection is that it is fundamentally an antiscientific philosophical outlook, and, at bottom, irrationalist. This objection can take several forms. First, it is often thought that hermeneutics is sceptical about the competence of modern science, as if science were incapable – according to the hermeneutic standpoint – of delivering genuine, objective knowledge of anything. Heidegger's talk of science as emerging from a "background" of practical concerns is seen as an objection to the validity of scientific theories, since it seems to present those theories as contingent on or relative to the background. If so, what makes science superior to, or more justified than, any other kind of practical engagement with the world? If natural science is ultimately just one way amongst others of dealing with the world, what authority does it really hold? Thinkers who put the issue in such terms tend to view the hermeneutic notion of the background as an avatar of what Popper termed the "myth of the framework"; that is, the misconstrual of scientific knowledge as relative to a particular "framework," "paradigm," or "language game."[16] This objection seriously misrepresents, however, the motivation behind the hermeneutic invocation of the background and Taylor does a service to the hermeneutic tradition by pointing out why. For far from casting doubt on the objectivity of science, the "background" argument is intended as an articulation of the conditions of possibility of the knowledge we do in fact have. It is not a sceptical argument at all. On the contrary, it is used to bolster a 'realist' theory of science, one that attributes the success of scientific theories to their ability to locate the causal powers that really do inhere in objects.[17] If anything, it is the positivist and falsificationist philosophies of science, rather than hermeneutics, that shortchange the explanatory competence of scientific theories.

Hermeneutics is also accused of being antiscientific or irrationalist because of the limits it draws to objective knowledge. On the one hand, the criticism is made that the "background" is artificially and arbitrarily excluded from scientific scrutiny. Again, however, this objection rests on a misunderstanding. For to say that objective knowledge is transcendentally conditioned by the background – that the background is required for knowledge claims to be intelligible – is to say nothing whatsoever about where, as a matter of fact, the empirical limits of scientific knowledge lie. On the other hand, the objection is often put that hermeneutics imposes arbitrary restrictions on the use of objective methods in the human sciences. Taylor's own account of the logic of the social sciences has been the target of such criticism.[18] Suffice it to note here that although Taylor has not elaborated in any detail the procedures by which interpretative social theories earn their claim to validity, it is consistent with his hermeneutic stance for him to doubt that there is much of worth to be said on this issue – at least by way of formal methodological rules – without abandoning a commitment to the distinction between validity and nonvalidity in the social sciences as such. If, as his critics allege, Taylor is an interpretative sceptic, he is a sceptic about the merits of formalism in the human sciences rather than validity in them.

Naturalists are not the only ones to object to the hermeneutic epistemology of the social sciences. There is also the camp of what could loosely be called "critical" social theorists. According to the standard classification, critical social theory is in the business not just of explaining (like natural science) or interpreting the world (like hermeneutics), but of transforming it.[19] The ultimate goal of social theory, according to the critical model, is emancipation. But the standard classification is misleading. This is because hermeneutic social science, as Taylor understands it, itself has the goal of emancipation in view, and its emancipatory power is integral to whatever validity it rightfully claims. According to Taylor, at their best social theories serve as "self-definitions": They reflect the purposes which the knowing agent, or the society in which the agent is embedded, takes as fundamental.[20] They also orient agents in their pursuit of their self-defining goals. By clarifying the conditions that have to be in place for these purposes to be more fully realised, and by clarifying the meaning of the purposes themselves, social theory can help bring about, in a more complete manner, the "selves" they define. And in successfully doing this – in helping to shape a self-formative process – they emancipate. Admittedly, such "self-realisation" may not be what other critical theorists have in mind when they refer to emancipation. But then the argument becomes a dispute about the meaning of emancipation, freedom, and kindred notions, rather than an argument between hermeneutics and an opposed "critical" conception of the ends of social science.

## THE LINGUISTIC TURN

Philosophical hermeneutics is closely associated with the "linguistic turn" in twentieth-century philosophy. For Heidegger, Gadamer, and Ricoeur, as well as for nonhermeneutic philosophers linked with the linguistic turn (such as Wittgenstein, Austin, and Derrida), a (if not the) chief challenge facing philosophy is to think about language the right way: If we go wrong here, philosophical reflection will be at best fruitless, at worst (and more likely) a source of grievous illusion. Taylor agrees. But more explicitly than his fellow hermeneutic philosophers, Taylor presents the challenge of thinking about language in the right way as a task for philosophical anthropology. At the core of the linguistic turn, as Taylor interprets it, is the proposition "that the question of language is somehow strategic for the question of human nature, that man is above all the language animal."[21] Taylor's investigations into language are guided by the conviction that we must first think about language in the right way if we are really to grasp what it is to be human, and that if we go astray in the former endeavour, we will grievously misconstrue the kind of being we are. Although this conviction certainly fits comfortably within post-Heideggerian hermeneutics, it is more prominent in Taylor than in other hermeneutic thinkers, and it contributes to the distinctive voice Taylor has within the hermeneutic tradition.

Human beings are not the only living species to use language, and a philosophy of language that has the strategic importance hermeneutics attaches to it must recognise both the continuity that exists between the human and other forms of life, and the role language plays in differentiating the human life-form. Taylor notes that at a rudimentary, cross-specific level, language functions as a mechanism for coordinating behaviour and as a mechanism for primitive socialisation.[22] By emitting and responding to signals, animals convey information to each other in ways that are beneficial to the survival of the species as a whole. Higher animals (including humans) are also able to bond together into groups by communicative means. In both these cases, Taylor maintains, language serves some nonlinguistically defined purpose. Language, at this level, is intelligible just in terms of biological imperatives; its intelligibility is not dependent on standards that are internal to language itself. But this changes once we move into what Taylor calls "the semantic dimension."[23] At this level of language use, it becomes possible to talk about the "rightness" of linguistic expressions. That is to say, a linguistic expression, when operative within the semantic dimension, is subject to norms. And it is only when the use of linguistic expressions is governed by norms that the issue of their meaning or significance arises, as distinct from their causal role. "Success" in the semantic dimension is not a matter of being causally instrumental in bringing about some nonlinguistically defined end, but of being right, of satisfying a standard internal to language, in whatever manner is appropriate. Although the semantic dimension has its genesis in nonhuman uses of language – it realises a potential that is already there in animal life – it exhibits a distinct mode of intelligibility. For Taylor, to acknowledge this qualitative shift is to take the first crucial step towards understanding how language and the distinctively human form of life are related.

The second step is to appreciate the full range of norms, or the many ways of "getting things right," within the semantic dimension. We need to be alert to this, Taylor thinks, in view of the prevalence of what he terms "designative" theories in modern philosophy of language and the taken-for-granted assumptions such theories build on.[24] Designative theories accept that language is normative. They agree that there is a qualitative difference between getting something right in language and participating in some causal chain, but the normativity they recognise has just one source: truth as the correspondence between a representation or literal description and its object. That is to say, it is the norm of designation, of the ability of a word or sentence to designate or represent an object or state of affairs, that enables words or sentences to mean something. Getting things right in language is thus essentially a matter of having the designative function in order. But Taylor is convinced that this is a much too narrow view of the semantic dimension. We are able to "get things right" in language in a host of ways – for instance, by articulating a feeling properly, by evoking the right mood, or by establishing an appropriate interpersonal relation – many of which are not at all a matter of designating things. Furthermore, unlike the designative use of language, these forms of language use are not "about" something that stands independently of the articulation itself. Taylor is impressed by the fact that an articulation can constitute the emotion, or mood, or social relation it expresses. New kinds of feeling and sociality are brought into being through language. But this does not prevent such modes of articulation from being right (when they are right). In other words, there are forms of language use that are constitutive and productive of their objects, and productive in a way that is "true to" or "right for" them. Inevitably, Taylor points out, such forms of articulation get screened off within the designative paradigm.

Creatures whose feelings, actions, and social relations are constituted by the ways they are articulated in language are in a clear sense "self-interpreting animals": what they are as animals – the quality of their experience, they ways they act, and how they behave together – is inseparable from how they interpret themselves. For Taylor, this is the core truth of philosophical hermeneutics. In order to be able to articulate this truth, hermeneutics must obviously have access to a more expansive theory of meaning than the designative one. But Taylor, in line with other hermeneutic theorists, does not simply claim that the expressive/constitutive capacity of language sits alongside the designative capacity. The claim is that the power of expression – the power of disclosing and constituting a human "world" – is fundamental and originary. The capacity of language to designate things is one amongst a series of possibilities immanent to the power of expression itself. Theories that put designation first in the order of intelligibility, in Taylor's view, suffer from a parallel flaw to the representationalist epistemology considered earlier. Just as the rational processing of neutral input has its genesis and intelligibility-condition in agent-knowledge, so neutral talk about objects, or true descriptions of states of affairs, draws on a prior, more fundamental capacity for expression, which is "always already" in place whenever we describe literally, neutrally, and

accurately. Taylor thus draws attention to an insight which is crucial to the
hermeneutic tradition but which, perhaps more than anything else, baffles
and bewilders antihermeneutic philosophers, especially those working in
the analytic tradition: the equiprimordiality of normativity and productive
world-disclosure. For hermeneutics, language is at once and indivisibly the
medium through which we think about the world (the semantic dimension
in which truth and other norms hold sway) and the medium through which
we create a world. According to Taylor's hermeneutic theory of meaning,
literal truth and plainspeaking prose domesticate, without ever eliminating,
primordial expressive powers.

If one looks at Taylor's work on language from the perspective of recent Anglo-American analytic philosophy, one is likely be as disappointed
about what Taylor does not say as perplexed by what he does. Taylor has
written very little about the issues that take centre stage in mainstream
philosophy of language in the English-speaking world. For instance, there
is no worked-out "theory of reference" in Taylor's writings, and there is
hardly any account of the "pragmatics" of speech that many contemporary
philosophers take to be decisive for the theory of meaning. It is notable
that, unlike Ricoeur and some other contemporary hermeneutic thinkers,
Taylor is downbeat about Donald Davidson's seminal work in philosophy of language, and shows little inclination to contribute to the debates
Davidson initiated.[25] This is because, in Taylor's view (and here he is closer
to Gadamer than Ricoeur) such debates fail to focus on the philosophically crucial issue: the nature of the expressive power. The debates which
do focus on this issue, Taylor shows, occur not in analytic philosophy of
language, but in and between the "post-Romantic" traditions of Continental philosophy. Taylor has constructed an intriguing and helpful map for
finding our way about in these debates.[26] He distinguishes, for instance,
between various types of subjectivism and antisubjectivism regarding the
expressive power, whatever is made manifest in it, and the subject or agent
responsible for bringing the expression about. On all these issues, Taylor,
along with the late Heidegger and Gadamer, commends the antisubjec-
tivist stance. Although Taylor's commendations may not always be backed
up with as much argument as one would wish – his polemic with Derrida is
a case in point – Taylor has at least shown that there are arguments here to
be made, and that they are well worth making wherever one stands in the
debate.[27]

Taylor thus contrasts the hermeneutic theory of meaning he shares with
Heidegger and Gadamer with the designative theories popular amongst analytic philosophers on the one hand, and subjectivist constructions of the

expressive power in Continental philosophy on the other. For Taylor, these are not just different approaches to language; they also, if sometimes only implicitly, come packaged with different theories of human nature. At first sight Taylor's view might seem far-fetched: Can't one take the designative relation between language and the world to be decisive for the theory of meaning without getting embroiled in controversies about human nature? Taylor's view becomes less implausible, however, when one considers that a philosophy of language cannot be neutral with regard to human nature. The very idea of "self-interpreting animals" cannot even be formulated within a theory of meaning that has no room for the expressive or constitutive power of language – hardly a neutral outcome from an anthropological point of view. But Taylor's claim is in fact stronger than this: It is not just that designative theories are not neutral about human nature; such theories actually give positive support to a rival, anti-expressive anthropology of their own. Taylor here brings out some often neglected features of the early modern theories of meaning that continue to shape contemporary debates. The classical designative theories, Taylor shows, were driven by a powerful ideal of self-transparency and instrumental freedom. They presented language as a tool or resource which human beings potentially have the freedom to do with as they will. On this account, humans are not only capable of manipulating and reshaping language according to their own designs and purposes; they have a responsibility to achieve such mastery and control, for otherwise they are led into error and illusion about the world and themselves. The classical designative theories depicted nondesignative elements as sources of such error and bewitchment, and thus as hindrances to the subject's self-defining instrumental freedom. Taylor is convinced that a disengaged notion of freedom – or an "anthropology of disengagement" – also informs those expressivist theories that take a subjectivist approach to the expressive power.

For nonsubjectivist expressivism, by contrast, the fact that human beings are language animals means that they can never achieve full self-possession. The thinking and acting subject is always already situated in the semantic dimension, and so subject to norms that are in some sense "given." The semantic dimension is, in principle, independent of the will and must escape objectification by the will. The constitutive power of language also militates against the ideal of absolute cognitive self-possession. For if there are experiences, feelings, and social relations that are constituted by the way we express or interpret them, and these things help define who we are, our self-understanding can never be complete. These features of human existence are not objects waiting to be represented by the right kind of designative language. There is no final, "self-authenticating" vocabulary for them; and relatedly, there is always more "meaning" to them than is expressed in any particular self-interpretation. The meaning of human existence insofar as it inhabits the semantic dimension or is constituted by language qua expressive power can never be finalised. In addition, the language of self-interpretation is beyond the individual's control because language has an inherently intersubjective character. The language "I" speak, if it is to say anything, is always the language of a "we." In general, then, we can say that the hermeneutic theory of meaning Taylor sympathetically reconstructs helps articulate a nonvoluntarist ontology of human finitude. It at once points to certain defining characteristics of human nature and draws limits to what we can know about ourselves given this nature. In this way, the question of language is strategic for the question of human nature not just for suggesting what human nature is like, but also for revealing the mode of articulation that is suitable for the theory or "science" of human nature as such.

## THE MORAL SUBJECT

One of the central issues in the tradition of post-Heideggerian hermeneutics has been the question of its relation to ethics. Notoriously, Heidegger seemed to think that ethics could be left to itself once we situated ourselves properly in relation to Being, or as he also formulated it in his earlier writings, once we achieved genuine (that is, "nonsubjectivist") authenticity in our thought and action.[28] If human beings are self-interpreting animals, our natures are not simply given to us. We must assume responsibility for our own existence, and whatever ethical orientation we have is only properly viewed in light of this self-responsibility. To exist authentically, in proper relation to Being, is thus a kind of injunction based in our self-interpreting nature. But whether this insight could back up or justify one ethical orientation amongst others remained unclear. Sartre also drew attention to the unavoidability of taking responsibility for ourselves – however, in "bad faith," it might seem otherwise. And although Sartre did acknowledge the need to develop a positive, substantive ethics of authenticity from his hermeneutic point of departure, he was unable to satisfy it.[29] The problematic relation between post-Heideggerian hermeneutics and ethics is even more evident in Levinas's work.[30] Levinas accepts the thesis that human beings are self-interpreting animals, but for him the injunction to become oneself (authentically) is paradoxically fulfilled only in the self-negating stance of being "for another." For Levinas, ethics is not about authenticity at all. It is about giving oneself over to the other human being or "substituting" for the Other. Levinas is convinced that this relation, rather than the self-relation or the relation to Being, is primordial. But for all Levinas's concern with articulating the "for-the-other" relation, with "showing up" the priority of ethics over ontology in a philosophical discourse, it is far from clear how we are to interpret the concrete ethical implications of his hermeneutic endeavour – if indeed there are any. Like Heidegger and Sartre, Levinas is at most a reluctant "ethicist," and he is just as averse as they are to talking about moral "values" or "agency."

The distinctiveness of Taylor's voice in the hermeneutic tradition owes much to the explicitly moral perspective he brings to the post-Heideggerian thesis that human beings are self-interpreting animals. We have to bring such a perspective, Taylor argues, because self-interpretations are conducted in languages that cannot but instantiate distinctions of worth. As Taylor puts his claim,

> our self-understanding essentially incorporates our seeing ourselves against a background of what I have called "strong evaluation." I mean by that a background of distinctions between things which are recognised as of categoric or unconditioned or higher importance or worth, and things which lack this or are of lesser value.[31]

We have already seen that, for Taylor, in important cases our self-understanding constitutes who we are. There are feelings, moods, and social relations that are shaped through the way we articulate or express them. Articulation, once we are in the semantic dimension, is not an arbitrary matter: It is responsive to, or guided by, standards that are normative for the subject. Taylor then points out that amongst the things we articulate this way are our "moral" feelings, for example, shame, pride, indignation, dignity, self-respect, injustice, and so forth. In Taylor's view, the norm-guidedness that is necessary for the proper articulation of such feelings is a responsiveness to the categoric worth of the thing at hand. Taylor's next step is to argue that it is impossible to conceive a recognisably human life lived without some apprehension of the distinction between a thing having such worth or not. If this argument is successful, he will have shown that the articulations that contribute to human self-understanding are necessarily framed by a background set of qualitative distinctions of worth.

Whether or not we take the argument to be successful,[32] we must be careful not to misrepresent the conclusion it purportedly reaches. Taylor's claim is that human subjectivity has a "moral" dimension because of its noncontingent connection to frameworks of strong value. The idea is that a human identity is intelligible only in relation to "the good." This has led some critics to argue that Taylor has a "moralistic," "intellectualist," and exaggeratedly "linguistic" conception of the self.[33] The objection is that agents need not define themselves in terms of moral self-interpretations (they can be self-interpreting without being moral or caring much about morality), and they can be moral or concerned by morality without articulating those concerns linguistically (that is, without possessing or exercising an intellectual capacity for reflective articulation). The force of the criticism is considerably weakened, however, by the broad way in which Taylor uses the expressions "moral," "the good," and "articulation." All that is needed to have a self or identity constituted by moral concerns is for some desires and purposes to matter because of their worth. But that worth need not be "moral" in the narrow sense, say, of being dutiful, or altruistic, or benevolent. Likewise, articulations can take a variety of expressive forms, and certainly need not be "rationalistic" or "intellectualist." No doubt Taylor's employment of the term "strong evaluation" contributed to the confusion over this issue, since the strong evaluator does assume a reflective, rational stance. But strong values can direct a subject's activity without the mediation of reflection, and indeed it is this prereflective, inchoate orientation to good that constitutes the "moral dimension" of human subjectivity for the large part. Unless we see that strong value rather than strong evaluation is the decisive feature, Taylor's hermeneutic conception of the self will indeed seem falsely linguistic, reflective, and intellectualist.

Taylor thus extracts a more explicitly moral meaning from the insight that human beings are self-interpreting animals than other thinkers in the hermeneutic tradition. He makes a parallel move in his appropriation of the hermeneutic idea that narratives are crucial to human identity. Drawing on Heidegger's famous analysis of the temporal structure of *Dasein*, Taylor argues that self-understanding is impossible without some grasp of how the self unfolds in time, of how it constitutes a temporal totality.[34] Self-interpretation must bring past, present, and future together, a synthesis that only narratives can achieve. For Taylor, we must not think of this synthesis as separate from the frameworks of strong value that articulate distinctions of worth; rather, we should think of the synthesis as disclosing possibilities for the meaning of a life as a whole. Self-interpretation thus requires some temporal framework within which the direction of a life in relation to the good can be articulated. At this point Taylor imports aspects of Alasdair MacIntyre's account of human life as a "quest."[35] As self-interpreters and thus also self-narrators, we find ourselves having to make sense of our lives as a sequence of "maturations and regressions, overcomings and defeats"[36] in realising the good. It is arguable, however, that this is one step too many in the passage from hermeneutics to moral ontology. Ricoeur suggests so: He draws attention to significant disanalogies between the unity of a good life, a life gathered together as a singular totality, and the narrative unity of a piece of fiction.[37] And Taylor himself equivocates on the matter when he acknowledges the power of narrative (particularly in modernist literature) to subvert the very notions of unity and identity on which the conception of life as a "quest" seems to rest.[38]

The hermeneutic provenance of Taylor's conception of practical reason, however, is beyond dispute. Like Heidegger, and especially Gadamer before him, Taylor is hugely impressed by Aristotle's thinking on this topic.[39] For Aristotle, practical reason is fundamentally a matter of being sensitive or responsive to the ethical demands of a particular situation. Although a natural capacity, this sensitivity or responsiveness is acquired through socialisation into a form of life. In the course of our socialisation, we develop characters, a sense of self, and a way of seeing the world that enables us to tell the difference between correct and incorrect modes of conduct. This difference is not something that can be discerned independently of our socialised, and so historically mediated, practical point of view. And it is not something that can be established by purely theoretical inquiry. Rather, when reasoning about practical matters we have to work with the inherited language and norms we share with similarly socialised subjects, and rely on our judgement about what is appropriate to the given situation. For Gadamer, this focus on judgement and application enabled Aristotle to avoid the abstract formalism that afflicts modern approaches to practical reason, and it also provides the focus of Gadamer's own approach.[40]

Taylor shares Gadamer's dissatisfaction with moral formalism, but his Aristotelian alternative takes a rather different direction. Less informed by the tradition of legal hermeneutics than Gadamer, and more concerned by issues in moral psychology, Taylor seeks to make better sense of the link between practical reason and motivation rather than to reinstate the humanist paradigm of judgement.[41] He does this by proposing that practical reason involves transitions in the interpretation of motivationally potent, identity-expressive strong values.[42] The practical judgement favoured by reason, according to Taylor, is an interpretation of the good that compares favourably with the interpretation we began with. The justification is not done by a formalisable procedure – such as the maximisation of general happiness or the universalisation of a maxim – as modern formalist theories claim. Rather it is done by the content of the strong value as revealed by the better interpretation. Furthermore, that content is not abstracted from the motivational set of the practical reasoner – otherwise a further reason would be needed to make the reasoning matter to the agent – since strong values are integral to the subject's sense of self. Admittedly, it follows that practical reason has a limited scope: It is always addressed from and to particular lived points of view. And because of this, it is powerless when faced either with the sceptic who claims not to have a strongly evaluated starting point at all, or with the dogmatist who believes that his starting point is immune from the possibility of reflective revision and improvement.

For some philosophers, however, particularly those in the Kantian tradition, a more serious drawback in Taylor's hermeneutic model of practical reason is that it does not distinguish between the kind of validity possessed by a soundly interpreted strong value and the kind of validity possessed by a legitimate moral principle. Kantians such as Habermas want to uphold a distinction of this sort in order to preserve the intuition that there are some norms – strictly speaking "moral" ones – that apply to all of us, irrespective of the "ethical" values we identify with.[43] In short, the idea is that moral duties and obligations are both universal and uniquely binding on us, that we have, for instance, a duty to respect other people's basic rights whatever personal aspirations we (or they) may uphold, and that this duty ought to override those aspirations. Thus, although the "ethical" use of practical reason, as Taylor shows, is a matter of "hermeneutic self-clarification," Habermas argues that its "moral use" involves a different kind of procedure: the testing of a norm for its universalisability. The participants in practical reason in this sense must abstract from their conception of the good (their strong values) in order to test the validity of claims about what "morality" as such requires. Practical reason can thus be used to settle conflicts arising between people with rival strong values – to settle them on strictly speaking moral grounds – and it can be used to criticise forms of life that fail to respect basic principles of justice.

It is hard to argue with Habermas's point that Taylor's model of practical reason as "hermeneutic self-clarification" is better suited to some practical circumstances than others. Certainly, it does little to explicate what a fair or impartial resolution of a practical dispute requires – not a negligible shortcoming for many moral theorists.[44] Taylor does, however, provide a response to the criticism that a hermeneutic approach to ethics is unable to make sense of the peculiar binding force of moral demands. For Taylor, the injunctions to treat other people as "ends" and not "means," to respect basic human rights, and to minimise suffering rightly take precedence over other values in the modern world. And it is important that a conception of ethics be able to articulate this priority of the "right" over the "good." But rather than do this by abstracting the right from the good, and by demarcating a logically distinct realm of "morality," Taylor urges us to consider autonomy, universal justice, and the minimisation of suffering as "hypergoods," that is, "higher-order" goods from the standpoint of which judgements about other goods become possible.[45] "Moral" values, according to Taylor, owe their peculiar stature not to some putatively unique proximity to the structure of agency, language, or reason, but on the one hand to the anthropological fact that values of that kind are crucial for stabilising social relations everywhere, and on the other to the historical fact that in modern societies they matter to people enormously. "Morality" in its strict sense is thus one expression – albeit fundamental – of the modern identity. In line with the hermeneutic tradition Taylor thereby "historicises" the moral subject. But this by no means implies that the historically contingent standards that define the modern subject cannot be rationally redeemed. And just as important, it does nothing to protect those standards from being the object of rational criticism themselves.

This raises a number of issues about whether hermeneutics can provide a suitable standpoint from which to give a philosophical critique of oppressive or alienating practices. I believe that it can, and that in general it can help justify and especially sustain a progressive politics. I also think that Taylor, more than anyone else in the hermeneutic tradition, shows us why. Unfortunately, I do not have space to explore these issues, which would require a discussion of Taylor's social and political theory in relation to that of other hermeneutic thinkers.[46] In this essay I have only tried to indicate the hermeneutic provenance of Taylor's thinking about knowledge, language, and ethics, and I have suggested some ways in which Taylor's thinking on these matters makes a distinctive contribution to the hermeneutic tradition.

## Notes

1. For a more detailed account of the various ways of defining hermeneutics than the one sketched here, see Richard E. Palmer, *Hermeneutics*, Evanston, IL: Northwestern University Press, 1969.
2. On the complex of cultural and philosophical associations between hermeneutics and relativism, see Ernest Gellner, *Relativism and the Social Sciences*, Cambridge, U.K.: Cambridge University Press, 1985.
3. See especially Charles Taylor, "Interpretation and the Sciences of Man" in *Philosophy and the Human Sciences. Philosophical Papers 2*, Cambridge, U.K.: Cambridge University Press, 1985, pp. 15–57.

4. On this idea of metaphysical "queerness," see J. L. Mackie, *Ethics: Inventing Right and Wrong*, Harmondsworth: Penguin, 1977.

5. The currency of this expression is largely due to Christine Korsgaard's use of it, which in fact differs from the meaning I intend to convey here. See Christine Korsgaard, *The Sources of Normativity*, Cambridge, U.K.: Cambridge University Press, 1996.

6. It has been suggested that Hegelian Idealism and Pragmatism should be read as developing this post-Kantian theme in a different direction. See, for instance, Robert Pippin, *Hegel's Idealism*, Cambridge, U.K.: Cambridge University Press, 1989, and Robert Brandom, *Making it Explicit: Reasoning, Representing and Discursive Commitment*, Cambridge, MA: Harvard University Press, 1994.

7. Martin Heidegger, *Being and Time*. John Macquarrie and Edward Robinson (trans.), Oxford: Blackwell, 1962.

8. Charles Taylor, *Human Agency and Language. Philosophical Papers 1*. Cambridge, U.K.: Cambridge University Press, 1985: p. 3.

9. Ibid, p. 45.

10. I certainly do not mean to suggest here that either Dilthey or Gadamer neglects prereflexive modes of understanding – that would be absurd. The problem is rather that the concept of interpretation in its ordinary use generally refers to a reflective act, and that a hermeneutics that defined human beings as self-interpreting just in that sense would be open to phenomenological correction.

11. See, among other places, "Overcoming Epistemology" and "Lichtung or Lebensform: Parallels between Heidegger and Wittgenstein" in Charles Taylor, *Philosophical Arguments*, Cambridge, MA: Harvard University Press, 1995, pp. 1–19 and 61–78 respectively.

12. See Maurice Merleau-Ponty, *Phenomenology of Perception*. Christopher Smith (trans.), London: Routledge, 1962. See also the commentary on this text by Charles Taylor and Michael Kullman, "The Pre-Objective World," *Review of Metaphysics* 12 (1958): 103–32.

13. Charles Taylor, *Philosophical Arguments*, Cambridge MA: Harvard University Press, 1995, p. 10.

14. Ibid, p. 61.

15. See Hans-Georg Gadamer, *Truth and Method*. Joel Weinsheimer and Donald G. Marshall (trans.), London: Sheed and Ward, 1993. See also Taylor's discussion of Gadamer in "Comparison, History, Truth" in *Philosophical Arguments*, Cambridge MA: Harvard University Press, 1995, pp. 146–64.

16. Karl R. Popper. "Normal Science and its Dangers" in Imre Lakatos, and Alan Musgrave (eds.), *Criticism and the Growth of Knowledge*, Cambridge, U.K.: Cambridge University Press, 1970, p. 56.

17. See, for instance, Charles Taylor, "Understanding in Human Science," *Review of Metaphysics*, 34, 1 (1980): 25–38. See also his "Rorty in the Epistemological Tradition" in Alan Malachowski (ed.), *Reading Rorty*, Oxford: Blackwell, 1990. See also his "What's Wrong with Foundationalism? Knowledge, Agency and World" in Mark Wrathall and Jeff Malpass (eds.), *Heidegger, Coping and Cognitive Science*. Cambridge, MA: MIT Press, 2000. For further discussion of Taylor's

hermeneutic realism see Nicholas H. Smith. *Strong Hermeneutics: Contingency and Moral Identity*, London: Routledge, 1997, and Ruth Abbey, *Charles Taylor*, Princeton: Princeton University Press; Teddington, UK.: Acumen Publishing, 2000.

18. See, for instance, James Bohman, *New Philosophy of Social Science: Problems of Indeterminacy*, Cambridge, MA: MIT Press, 1991, and Michael Martin, "Taylor on Interpretation and the Sciences of Man" in M. Martin and L. C. McIntyre (eds.), *Readings in the Philosophy of Social Science*, Cambridge, MA: MIT Press, 1994.

19. See, for instance, William Outhwaite, *New Philosophies of Social Science: Realism, Hermeneutics and Critical Theory*, New York: St. Martin's, 1987, and Jurgen Habermas, *On the Logic of the Social Sciences*, S. W. Nicholsen and J. A. Stark (trans.), Cambridge, MA: MIT Press, 1988.

20. Charles Taylor, *Philosophy and the Human Sciences. Philosophical Papers 2*, Cambridge, U.K.: Cambridge University Press, 1985.

21. Charles Taylor, "Language and Human Nature" in *Human Agency and Language. Philosophical Papers 1*, Cambridge: Cambridge University Press, 1985, p. 216.

22. Charles Taylor, "The Importance of Herder" in *Philosophical Arguments*, Cambridge, MA: Harvard University Press, 1995, pp. 83–7.

23. Charles Taylor, "Heidegger, Language, Ecology" in *Philosophical Arguments*, Cambridge, MA: Harvard University Press, 1995, p. 103

24. For Taylor's take on designative theories, see his "Language and Human Nature" and "Theories of Meaning" in *Human Agency and Language. Philosophical Papers 1*, Cambridge, U.K.: Cambridge University Press, 1985, pp. 215–47 and 248–92 respectively. See also his "Heidegger, Language, Ecology" in *Philosophical Arguments*. Cambridge, MA: Harvard University Press, 1995, pp. 100–26.

25. Ricoeur engages with Davidson's work in some detail (in a qualifiedly sympathetic spirit) in Paul Ricoeur, *Oneself as Another*, Kathleen Blamey (trans.), Chicago: University of Chicago Press, 1992. The relevance of Davidson's philosophy of language for hermeneutics is pressed by, amongst others, Andrew Bowie. See his "The Meaning of the Hermeneutic Tradition in Contemporary Philosophy" in A. O'Hear, (ed.), *Verstehen and Humane Understanding*, Cambridge, U.K.: Cambridge University Press, 1996, pp. 121–44.

26. See Charles Taylor, "Heidegger, Language, Ecology" in *Philosophical Arguments*, Cambridge, MA: Harvard University Press, 1995. See especially pp. 111–26.

27. I discuss this point further in Nicholas H. Smith, "Reason after Meaning," *Philosophy and Social Criticism*, 23 1 (1997): 131–40 and *Charles Taylor: Meaning, Morals and Modernity*. Cambridge, U.K.: Polity, 2002.

28. On the notion of authenticity see Martin Heidegger, *Being and Time*. John Macquarrie and Edward Robinson (trans.), Oxford: Blackwell, 1962. For his cautious remarks about ethics see his "Letter on Humanism" in *Basic Writings*, David Farell Krell (trans.), London: Routledge, 1993. See especially pp. 250–9.

29. Sartre never managed to write the "future work" on ethics alluded to in the final sentence of *Being and Nothingness*. See Jean-Paul Sartre, *Being and Nothingness*, Hazel Barnes (trans.), London: Methuen, 1957.

30. See, for instance, Emmanuel Levinas, *Totality and Infinity*. Alphonso Lingis (trans.), Pittsburgh: Duquesne University Press, 1969.

31. *Human Agency and Language. Philosophical Papers 1*, Cambridge, U.K.: Cambridge University Press, 1985, p. 3.

32. I do not have space to consider the details of the argument here. For further discussion see my *Strong Hermeneutics: Contingency and Moral Identity*, London: Routledge, 1997, and *Charles Taylor: Meaning, Morals and Modernity*, Cambridge, U.K.: Polity, 2002.

33. See, for example, Owen Flanagan, "Identity and Strong and Weak Evaluation," and A. O. Rorty and D. Wong, "Aspects of Identity and Agency," both in O. Flanagan, and A. O. Rorty (eds.), *Identity, Character and Morality*, Cambridge MA: MIT Press, 1990.

34. See Martin Heidegger. *Being and Time*. John Macquarrie and Edward Robinson (trans.), Oxford: Blackwell, 1962.

35. Alasdair MacIntyre, *After Virtue*, second edition, Notre Dame: Notre Dame University Press, 1984, p. 219.

36. Charles Taylor. *Sources of the Self: The Making of the Modern Identity*, Cambridge, MA: Harvard University Press, 1989, p. 50.

37. See Paul Ricoeur, *Oneself as Another*. Kathleen Blamey (trans.), Chicago: University of Chicago Press, 1992, pp. 158–63.

38. Again, let me refer the interested reader to further discussion of this point in *Charles Taylor: Meaning, Morals and Modernity*. Cambridge, U.K.: Polity, 2002, pp. 100–2.

39. Aristotle, *Nicomachean Ethics*, D. Ross (trans.), Oxford: Oxford University Press, 1980.

40. Hans-Georg Gadamer, *Truth and Method*. Joel Weinsheimer and Donald G. Marshall (trans.), London: Sheed and Ward, 1993. See also Gadamer's "On the Possibility of a Philosophical Ethics" in *Hermeneutics, Religion and Ethics*. Joel Weinsheimer (trans.), New Haven: Yale University Press, 1999.

41. This is by no means to say that Taylor has no use for the Aristotelian-humanist concept of judgement; the point is rather that he does not thematise this concept as other hermeneutic thinkers do.

42. See Charles Taylor, *Sources of the Self: the Making of the Modern Identity*, Cambridge, MA: Harvard University Press. 1989. See also his "Explanation and Practical Reason" in *Philosophical Arguments*, Cambridge, MA: Harvard University Press, 1995, pp. 34–60.

43. See "On the Pragmatic, the Ethical, and the Moral Employments of Practical Reason" in Jurgen Habermas. *Justification and Application*. Ciaran Cronin (trans.), Cambridge, U.K.: Polity, 1993.

44. Whether this reflects Taylor's failure – allegedly typical of hermeneutics – to define morality in a precise manner, and so differentiate the rationality of moral argumentation from other kinds of practical discourse, is another matter. The thought that the hermeneutic-Aristotelian approach to practical reason is fatally compromised by its unwillingness or inability to circumscribe the moral is

elaborated by Axel Honneth in his "Between Hermeneutics and Hegelianism: John McDowell and the Challenge of Moral Realism" in N. Smith (ed.), *Reading McDowell on Mind and World*, London: Routledge, 2002.

45. Charles Taylor. *Sources of the Self: The Making of the Modern Identity*. Cambridge, MA: Harvard University Press, 1989, p. 63.

46. For such discussion, see my *Strong Hermeneutics: Contingency and Moral Identity*, London: Routledge, 1997, and *Charles Taylor: Meaning, Morals and Modernity*, Cambridge, U.K.: Polity, 2002.

# 2 | Taylor's (Anti-) Epistemology
HUBERT L. DREYFUS

## INTRODUCTION

Epistemology, as Charles Taylor understands it, is a discipline that arises along with the subject/object ontology introduced by Descartes. This ontology understands the subject as a self-sufficient mind related to the objects in the world by way of internal mental states that in some way represent those objects but in no essential way depend on them. The radical gap between what is inside the mind and what is outside in the world must be mediated in order for a subject to have knowledge of the world, and epistemology is the study of this mediation.

In opposition to this Cartesian picture, Taylor describes the positive role our bodily skills and taken-for-granted background practices play in making sense of the world and in putting us in direct touch with everyday reality. But, at the same time, he stresses the negative role our modern taken-for-granted background framework plays in blinding philosophers to these phenomena. This blindness is characteristic not only of earlier versions of epistemology such as sense data theory, Kant's scheme-content analytic, and Husserl's phenomenological account of the mediational role of intentional content; it also casts doubt, Taylor seeks to show, on the claims of contemporary thinkers such as Donald Davidson and Richard Rorty, to have overcome epistemology. According to Taylor, these philosophers are still thinking within the inner/outer picture of our epistemic situation. In their version of it, we have access to the meaningful world and to the physical universe only insofar as it causally impinges on our sense organs and, thereby, produces our beliefs.

In discussing Taylor's anti-epistemology, I lay out, defend, and show the current relevance of his persuasive account of our direct encounter with the things in the world, and how this encounter grounds our knowledge. I then consider two challenges to this view: (1) The possibility that we are brains in vats, fooled by an evil computer scientist into thinking we are in direct contact with the real world, whereas, in fact, there is no such world and (2) Rorty's implicit critique that Taylor's account of our embedding in the everyday world introduces a new version of the inner/outer distinction that undermines Taylor's realist claim that natural science, at least in principle, is able to get outside our everyday experience and describe the physical universe as it is in itself.

In response to these challenges, I argue that Taylor could accept the brain in the vat as a possibility, and, nonetheless, defend his basic anti-epistemological argument. Second, I suggest that Taylor's realism regarding the everyday world, far from standing in the way of scientific realism, enables him to counter Rorty's antirealism with a robust realism concerning the entities described by physical theory.

## OVERCOMING THE MEDIATIONAL PICTURE

Taylor argues that no mental representations, be they sense data, visual experiences, or intentional content, and so forth, mediate our relation to everyday reality. The most recent and general version of the view Taylor opposes is found in Husserl's *Cartesian Meditations*.[1] As Husserl saw, and John Searle states clearly, all propositional intentional content is inner in the sense that the conditions of satisfaction formulated in the content depend on the mind and are independent of whether anything in the world satisfies them. In response, Taylor boldly states his thesis

> There is a big mistake operating in our culture, a (mis)understanding of what it is to know, which has had dire effects on both theory and practice in a host of domains. To sum it up in a pithy formula, we might say that we (mis)understand knowledge as "mediational". In its original form, this emerged in the idea that we grasp external reality through internal rep-resentations. Descartes in one of his letters, declared himself "assuré que je ne puis avoir aucune connaissance de ce qui est hors de moi, que par l'entremise des idées que j'ai eu en moi".[2] When states of mind correctly and reliably represent what is out there, there is knowledge.[3]

Taylor's goal is to reveal the inner/outer structure of all epistemologies, even recent would-be anti-epistemologies, and to present and defend an opposed view, a view that denies that the inner/outer dichotomy in any form correctly describes our basic relation to reality. In response to the reigning mediational view, he draws on and elaborates Heidegger's phenomenology of being-in-the-world, Merleau-Ponty's account of our bodily being-devoted-to-the-world (*être au monde*), and Samuel Todes's detailed description of how our body's structure and its capacity for self-movement structures the everyday world.[4] These thinkers argue that nothing – not even propositional content – mediates our relation to everyday reality; that, at a level of involvement more basic than belief, we are directly at grips with the things and people that make up our world.

Taylor elaborates an account of our direct interaction with the world in contrast to the mediational view: He notes that my ability to get around in this city or this house comes out only in getting around in this city or house. This important observation holds for the most global skills as well as the most local ones. Globally, it could be said, and, indeed, was said by Wittgenstein and Heidegger, concerning my ability to find my way about in the world.[5] Taylor illustrates the antimediational point with a football:

> We can draw a neat line between my *picture* of an object and that object, but not between my *dealing* with the object and that object. It may make sense to ask us to focus on what we *believe* about something, say a football, even in the absence of that thing; but when it comes to *playing* football, the corresponding suggestion would be absurd. The actions involved in the game can't be done without the object; they include the object.[6]

More locally, one might add, I can't go through the motions of tying my shoelaces without holding on to the item in question, and I can't tell which finger I use to type the letter "e" except by typing it. In general, unlike mental content, which can exist independently of its referent, my coping abilities cannot be actualized or, often, even entertained in the absence of what I am coping with.

This is not to say that we can't be mistaken. It's hard to see how I could succeed in getting around in a city or in tying a shoe without the existence of the city or the lace, but I could be mistaken for a while, and, in the light of my failure to cope successfully, I may have to retroactively cross off what I seemingly encountered and replace it with a new understanding that amounts to directly encountering something else.

Taylor's originality and importance consist not only in his combining and drawing out the consequences of the best phenomenological accounts of involved coping; they also consist in his controversial claim that the mediational view he is attacking is still taken for granted by those who, in opposition to functionalism, defend qualia, and even those, like Donald Davidson and Richard Rorty, who claim to oppose all forms of subject/object, mind/world dichotomies. Taylor claims that these thinkers are still imprisoned unawares in Descartes' inner/outer picture. He points out that

> [Although] Quine denies Cartesian dualism by denying one of its terms – there is no "mental substance", everything is matter, and thinking itself arises out of matter – [he] recreates a similar structure in the new metaphysical context. Our knowledge comes to us through "surface irritations", the points in our receptors where the various stimuli from the environment impinge. Alternatively, he sometimes takes the immediate description of what is impinging, observation sentences, as basic, and he sees the edifice of science as built under the requirement that shows how (most of) these hold. In either variant, there is a mediational, or "only through" structure here.

Taylor goes on to show that those who at first sight seem to be opposed to Quine still hold that our knowledge of reality is necessarily mediated by propositional representations such as beliefs. He notes that Davidson quotes approvingly Rorty's claim that nothing counts as justification unless by reference to what we already accept, and there is no way to get outside our beliefs and language so as to find some test other than coherence.[7] And Davidson adds, "what distinguishes a coherence theory is simply the claim that nothing can count as a reason for holding a belief except another belief."[8] Indeed, Davidson explicitly "rejects as unintelligible the request for a ground or source of justification of another ilk [than belief]."[9]

An assurance that one's view is self-evident, Taylor notes, is characteristic of what Wittgenstein calls a picture – a largely unreflected background understanding, that is, a way of seeing things, that seems so obvious, so commonsensical, as to be unchallengeable. That Davidson and Rorty are stuck in the Cartesian picture, Taylor claims, is evident in the way they assume, without argument, that the only way to ground a belief is to justify it rationally, on the basis of another belief.

To help us appreciate what Davidson and Rorty miss, Taylor elaborates an account of our basic, preconceptual way of being in the world.

> [T]hings figure for us in their meaning or relevance for our purposes, desires, activities. As I navigate my way along the path up the hill, my mind totally absorbed anticipating the difficult conversation I'm going to have at my destination, I treat the different features of the terrain as obstacles, supports, openings, invitations to tread more warily, or run freely, etc. Even when I'm not thinking of them these things have those relevances for me; I know my way about among them. This is non-conceptual; or put another way, language isn't playing any direct role.[10]

Taylor explains in a personal communication that

> These relevances, which J. J. Gibson calls affordances – that the ground
> affords walking, water affords drinking, holes afford hiding, and so forth –
> are clearly meaningful relative to one's interests and the structure of one's
> body, yet they do not have to be experienced conceptually, i.e. our response
> to them need not be based on beliefs. We can, on reflection, note that
> boulders are obstacles, but we can just as well respond to their current
> relevance like non-linguistic animals.

On the basis of his description of our nonconceptual coping, Taylor objects to the Davidson/Rorty claim that knowledge consists solely of beliefs
that are justified by other beliefs. He responds by contrasting this conceptual, and thus mediational, picture with a convincing description of how we
acquire perceptual knowledge that is, how our perception-based beliefs are
formed and come to be relied on.

> To show how the coherentist claim that reasoning from other beliefs is the
> only way particular beliefs can be grounded is so far from obvious as to be
> plain false, we need to step outside the mediational picture, and think in
> terms of the kind of embedded knowing which Heidegger, Merleau-Ponty,
> and Todes have thematized. Of course, we check our claims against reality.
> "Johnny go into the room and tell me whether the picture is crooked".
> Johnny emerges from the room with a view of the matter, but checking
> isn't comparing the problematized belief with his belief about the matter;
> checking is forming a belief about the matter, in this case by going and
> looking. What is assumed when we give the order is that Johnny knows,
> as most of us do, how to form a reliable view of this kind of matter. He
> knows how to go and stand at the appropriate distance and in the right
> orientation, to get what Merleau-Ponty calls a maximal grip on the object.
> What justifies[11] Johnny's belief is his being able to deal with objects in this
> way, which is, of course, inseparable from the other ways he is able to use
> them, manipulate, get around among them, etc. When he goes and checks
> he uses this multiple ability to cope, and his sense of his ability to cope gives
> him confidence in his judgment as he reports it to us.

Here Taylor is at his best. He shows that a description of our direct involvement with things is a convincing phenomenological answer to the
dogmatic claim that the mind's relation to the world must be mediated
by beliefs caused by the things in the world. Perception provides reliable
prepropositional bases for action and for accepting beliefs.

## HOW TAYLOR'S PHENOMENOLOGY SUPPORTS AND EXTENDS THE WORK OF JOHN MCDOWELL

Taylor notes the relevance of his phenomenological descriptions of everyday coping to the powerful critique of dualist epistemology mounted by John McDowell.[12]

> McDowell is struggling directly with the inner/outer split implicit in Davidson's and Rorty's account of knowledge. He argues that beliefs alone cannot have content and connect with the world, and that only perception supplies the content of beliefs about reality. He therefore attacks the sharp demarcation between the space of reasons and the space of causes.

Taylor's anti-epistemology has no place for this boundary either. His account of the formation of beliefs is meant to explain, as is McDowell's, "how it can be that the places at which our view is shaped by the world, in perception, are not just causal impingings, but are sites of the persuasive acquisition of belief."[13]

To begin with Taylor notes that:

> McDowell acknowledges that our perceptually formed beliefs are not just there as brute givens. Perception is precisely the activity whereby we have and can acquire more insight into why we have the beliefs we do. As McDowell says, the inclination "to apply some concept in judgment . . . does not just inexplicably set in. If one does make a judgment, it is wrung from one by the experience, which serves as one's reason for the judgment. In a picture in which all there is behind the judgment is a disposition to make it, the experience itself goes missing."[14]

Taylor endorses McDowell's view: "Here is a phenomenological truth; and it points up something essential in the logic of the justification of our empirical beliefs; they do not start from pure givens that we cannot get behind." This was the message in Taylor's argument centering around Johnny checking the picture.

Thus, in his description of the perceptual grounding, Taylor is entirely in agreement with McDowell. McDowell assumes, however, that to enter the space of reasons, perception must not only motivate beliefs but must justify beliefs by counting, as reasons for holding them, and so must be conceptual.[15] But, Taylor asks, if, as McDowell seems to suppose, conceptually articulated perceptions just pop into our mind, the way beliefs do for Davidson and Rorty, why should we trust some of our perceptions more than others? For example, McDowell's account does not help us understand why Johnny's belief that the picture is askew, based as it is on his getting a maximal grip on the scene, is more reliable than Johnny's belief that the moon, on which he can get no such grip, is bigger on the horizon than at the zenith.

Taylor, therefore, seeks to show how an account of the basic levels of perception and the epistemic skills involved in forming a belief would enable McDowell to understand that there are degrees of perceptual support beneath rational justification – that our propositionally formed beliefs can only arise on the basis of a more basic skillful contact with the world that is prepropositional and in part even preconceptual.

Taylor agrees with McDowell that reasoning is an exercise of a norm-guided capacity; it is thus an exercise of spontaneity in us, or otherwise put, of freedom. He notes that here McDowell is endorsing Kant: "When Kant describes the understanding as a faculty of spontaneity, that reflects his view of the relation between reason and freedom; rational necessitation is not just compatible with freedom but constitutive of it. In a slogan, the space of reasons is the realm of freedom."[16] Taylor continues to paraphrase and quote McDowell:

> Once we see the emptiness of the myth of the Given, our problem is somehow to bring this free spontaneity together with constraint. In order to stop the oscillation between the need for grounding which generates the myth of the Given, and the debunking of this myth, which leaves us with the need unfulfilled, "we need to recognize that experiences themselves are states or occurrences that inextricably combine receptivity and spontaneity";[17] we have to be able "to speak of experience as openness to the lay-out of reality. Experience enables the lay-out of reality itself to exert a rational influence on what a subject thinks."[18]

Taylor agrees with McDowell that if we want to see how constraint and spontaneity come together, we have to find this in perception. But Taylor insists that to do so, we have to bring out how our ability to form beliefs like "the picture is crooked" draw on preconceptual epistemic skills. In Taylor's estimation, the difference between him and McDowell

> seems to come down to this. We both give a crucial place to spontaneity in our most basic contact with the world; but McDowell doesn't envisage any spontaneity which is not the exercise of concepts; whereas, following Merleau-Ponty, I have been describing precisely such a sub-conceptual exercise of spontaneity in our original grasp of our world.

To make his point, Taylor transposes the basic holistic arguments drawn from Kant from their original register into the preconceptual:

> Kant developed the original holistic argument on which all previous deconstructions of mediationalism have drawn. This is the argument against the atomism of the input, which consists in showing that any particulate percept has to be related to the world in which it figures, that we have necessarily to relate bits of knowledge [*Erkenntnisse*] to their object [*Gegenstand*]. McDowell makes this same point: "The object of experience is understood as integrated into a wider reality, a reality that is all embraceable in thought but not all available in this experience".[19]

But McDowell understands this holism as based on the way our "conceptual capacities" operate, whereas for Taylor, this kind of holism already functions on the level of preconceptual experience. As evidence Taylor cites Merleau-Ponty's description of the skilled football player:

> For the player in action the football field is . . . pervaded with lines of force (the "yard lines"; those which demarcate the "penalty area") and articulated in sectors (for example, the "openings" between the adversaries) which call for a certain mode of action and which initiate and guide the action as if the player were unaware of it. The field itself is not given to him, but present as the immanent term of his practical intentions; the player becomes one with it and feels the direction of the "goal," for example, just as immediately as the vertical and the horizontal planes of his own body.[20]

For Taylor this description provides a good example of preconceptual spontaneity.

> Kant and McDowell speak of "spontaneity", because they see the knowing agent not just passively receiving impressions from the outside world, but actively construing her surroundings, making sense of them. This we certainly do by applying concepts much of the time. But clearly not all the time. The football player is actively "making sense" of the field before him, articulating it into sectors, impregnable zones, possible "openings" between adversaries, vectors of vulnerability where the other team can break through; all without benefit of concepts – the terms we've applied here are ours, not drawn from his vocabulary.

Taylor concludes:

> Spontaneity at all levels is guided by the goal of getting it right; being clearly "forced" to come to some conclusion is not its negation, but its highest fulfillment. The same intrinsic relation between spontaneity and

necessity that we see in the Kantian moral sage, and the Polanyian scientist, is visible in the lowly football player. He too is straining every faculty to get an accurate take on the ever-changing lines of force in the field. But the medium here is not moral reflection or theoretical representation, but the behavioral affordances of attack and defense.

Thus Davidson and Rorty may well be right that it is obvious that only beliefs can be *reasons* for accepting other beliefs, and maybe they are right that only beliefs can *justify* other beliefs, but McDowell and Taylor are surely right that it is a mistake to think that this shows that our only direct relation to the world is a causal one. Insofar as Davidson and Rorty ignore the actual evidence given by perceiving and take for granted that knowledge consists only in beliefs being justified by other beliefs, they seem to be captured by a form of the inner/outer mediational picture in which our beliefs are cut off from the external world. As McDowell complains, for Davidson, our beliefs are left frictionlessly "spinning in a void."[21]

In sum, McDowell sees that beliefs alone cannot have content and connect with the world; that perception is necessary to connect beliefs to reality. In assuming, however, that perception must have conceptual content in order also to connect to the spontaneity of the space of reasons, he passes over the basic epistemological skills that make the conceptual content of perception possible in the first place. If McDowell wants a full account of the relation of mind and world, including why some perceptions are more reliable than others, he needs to take on board phenomenologists such as Merleau-Ponty, Todes, and Taylor. Their account of the basic levels of perception would enable him to make the last step to an account of the reliability of our direct perceptual contact with everyday reality.

## DOES THE BRAIN-IN-A-VAT FANTASY POSE A PROBLEM FOR THE CONTACT REALIST?

So far Taylor's argument against the mind/world, inner/outer, dichotomy is on solid phenomenological ground, but he would like to go further. He would like to use the phenomenon of being-in-the-world he so convincingly describes, to cast doubt on the Descartes-inspired argument that we might, nonetheless, be brains in vats. It looks as though neuroscience calls into question any phenomenological account of our unmediated contact with an independent reality. It seems plausible to suppose that, as long as the impulses to and from the nervous system reproduce the complex feedback loop between the brain's outgoing behavior-producing impulses and the incoming perceptual ones, the person whose brain was being so stimulated would have the false belief that he was directly coming to grips with the things in the world.

To defend his view that, in coping, the agent always directly encounters the real world, Taylor thinks he has to keep open the possibility that the causal basis of being-in-the-world is not in the head, or in the whole organism, or even the organism plus a whole virtual world, but that it might turn out that the basis of our experience of coping must be in the nervous system plus the whole actual world.

To meet this challenge, Taylor begins by repeating his well taken phenomenological critique of behaviorism and cognitivism.[22] "The idea is deeply wrong that you can give a state description of the agent without any reference to his/her world (or a description of the world qua world without saying a lot about the agent)." But he then moves from the agent to the causal level:

> That's why I find the brain-in-a-vat supposition so unconvincing. It seems to me to rely on the old Cartesian separation mind/world, and just to transfer the first term into a material register. But once you take account of the embedding of practice in body-world, the whole idea gets less convincing.

Taylor therefore questions the generally accepted belief that the experience of being-in-the-world, like any experience, must be, as Searle puts it, "caused by and realized in the nervous system."[23] He responds that "maybe the minimum system which can duplicate the experience of a human being in the world is a human being in a world." But, granted that our skill for getting around in the world can only be experienced as functioning in direct contact with concrete situations, why should we need more than a virtual world to reproduce this experience? As Searle says, "[E]ach of us is precisely a brain in a vat; the vat is a skull and the 'messages' coming in are coming in by way of impacts on the nervous system."[24]

Taylor's response is that

> Experience supervenes on a whole human organism operating in its environment; that we know. Now maybe we can show that it supervenes on something less than this. But how can we know this? ... Knowing that the bodily medium is crucial doesn't tell us how it is, and therefore gives us no way of knowing how to identify bits which are crucial.

Taylor is right that the Descartes/Searle picture is by no means as obvious as current philosophers seem to suppose. But as long as Taylor admits that determining what conscious experience supervenes on is an empirical question, we have to take seriously the (admittedly far-fetched) possibility that experience could supervene on a nervous system connected to a virtual world – that, therefore, we may be brains in vats whose experiences are produced and coordinated by an intelligent computer, as in the movie *The Matrix*.[25] If this scenario is even a wildly remote empirical possibility, indeed, even if is understood only to be an intelligible possibility, it appears that the phenomenology of direct coping cannot be used to counter the epistemological claim that all of our experience of the world is indirect.[26]

This seeming conflict between neuroscience and phenomenology arises because, in Taylor's description of perception as unmediated contact with reality, he claims too much. Remember that, according to him, we can't get around in a house, a city, or the world without interacting with that house or that city. But in the brain-in-the-vat fantasy, there is no house and no city, indeed, no real world, to interact with. It seems that it is not strictly true that, as Taylor likes to quote Merleau-Ponty, "To ask if the world is real is to fail to understand what one is asking."[27] Once one has read Descartes or seen *The Matrix*, the question seems at least to make sense.

But it seems to me Taylor should not worry. Whether an agent's relation to the world is direct or mediated is a phenomenological question. It could not possibly be supported or refuted by an answer to the empirical question as to whether the processing that underlies the experience of being-in-the-world takes place in the brain, the nervous system, the organism, or the whole physical universe. All Taylor can claim, and all he needs to claim to defend his antimediationalist view, on the basis of phenomenology, is that even in the case of the brain in the vat, the people whose brains are getting virtual reality inputs correlated with their action outputs are *directly coping* with *perceived reality*. Even in *The Matrix* world, people play football with footballs, relate to chairs by sitting on them, and find their way around in their world without representing it in their mind.

The important point is that, even in the world of a brain in a vat, coping is more direct than allowed in any of the mediational views that have been held from Descartes to Rorty. On these views, the content of our beliefs can be entertained without taking a stand on the existence of the objects that would make these beliefs true. But, even if the brain-in-the-vat fantasy makes sense, Taylor can still hold the radically antimediationalist view that, no matter whether the brain is in a cranial vat in an organism coping with the world, or a ceramic vat interacting with a computer, "[t]he very idea of an inner zone with an external boundary can't get started here, because our living things in a certain relevance can't be situated 'within' the agent; it is in the interaction itself."[28] So he should still conclude that, even in *The Matrix* world, "the idea is deeply wrong that you can give a state description of the agent without any reference to his/her world (or a description of the world qua world without saying a lot about the agent)."

Another way to make this point is that one should sharply distinguish the skeptical/epistemological problem as to whether our inner mental states accurately represent what is out there in the external world from a phenomenological description of an agent's relationship to the world. The issue for Taylor should not be whether the world is as we *believe* it to be. That is Cartesian doubt. The phenomenological point is that our direct contact with the perceptual world is more basic than belief. So when Merleau-Ponty says that to ask if the world is real is to fail to understand what one is asking, he must mean that, even in *The Matrix* world, at the basic level of involved skillful coping, people would still be "empty heads turned towards one single self-evident world where everything takes place."[29] Thus, Taylor's phenomenological account of being-in-the-world and his consequent critique of mediationalism is untouched by the conceivability of our being a brain in a vat.[30]

## THE REAL PROBLEM: ANTI-EPISTEMOLOGY AS ANTIREALISM

Paradoxically, however, once we recognize that in perception we directly encounter everyday perceptual objects on the background of our unmediated embedding in the everyday perceptual world, it looks as though we can no longer make sense of the idea that we are capable of knowing things as they are in themselves, that is, independently of the way they make sense to us in our embodied interaction with them. It seems that, at the primordial, preconceptual level of perception and action, we are confined to the cross-cultural clearing opened up by our ability to respond to affordances, and, at a higher level, we are imprisoned in the general style of our culture's coping practices. Indeed, just insofar as our everyday coping practices give us direct access to our world, they seem to block access to, indeed, make unintelligible, the very idea of access to the universe as it is in itself.

Rorty is happy to embrace this consequence. He holds that we are confined to what can be encountered on the basis of our coping practices.[31] We therefore shouldn't think of science as a way of discovering propositions that correspond to an independent reality, and, fortunately, we don't need to. Embedded coping is the only realism we can make sense of, and all the realism we need to make sense of science. Taylor, however, although following Merleau-Ponty in thinking of our relation to the everyday world as a "co-production,"[32] also wishes to defend a robust realist view of science as giving us access to things as they are in themselves, independent of their relation to our bodily and cultural coping skills. Rorty highlights his opposition to Taylor on this point:

> Realism becomes interesting only when we supplement plain speech and common sense with the "in itself" versus "to us" distinction. Taylor... thinks that this latter distinction cannot simply be walked away from but must be dealt with. I think neither he nor anyone else has explained why we cannot just walk away from it. Such an explanation would have to tell us more than we have ever before been told about what good the distinction is supposed to do us. I keep hoping that Taylor, as fervent an anti-Cartesian as I, will join me in abandoning it. Alas, he persists in agreeing with Bernard Williams, . . . and other admirers of Descartes that it is indispensable.[33]

Here we have the parting of the ways between two views. On the one hand we have Rorty's, which I shall call *deflationary realism*, that claims that the objects of science are only intelligible on the background of our embedded coping, so that the idea of a view from nowhere is literally unintelligible. On the other hand there is Taylor's view, which I shall call *robust realism*, which claims that, to understand the status of the structures studied by natural science, we have to make sense of an absolutely independent reality. From the perspective of the robust realist, deflationary realism is a kind of antirealism that succumbs to a new inner/outer distinction.

Rorty holds that stressing being-in-the-*world* blocks direct access to the *universe*. How can Taylor defend the seemingly contradictory claims that the primordial and unavoidable significances of things are or are connected to our bodily existence in the world, and that, nonetheless, we can make sense of a science of the components of the universe as they are in themselves, utterly independent of any relation to our embodiment?

Taylor responds that:

> Our humanity consists in our ability to decenter ourselves from our original mode of absorbed coping; to learn to see things in a disengaged fashion, in universal terms, or from an alien or "higher" point of view. The peculiar form that this takes in Western scientific culture is the attempt to achieve, at least notionally, a "view from nowhere", or to describe things from the "absolute standpoint". Only we have to see that this decentered mode,

whatever form it takes, is in an important sense derivative. The absorbed, engaged one is prior and pervasive.

But such a response raises more questions than it answers. If the engaged experience is primordial and the disengaged mode is derivative from the engaged one, what sort of view from nowhere can we hope to achieve or even approach? It seems to follow, rather, that whatever we can encounter is a function of the kinds of bodies and needs we ineluctably have. If, for example, our body structures our experience of spatiality and temporality as Merleau-Ponty contends, Todes works out, and Taylor accepts, how can we prescind from our bodily-relative sense of reality and still have a science of the motions of objects in the spacio-temporal universe? How could Taylor's view be anything but a refined variant of deflationary realism?[34]

Indeed, Taylor seems to make exactly the deflationary move he wants to resist when he says that:

> The mediational view provides the context in which the whole complex of issues around "realism" and "anti-realism" make sense. They lose this sense if you escape from this construal, as Heidegger and Merleau-Ponty have done. Or perhaps better put, one awakes to an unproblematic realism, no longer a daring philosophical "thesis".

This sounds exactly like Rorty's reading of Heidegger and Merleau-Ponty. Indeed, it looks as though Taylor's "unproblematic realism" concerning the things that we ordinarily cope with – things that would not be the sort of spacio-temporal things they are independent of our embodied coping – when made the basis of a "realism" concerning the universe, is precisely deflationary realism.

As Rorty puts it "Taylor thinks that once one gets out from under epistemology one comes to an 'uncompromising realism.' I think one comes to a position in which the only version of 'realism' one has left is the trivial, uninteresting, and commonsensical one which says that all true beliefs are true because things are as they are."[35] So, according to Rorty, there is nothing more one can say about what makes the propositions of science true than we can say about what makes the claims we make about baseballs true. They both report how things are, and they both depend on our embedding. It is, thus, not only false but unintelligible to hold, as Bernard Williams, Thomas Nagel, and Taylor do, that truths about baseballs depend on our bodies and our cultural agreements, whereas the truths of science describe things as they are totally independently of us and our everyday way of making sense of things.

If all we can say about our scientific truth claims is they are no more nor less relative to our sense-giving capacities than our everyday truth claims, it's hard to understand how Taylor's account of our direct embodied encounter with everyday reality is supposed to make the idea of a view from nowhere even notionally intelligible. The emphasis on a background of intelligibility correlative with our bodily structure would seem to argue for just the opposite conclusion – a view from somewhere, namely, from within our embodied embedding. In comparison with robust realism's thesis that science studies things as they are independently of us, unproblematic realism does not seem to be realism at all. Indeed, unproblematic realism with respect to the everyday world makes realism concerning the universe highly problematic.

This is where Taylor makes an original move that diverges not only from Rorty but also, in different ways, from the existential phenomenologists he generally agrees with, and even from some of his own claims. He tells us that:

> If we see that our grasp of things is primordially one of bodily engagement with them, then we can see that we are in contact with the reality which surrounds us *at a deeper level than any description or significance-attribution* we might make of this reality, and that this dissolves the temptations to anti-realism.

That is, significance depends on our coping, but, in coping, we sense we are in touch with a reality more basic than significance. It remains to be seen, however, if this reality beneath significance is more than the brute causality independent of any description invoked by Rorty; whether it has the structure attributed to it by science.

As we have seen, Taylor points out that even when I'm thinking about something else, my body takes account of obstacles such as boulders and the like without my needing to be aware of them at all. This gives us an ahistorical, cross-cultural commonality with all creatures that have bodies of roughly our size, shape, and power, no matter how, on reflection, they classify boulders – whether in their world boulders are sacred objects, lookout towers, or simply rocks that get in the way of climbing. But this still leaves unclear how a cross-cultural experience of obstruction, for example, could in any way justify the claim that, in responding to affordances, one is responding in a direct way to how the universe is in itself independent of all our significance attributions. No one could doubt that the significance of boulders as obstructions depends on our kinds of bodies and our kinds of desires.

So we still need to understand how, what is experienced in perception at a level deeper than significance, is the real as it is in itself. Taylor explains that "The most fundamental, rock-bottom feature of our general take on the world is that it surrounds us, gives us things, but also withholds, threatens to annihilate or hurt us sometimes, allows us to do some things, and resists others." But again one wonders why "surrounding," "giving," "withholding," "threatening," and "resisting" are the way things are in themselves rather than our way of making sense of them. A better case for our getting in touch with the way things are in themselves is offered by Todes. He points out that our experience of having to balance in a gravitational field gives us the sense of a force independent of us that we have to conform to, a force which sustains our coping only if, by balancing, we relate to it on its terms.[36] But again one can ask whether our relation to this force as something that pulls us down but also enables us to stand up, isn't our way of making sense of nature in our world, rather than an experience of how the universe is in itself.

In each of the above experiences we make sense of the experience as something that conditions us, sets boundary conditions on our ability to cope, and thereby reveals something outside our coping powers. But in so doing we have not yet arrived at a primordial bodily "contact with the reality which surrounds us *at a deeper level* than any description or significance-attribution we might make of this reality." We have only arrived at the paradoxical significance attribution of something that somehow exceeds our significance attribution. This is certainly not enough to dissolve "the temptations to anti-realism."

It looks as though whatever is independent of us is so inextricably bound up with our coping capacities that it can only be understood as a boundary condition on our activity. But natural science doesn't just run up against the boundaries of our coping, it claims to reveal the intelligible structure of the universe as it is in itself. If all that active perception gave us were a sense of something independent of us that set limits to our coping, we would not be able to describe the universe from nowhere, and we would be left with deflationary or internal realism – science at best describing what Merleau-Ponty calls "the in itself for us."[37]

But Taylor's novel approach only begins with the above account of our encounter with the sustaining and threatening phenomena that condition our coping. He turns from his description of the otherness revealed by all coping to an even-more-overlooked component of our primordial perceptual experience, namely, that, in skillful coping, as in balancing in the vertical field or climbing over boulders, our skill consists in getting in sync with the structure of the universe the better to cope with it. Consider what is involved in grasping and drinking from a glass that lies to hand. To begin with, I have to see the glass. This is no mean feat. To perceive at all, we have to align ourselves with the causal powers of the universe. As embodied beings, we have to face what we are looking at, move to an appropriate distance given the size of the object, and assure an unencumbered line of sight to it. In this way, our embodied skill spontaneously takes account of the fact that, as the causal theory of perception makes clear, in order to see an object, we have to be in a position for our eyes to be causally acted upon by light from it.

Thus, the universe constrains us, and rewards us with sight only insofar as we conform to its causal structures. But we are so skilled at getting an optimal take on things that, unless there is some disturbance, we overlook the fact that we once had to learn to align ourselves with the constraints of nature in order to perceive. In general, the universe solicits us to get a better and better grip on its causal structure, and rewards us with more and more successful coping. Our coping skills thus put us in touch with *the structure* of the causal powers of nature, not just its brute impinging, thereby bridging the gap between the meaningless brute causal influence acknowledged by Rorty and our perception of a meaningful perceptual world accepted by McDowell.

Taylor is thus able to specify the way in which perception gives us access to the causal structure of the universe, revealed in our way of making sense of things, but independent of our everyday significance attributions. One can only see this if one uses phenomenology to uncover the coping skills covered up by the conceptually permeated perceptual world where analysis normally starts. Only by accepting Rorty's challenge that he tell more than we have been told before in the history of philosophy, is Taylor able to show us what philosophers close to common sense like Aristotle have suspected all along: that we experience ourselves as perceptually in touch with the cosmos. But we can only understand how we are normally in touch with things in themselves when we see that we are not disembodied, detached contemplators, but rather, embodied, involved coping agents.[38]

## SUPERSESSION

To understand Taylor's robust realism vis-à-vis science, we now need to extend his claim that in our everyday coping experience we sense that we are in contact with a nature with a structure of its own that supports our coping, to the stronger claim that it makes sense to think we can correctly describe that structure and that, indeed, there is evidence that our current science may well be progressively getting it right about (at least some aspects of) the universe. To do so, we need to introduce and defend Taylor's account of supersession.

Taylor begins by reminding us that when we confront anomalies in our perceptual experience, we know how to find out what's wrong with our current understanding and improve it. If we enter a cafe that seems too large for the building it is in, we are confused until we resolve this anomaly by noting that the walls are covered by mirrors. Then things snap into place, and our confused, partial perceptual grasp becomes clear and secure. As we explore a city, we gain a more and more perspicuous understanding of it; we are no longer surprised and disoriented at each turn. In general, in our everyday perceptual encounters with the world, we are solicited to move toward an ever more clear and secure grasp of our surroundings.

In understanding other cultures, this process of moving from confusion to clarity is much more difficult. Thanks to our shared embodiment, however, we can make some progress toward an understanding of what is going on in another culture by noticing that its members respond to many of the same affordances we do. But we may nonetheless find that their understanding of the sacred, to take Taylor's favorite example, makes no sense to us. How could the Aztecs in a sacred service tear out and eat the heart of sacrificial victims, who, strangely, don't even think of themselves as victims, but seem to be honored by thus being killed? Taylor points out that we cannot even be sure that "sacred," "sacrifice," and "honor" are the appropriate terms here. He tells us that in such cases:

> What is needed is not the Davidsonian "principle of charity," which means: make the best sense of them in what we understand as sense; but rather: coming to understand that there is a very different way of understanding human life, the cosmos, the holy, etc. Somewhere along the line, you need some place in your ontology for something like "the Aztec way of seeing things", in contrast to "our way of seeing things"; in short, something like the scheme/content distinction.

But this pluralism need not lead to antirealism. According to Taylor, we have a sense that we are open to something that is independent of any of our interpretations – something that sets limits on what takes on reality are livable. We can thus accept that there are radically different cultural understandings of being, and yet rank their relation to reality. Thus Taylor continues:

> We can see how the embedded view offers resources for recognizing differences of scheme, without generating arguments for non-realism. There may be (and obviously are) differences, alternative takes on and construals of reality, which may even be systematic and far-reaching. Some of these will be, all may be, wrong. But any such take or construal is within the context of a basic engagement with or understanding of the world. It is in virtue of this contact with a common world that we always have something to say to each other, something to point to in disputes about reality.

All the various cultural interpretations are *for us*, so what Taylor rightly considers realism with respect to cultural styles, looks like antirealism with respect to science. But it turns out that science has its own internally generated way of progressing. Rather than accepting with Heidegger and Thomas Kuhn that the worlds of Aristotle and Galileo can't be compared because they were asking different questions, Taylor looks for the specific anomalies that Aristotelians ran up against that Galileo could account for – in this case that missiles from catapults and guns don't head straight for their natural place at the center of the earth, but follow a parabolic path. Or, to take a simpler example, by assuming that the earth moves rather than the sun, Copernicus could give a more perspicuous account of the motion of the heavenly bodies than epicycle theorists could, and astronomers could then see that the sun could better be understood as a star than as a planet.

Moreover, Taylor points out, even the cultural background understandings on which the methods of science are based can progress. He notes that Kepler's success in getting a more complete and clear grasp of astronomical phenomena showed that the Aristotelian background understanding that one could not, and should not, try to account for all phenomena – both terrestrial and superlunary – in the same way, could be improved on. That undermined the Greek understanding of science as *empiria*, just as Galileo's findings undermined the medieval idea of *scientia*, and eventually led to the modern understanding of science as research. As Heidegger points out, research differs from scientia and empiria in proposing a universal ground plan and then trying to fit all phenomena, even those that look like anomalies, into that plan, rather than just dismissing anomalies as unnatural events, monsters, or miracles.[39] This new understanding of science as world-picturing, in turn, gave us a more coherent and powerful understanding of nature. More phenomena could be lawfully related according to the Newtonian ground plan than by Aristotelian generalizations from everyday experience.

In this way, according to Taylor, we can see that scientific revolutions are cases of supersession. If new overall conceptions are not immediately accepted it is because the older view is entrenched, not because the proposed changes are not rationally motivated. The proof that one view is superior to another, Taylor holds, is that once one understands the new overall way of looking at things in science, as in the case of the mirrors on the café walls, there is no way of going back and accepting one's former understanding. Thus, the direct coping that gets us in touch with a shared everyday world, and gives us a sense of an independent nature that sets limits to what we can do unless we get in sync with it, puts us on a path that leads to theories that correspond more and more adequately to the structure of the universe.

## TAYLOR VERSUS RORTY ON TRUTH

Rorty, however, thinks one can accept Taylor's account of supersession in science, namely that science progresses by accounting for anomalies and thereby giving a more and more coherent account of the phenomena, without accepting Taylor's claim that science thereby arrives at theories that correspond better to an independent reality. As Rorty puts it, "Believers in the correspondence theory have to claim that some vocabularies (e.g. Newton's) do not just work better than others (e.g., Aristotle's) but do so because they represent reality more adequately. Taylor thinks that good sense can be made of this claim, and I do not."[40]

Taylor's first response to Rorty on this point is simply to defend the correspondence theory of truth as our unproblematic commonsense understanding of the way we check our assertions against the facts.

> Lots of simple everyday sentences are meant to communicate the way things are; they give a "picture" of how things stand, and they are correct if the way things really stand corresponds to this picture. It is in this common and well-understood sense that many ordinary indicative sentences "represent" what they're about: there are 15 chairs in this room. Well, are there really? – Count them.

This disarmingly simple example of counting the chairs in the room is full of problems, however, as Taylor, given his interest in Wittgenstein, surely recognizes. How many chairs there are in a given room depends on the interests of the one counting them. If I want to seat students right now, then I don't want to count broken chairs and those in boxes waiting to be assembled. Or maybe I'll count the broken chairs, too, if they are not so badly damaged that one can't sit on them in a normal way. But, if I'm determining how many students the classroom will seat next semester, I'll count the unassembled chairs, too (but still not the badly broken ones). Of course, I can always spell out the assertion whose truth I want to check so as to avoid this sort of contextual under-determination. "Johnny, how many *currently usable* chairs are there in the room?" But, as Wittgenstein points out, one can never build the whole background into the explicit proposition whose truth can be spelled out so that it is convincing. Truth amounts to correspondence between our description of the facts relative to our interests and the facts themselves.

As a deflationary realist, Rorty is happy to take over the way Taylor's realistic account of truth as simple correspondence seems to level the difference between truths about the things in the world like chairs that are relative to our background concerns, and truths about the stuff in the universe that allegedly are not. Rorty simply levels the difference in the opposite direction from Taylor and argues that, since the truth about chairs requires a shared commonsense background, so must the truth about neutrinos:

> Taylor seems to think that neither I nor any one else would feel any "serious temptation to deny that the no chairs claim ["There are no chairs in this room"] will be true or false in virtue of the way things are, or the nature of reality." But I do, in fact, feel tempted to deny this. I do so because I see two ways of interpreting "in virtue of the way things are." One is short for "in virtue of the way our current descriptions of things are used and the causal interactions we have with those things." The other is short for "simply in virtue of the way things are, quite apart from how we describe them." On the first interpretation, I think that true propositions about the presence of chairs, the existence of neutrinos, the desirability of respect for the dignity of our fellow human beings, and everything else are true "in virtue of the way things are." On the second interpretation, I think that no proposition is true "in virtue of the way things are."[41]

To resist Rorty's leveling of the world and the universe, Taylor would have to highlight the difference between the way correspondence works in the everyday world and in science. He could point out that, unlike the number of chairs, how many neutrinos there are in a given space does not depend on how they fit with our everyday practices or what anyone, even the scientist who makes the claim, wants to do with them. The development of science shows that science gets better and better at what Heidegger calls deworlding, and that, where science is concerned, supersession leads us from relatively contextually determined (worldly) truth claims to relatively context-free (deworlded) truth claims about features of the universe as it is in itself.[42] (Not that we can ever be certain that the entities dealt with by our current science are fully deworlded.)

It might have turned out that all we could know about the independent structure of the universe was relative to our background understanding of the boundary conditions it placed on our activity. But Taylor reminds us that Galileo and company discovered that we could bracket our direct, embodied experience of the everyday world, leaving out more and more of the significance of things that depends on our social practices; as well as prescinding (as Taylor puts it) from the properties of everyday things that depend on our senses and on the shape and capacities of our bodies. We are able thereby to discover and investigate a physical universe with no perceptible things with their colors, orientation, solidity, weight, and so forth, where there is no near and far, no up and down, and no earlier and later. Moreover, it happily turned out that this deworlding, as Heidegger calls it, was not merely a negative accomplishment, but that, when we left behind the world of everyday experience, we discovered universal causal laws, and natural kinds some of whose properties explained why the kinds in question were describable by just those causal laws.

But to see that some theories don't just "work better than others" in some general pragmatist way, but that we need to and can make sense of the claim that some theories fit the universe better than others, we again have to go back to our sense of embodied coping. Taylor notes that

> if we were to take our beliefs as given and warranted only by other beliefs and didn't investigate how these beliefs were formed, Rorty would be right that a correspondence theory of truth adds nothing to what we already say when we affirm the truths of science. But this doesn't mean that talk of correspondence doesn't say anything important. If it adds nothing, it is because the understanding that our claims to truth are grounded in our epistemic skills for getting a grip on reality is an implicit part of the background understanding that underlies our pursuit of science.

Taylor points out that "the things that show up for us as obstacles, supports, facilitators, in short as affordances, have as it were an ontic solidity and depth." They have what philosophy will later call their "nature," which we have to respect and adjust ourselves to. Just insofar as coping requires this adaptation, and our actions confirm that we are getting a better and better grip on nature, correspondence makes sense to us as a way of describing our relation to reality.

Only when our theories about nature have been arrived at step by superseding step, following the demand for clarity and control that was implicit in our original perceptual encounter with an independent reality, have we the right to claim correspondence for our theories. Approaching pure correspondence – the view from nowhere – means approaching the goal of getting a maximum grip on the universe, thus satisfying the call for a clairvoyant account of reality that, from the start, drew us toward an increasingly encompassing and refined grasp of the independent reality that supports our coping.

To sum up, Taylor holds that our experience of our body's engaged coping has four basic, interrelated, characteristics that ground intelligibility – both that of the everyday world and that of the universe as revealed by science. *First*, we experience ourselves as open to the real. As Taylor puts it: "The reality of contact with the real world is the inescapable fact of human (or animal) life, and can only be imagined away by erroneous philosophical argument."[43] *Second*, we experience whatever we encounter as having aspects that go beyond what we can grasp at present. This is not just a fact about the things we perceive but, as Merleau-Ponty points out, a fundamental structure of perception. *Third*, we are drawn to make sense of things, to move toward getting a more and more coherent, and encompassing grip on them – as Merleau-Ponty puts it, "we are condemned to meaning."[44] As we have seen, Taylor calls this progressive movement toward making more and more sense, not only of the everyday world but also of reality in general, supersession. *Fourth*, in the process of gaining a more and more clairvoyant grip on our everyday world, we have discovered that we can leave behind all body-relative properties such as accessibility, color, size, and even the sort of everyday spatiality and temporality that are intelligible only on the basis of our embodied coping. We thereby gain the possibility of a theoretical grasp of physical reality that is alien to our everyday embodied mode of perception of space, time, objects, and causality, and which, for that very reason, could claim to correspond to the universe as it is in itself.

Note that Taylor is arguing against the deflationary realist and so only needs to claim that, given our coping experience, robust realism concerning science is intelligible – that it makes sense to think of science as attempting to describe the universe as it is in itself. He does not have to hold that our current science is getting it right about the universe or that any science will ever get it right; nor does he have to claim that we could ever know for sure whether the current science is in fact on the right track. These are epistemological questions, whereas Taylor and Rorty are concerned with the ontological question as to the mode of being of the entities studied by science.

Taylor go further, however. As we have just seen, he argues convincingly that, given our science's supersession claims, it makes sense to hold that our science is in fact zeroing in on (one aspect of) the physical universe as it is in itself. Taylor goes beyond deflationary realism by showing how (1) our primordial embodied and embedded grasp of reality, far from standing in the way of robust realism, makes intelligible how our body, cultural history, and language give us access to a universe whose intelligibility in no way depends on any structures of our embodied way of being in the world; and (2) supersession supports the view that we may well be learning more and more about the causal structure of that universe as it is in itself.

## TAYLOR'S PLURALIST ROBUST REALISM

Still, deflationary realists such as Rorty can persist. It looks as though no description of our direct embodied encounter with everyday reality, even if that reality is experienced as independent and inexhaustible, could make the idea of a view from nowhere intelligible. Taylor's emphasis on a background of intelligibility correlative with our bodily structure would seem to argue for just the opposite – a view from within our embodied embedding. Rorty contends that, granted we experience the causal character of the boundary conditions to which we must conform, how the structure of these boundary conditions is to be described must always be relative to our vocabulary, practices, and bodily coping capacities. Thus Rorty thinks he has the right to reject Taylor's realism on the grounds that the idea of a correct description that corresponds to the structure of the universe as it is in itself makes no sense. His actual argument, however, consists in ridiculing the idea that the universe has a language of its own. And, of course, the universe doesn't speak. But, all the same, the universe could have a structure whose essential properties were definable in a language it led scientists to adopt.

But how could the universe possibly have its own proper description? And how could it lead us to better and better ones? Taylor answers that it could if there were natural kinds with essential properties, and if we could designate the kinds we encounter by means of a provisional mode of reference using everyday language that remained noncommittal as to which, if any, of the descriptions we use to refer to the kind in question were essential to it. Both Heidegger and Saul Kripke have defended versions of this idea.[45]

So, to take two of Kripke's well-known examples, we could start by investigating some shiny gold-colored stuff and eventually find out that its essence is to have an atomic number of 79, regardless of whether or not it is gold-colored. Or we could provisionally identify lightning as a flash of light in the night sky and eventually find out that it is essentially an electrical discharge even when we can't see it. Thus, a purported natural kind is first designated by a description that points out an instance of it – that yellow stuff. This pointing fixes the reference but does not commit the designator to the claim that the description used in pointing out the kind has grasped the kind's essential property – the property that causally explains all the other physical properties. Thus, the initial description, although relative to our everyday language, interests, and capacities, leaves open the possibility that investigation may discover the kind's essential properties. In this way, Kripke shows that the way demonstrative reference works makes intelligible the idea of an access to natural kinds (if there are any) whose essential properties we can describe in a language appropriate to them.

Rorty would be quick to point out, however, that the question of the relativity of descriptions reappears in our understanding of what counts as an essential property. Must an essential property of a kind explain all and only the causal properties interesting to physics? If so, the essential property of gold may well, indeed, be having an atomic number of 79. But Taylor, with his openness to other cultures having an understanding of nature different from ours, would not want to accept this Kripkean view, since it follows from it that most of the beliefs about nature held by people in other cultures are false. Take gold, for example. For our science, its essential property is the one that explains how it falls under a large number of universal causal laws that explain its ductility, conductivity, malleability, solubility, capacity to form certain compounds and not others, and so forth. But for another culture, say the Ancient Egyptians, gold's essential property might have been that it was sacred and so shone with divine radiance. How can Taylor claim that true scientific assertions pick out the essential properties of things as they are in themselves, without accepting the implication of Kripke's scientific realism, that, insofar as our scientific understanding of nature is true, the understanding of nature of cultures that don't share our understanding must be false, that, for example, the Ancient Egyptian understanding that the essential property of gold is the sacred powers that cause its radiance is simply mistaken?

To begin with, we have to remember that ours may well be the only culture that claims that, if true, our theories concerning the kinds of entities in the universe correspond to those kinds as they are in themselves. Other cultures do not ask about the universe as it is in itself, in the sense of modern Western science. They have no notion of a view from nowhere. Only because we have such a notion are we committed to the claim that our definition of natural kind terms captures the meaning of these terms for anyone correctly using them any time anywhere.

Granted that our scientific understanding, if true, would be true in the world of the Egyptians even though they couldn't understand it, it doesn't follow, that what they meant by gold is determined by our science. Not that they had a rival universal account of gold as a natural kind. but neither were they deflationary realists *avant la lettre*. Gold being sacred presumably was not understood as relative to their description of it, but neither was gold's sacredness understood as a universal truth about gold that all must acknowledge. Presumably, for them, gold being sacred revealed one aspect of it not necessarily revealed from any other perspective. This is presumably how the Homeric Greeks and the Native American tribes viewed the different gods worshipped by themselves and their neighbors. They presumably sensed that they neither discovered nor invented their classification of things and their gods, but drew on their form of life to reveal nature and its kinds from their own perspective. They thus implicitly took for granted that the way nature is revealed depends on what Heidegger calls "different kinds of seeing and questioning natural events."[46]

The deflationary realist correctly believes that once world disclosing is recognized it would be mistaken to claim, as Kripke does, that the descriptions of natural kinds relied on in each particular world must either correspond to the structure of the universe as it is in itself, or be false.[47] But it doesn't follow that one has to give up a robust understanding of correspondence. Our scientific theory, if true, tells us what the property of gold that accounts for its other physical properties is, but this needn't be the whole story. As Heidegger puts it: "The statements of physics are correct. By means of them, science represents something real, by which it is objectively controlled. But . . . science always encounters only what *its* kind of representation has admitted beforehand as an object possible for science."[48] On this view, the Egyptians' understanding of the essential property of gold, if true, would also correspond to or reveal an aspect of nature.

Given his understanding of supersession, Taylor would claim that we could, at least in principle, have taught the Ancient Egyptians our science, and with it the distinction between the in-itself and the for-us. They could then see both that gold is a natural kind in our sense with its essential property being an atomic number of 79, and that our disenchanted understanding of nature overlooks the fact that nature is sacred, and its kinds have a sacred essence our science can't see. Even a view from nowhere of things as they are in themselves is only one limited way of disclosing them. Again, as Heidegger puts it, "What is represented by physics is indeed nature itself, but undeniably it is only nature as the object-area, whose objectness is first defined and determined through the refining that is characteristic of physics."[49]

Thus, whereas gold's physical property of being untarnishable is *causally* explained in terms of universal laws by our science and its view from nowhere, gold's essential sacred property of shining with divine radiance may only be accessible to Egyptian religious practices.[50] The kind of correspondence claim implicit in the practices of premodern cultures, if spelled out, would then amount to the claim that they have practices for gaining a perspective on reality that corresponds to one aspect of reality without claiming to have a view from nowhere that reveals objective reality as it is in itself. The aspect such practices revealed might have causal properties that could only be activated by those specific practices, and so would not be discoverable by a disenchanted science with a view from nowhere. Hence, what might seem a mystery or even an impossibility from the standpoint of our science might have a causal explanation within a given set of practices that reveal another type of causality. In the most extreme conceivable case, these culturally activated causal properties might even override the causal properties discovered by our science. If confirmed, repeatable levitation would be such a case and, our physics would then have to be revised to take account of such a phenomenon.[51]

All this leads to the conclusion that, although according to our disenchanted science it is true everywhere, whether or not anyone knows or cares about it, that gold has an atomic number of 79 since this property explains all the causal properties our science can see, it is only relative to our disenchanted way of questioning natural events that having an atomic weight of 79 is taken to be the essential property of gold. More generally, there is no single essential property of gold. Given the above considerations one has to be a plural realist where essences are concerned.

Furthermore, although we don't at present know of any alternative irreducible theories of nature as it is in itself, there is much we don't understand, and there may be other ways of getting at universal causal properties that Western science can't grasp. The success of acupuncture has so far resisted all attempts to understand it in terms of Western medicine, and we may simply have to accept two accounts of the body, one in terms of molecules and electrical impulses, and another that plots the paths of a kind of energy that can't be understood in terms of our current physics. We may also be seeing signs of a need for two independent accounts of reality, one describing those aspects of nature revealed to detached observors as it is in itself and another account of reality as it is revealed to involved human beings. Scientists and philosophers have, after all, so far failed to reconcile mechanical theories of physical reality with the seemingly undeniable facts of free will, consciousness, and meaning. Convergence in all these cases would certainly be satisfying and would reassure us that our theories describe an independent reality, but we have to leave open the possibly that there is no single privileged way the universe works.

Because he has broken free of the last version of the inner/outer mediational picture – the claim that we must be imprisoned in our description of reality – Taylor can agree with Rorty that there is no *one* language for correctly describing the universe, while holding, contra Rorty, that there could well be *many* languages each correctly describing a different aspect of reality. Taylor's anti-epistemology could then be characterized as pluralistic robust realism.

### Notes

1. Edmund Husserl, *Cartesian Meditations: An Introduction to Phenomenology*. Dorion Cairns (trans.), The Hague: Martinus Nijhoff, 1960.
2. Letter to Gibieuf of 19 January 1642; English version in *Descartes: Philosophical Letters*. Anthony Kenny (trans.), Oxford: Oxford University Press 1970, p. 123.
3. As Taylor has not yet published his detailed phenomenological alternative to current epistemology, which is tentatively entitled *Retrieving Realism*, I'll be quoting at length from personal communications on the subject unless otherwise noted.
4. See Martin Heidegger, *Being and Time*. J. Macquarrie and E. Robinson (trans.), Oxford: Blackwell, 1962; Maurice Merleau-Ponty, *Phenomenology of Perception*. C. Smith (trans.), London: Routledge, 1962, and Samuel Todes, *Body and World*. Cambridge, MA: M.I.T. Press, 2001.
5. Martin Heidegger, *Being and Time*. J. Macquarrie and E. Robinson (trans.), Oxford: Blackwell, 1962, p. 405.
6. Charles Taylor, "Overcoming Epistemology" in *Philosophical Arguments*, Cambridge, MA: Harvard University Press, 1995, p. 12. Emphasis in the original.
7. Richard Rorty. *Philosophy and the Mirror of Nature*, Princeton: Princeton University Press, 1979, p. 178.
8. "A Coherence Theory of Truth and Knowledge" in Ernest Lepore (ed.), *Truth and Interpretation: Perspectives on the Philosophy of Donald Davidson*, Oxford: Blackwell, 1992, p. 310.
9. Ibid.

10. Charles Taylor, "Foundationalism and the Inner-Outer Distinction" in *Reading McDowell on Mind and World*. Nicholas H. Smith (ed.), London: Routledge, 2002, p. 111.

11. If one takes justifying to be giving reasons for holding his belief, it does seem plausible to hold with philosophers like Davidson and Rorty that, in using his perceptual skill, Johnny would not be justifying his assertion that the picture was crooked, but, rather, Johnny has acquired the nonpropositional perceptual experience of the picture's being askew, and the disposition to act and judge accordingly. What is at stake philosophically is whether or not there is another way of *grounding* a belief than basing it on another already-accepted belief. On the view Taylor is defending, beliefs concerning the perceived world are grounded when we achieve a maximal grip on the object in question. Merleau-Ponty calls this relation of support "motivation." See Mark Wrathall, "Motives, Reasons and Causes," *Cambridge Companion to Merleau-Ponty*. Taylor Carman (ed.), Cambridge, U.K.: Cambridge University Press, forthcoming.

12. John McDowell, *Mind and World*, Cambridge, MA: Harvard University Press, 1993.

13. "Foundationalism and the Inner-Outer Distinction" in *Reading McDowell on Mind and World* Nicholas H. Smith (ed.), London: Routledge, 2002, p. 113.

14. John McDowell, *Mind and World*, Cambridge, MA:. Harvard University Press, 1993, p. 61. McDowell's description helps one understand why Merleau-Ponty calls this kind of grounding, "motivation." His argument also runs very close to Taylor's here, including his critical treatment of the same paper by Davidson, and even his citing the same quotations about the impossibility of getting beyond beliefs, and not being able to jump out of our skins. Ibid. Lecture I, sect 6. For Davidson, see "A Coherence Theory of Truth and Knowledge" in Ernest Lepore (ed.), *Truth and Interpretation: Perspectives on the Philosophy of Donald Davidson*, Oxford: Blackwell, 1992, pp. 307–19.

15. For instance, when he says things like the following: "But we really cannot understand the relations in virtue of which a judgment is warranted except as relations within the space of concepts: relations such as implication or proba-bilification, which hold between potential exercises of conceptual capacities." John McDowell, *Mind and World*, Cambridge, MA: Harvard University Press, 1993, p. 7. The "exercises" referred to here surely must be propositional.

16. Ibid., p. 5.

17. Ibid., p. 24.

18. Ibid., p. 26.

19. Ibid., p. 32.

20. Maurice Merleau-Ponty, *The Structure of Behavior*. A. L. Fisher (trans.), Pittsburgh: Duquesne University Press, 1983.

21. John McDowell, *Mind and World*, Cambridge, MA: Harvard University Press, 1993, p. 66.

22. See Charles Taylor, *The Explanation of Behavior*, London: Routledge and Kegan Paul, 1964, and "Overcoming Epistemology" in *Philosophical Arguments*, Cambridge, MA: Harvard University Press, 1995, pp. 1–19.

23. John Searle, *Minds, Brains, and Science*, London: Penguin, 1989, p. 21.

24. John Searle, *Intentionality: An Essay in the Philosophy of Mind*, Cambridge, U.K.: Cambridge University Press, 1983, p. 230.

25. As far as the issues here are concerned, we can ignore the question whether what is doing the processing is the brain or the whole nervous system. So, for the sake of simplicity, I'll refer to the brain.

26. Phenomenological evidence could perhaps be used to argue that the action/perception feedback loop between the agent and the world (what Merleau-Ponty calls the intentional arc) and the sense of relevance it generates is too ramified and open-ended to be simulated by a virtual reality program. Taylor's holistic doubts on this point are certainly well taken but not relevant here.

27. Maurice Merleau-Ponty, *Phenomenology of Perception*. Christopher Smith (trans.), London: Routledge, 1962, p. 344.

28. Charles Taylor, "Foundationalism and the Inner-Outer distinction" in *Reading McDowell on Mind and World* Nicholas H. Smith (ed.), London: Routledge, 2002, p. 114.

29. Maurice Merleau-Ponty, *Phenomenology of Perception*. Christopher Smith (trans.), London: Routledge, 1962, p. 355.

30. Whether the *beliefs* of a brain in a vat would be *false*, and if so, what the implications for the contact realist are, is a separate and more complicated question that must await my discussion of Taylor's account of truth.

31. Rorty insists that speaking of *propositions* corresponding to reality is a misleading way of speaking of our everyday activity in that it calls up a representationalist picture that pragmatists can and should leave behind. He says: "I do not think that either language or knowledge has anything to do with picturing, representing, or corresponding, and so I see formulating and verifying propositions as just a special case of what Taylor calls 'dealing' and I call 'coping.' "Charles Taylor on Truth," *Truth and Progress: Philosophical Papers*, Vol. 3, Cambridge, U.K.: Cambridge University Press, 1998, p. 95. But, if Taylor is right, this assimilation of propositions to modes of coping begs precisely the question at the heart of the mediational issue and confronts Rorty with a dilemma. Either propositions, as opposed to coping practices, must in some sense be inner and represent the world in that they have content and one can separate their conditions of satisfaction from whether these conditions are satisfied, or beliefs don't have propositional content, in which case, according to Rorty, they cannot provide rational justification for other beliefs.

32. We've already seen that Taylor's rejection of mediational antirealism turns on his account of how the embodied agent both shapes the world and is open to what shows up in it. He tells us:

> We need (i) to allow for a kind of understanding which is pre-conceptual, on the basis of which concepts can be predicated of things. For this, we need (ii) to see this understanding as that of an engaged agent, determining the significances (*sens, Sinne*) of things from out of its aims, needs, purposes, desires, and (iii) to see that the most primordial and unavoidable significances of things are or are connected to those involved in our bodily existence in the world: that our field is shaped in terms of up or down, near or far, easily accessible or out of reach, graspable, avoidable, and

so on. This is where Merleau-Ponty's contribution, enlarged and developed recently by Todes, has been so crucial.

Thus, according to Taylor, we have direct access to the everyday world precisely because it is organized by and for embodied beings like ourselves.

33. Richard Rorty, "Charles Taylor on Truth," *Truth and Progress: Philosophical Papers*, Vol. 3, Cambridge, U.K.: Cambridge University Press, 1998, pp. 93–4.

34. Taylor sometimes seems to undermine any hope of saving himself from antirealism, as in the following comment in "Foundationalism and the Inner-Outer Distinction" in N. Smith (ed.), *Reading McDowell on Mind and* World, London: Routledge, 2002, p. 113.

> ... I might lay out the environment I normally walk about in by drawing a map. But this wouldn't end the embedding of reflective knowledge in ordinary coping. The map becomes useless, indeed ceases to be a map in any meaningful sense for me, unless I can use it to help me get around. Theoretical knowledge has to be situated in relation to everyday coping to be the knowledge that it is.

With the claim that theory, like a map, must be abstracted from everyday practices yet gets its intelligibility only through its relation to them, Taylor seems committed to a kind of "only through" mediational antirealism. Merleau-Ponty makes a similar claim about maps at the beginning of *Phenomenology of Perception*: "Every scientific schematization is an abstract and derivative sign-language, as is geography in relation the countryside." Christopher Smith (trans.), London: Routledge, p. ix. And he draws a Rorty-like conclusion. "L'objectivité absolue et dernière est un rêve.... Nous ne pouvons pas nous flatter, dans la science, de parvenir...à un objet pur de toute trace humaine." Maurice Merleau-Ponty, *Causeries 1948*, Paris: Seuil: 2002, pp. 15–16.

35. Richard Rorty, "Charles Taylor on Truth," *Truth and Progress: Philosophical Papers*, Vol. 3, Cambridge, U.K.: Cambridge University Press, 1998, pp. 93–4.

36. Samuel Todes, *Body and World*, Cambridge, MA: M.I.T. Press, 2001. One needn't bring in gravity. We can simply point to whatever pulls everything, including us, down; something we have to get aligned with in order to cope successfully. See Piotr Hoffman's introduction to *Body and World* on the use Todes makes of his observations concerning the vertical field of influence.

37. Maurice Merleau-Ponty, *Phenomenology of Perception*. Christopher Smith (trans.), London: Routledge, p. 322.

38. We need to add "normally" here because, if Taylor admits the conceivability of the brain-in-the-vat, as I think he should, it might turn out that there is no Cosmos. But that is not an objection to Taylor's claim that prima facie we experience having to get in sync with something independent of us that both defeats and supports our activity and that, in so doing, we reveal its structure. More on the status of the truth claims based on this experience in Section VII.

39. Martin Heidegger, "The Age of the World Picture," *The Question Concerning Technology and Other Essays*. W. Lovitt (trans.), New York: Harper Torchbooks, 1977.

40. Richard Rorty, "Charles Taylor on Truth," *Truth and Progress: Philosophical Papers*, Vol. 3, Cambridge, U.K.: Cambridge University Press, 1998, p. 86.

41. Ibid., pp. 86–7.

42. In science the new context that replaces the world is the theory itself. As Heidegger points out, and Taylor agrees, scientific facts are always theory laden; they are, however, deworlded, that is, disconnected from our purposes.

43. Charles Taylor, "Foundationalism and the Inner-Outer Distinction" in *Reading McDowell on Mind and World*. Nicholas H. Smith (ed.), London: Routledge, 2002, p. 115.

44. Maurice Merleau-Ponty. *Sense and Non-Sense*. H. L. Dreyfus and P. Allen Dreyfus (trans.), Evanston, IL: Northwestern University Press, 1964.

45. See Hubert L. Dreyfus, "Comments on Cristina Lafont's Interpretation of *Being and Time*," *Inquiry*. A. Hannay (ed.), Vol. 45, No. 2, June 2002. Saul A. Kripke, *Naming and Necessity*, Cambridge, MA: Harvard University Press, 1972, p. 132.

46. Martin Heidegger, "The Age of the World Picture" in *The Question Concerning Technology and Other Essays*. W. Lovitt (trans.), New York: Harper Torchbooks, 1977, p. 117.

47. That doesn't mean that what a culture's natural kind terms mean is up for grabs. Rorty had it when he spoke of a culture's fundamental vocabulary. A culture's way of understanding nature, for example, is too bound up with its other practices to be changed at will. See Richard Rorty, *Contingency, Irony, Solidarity*, Cambridge, U.K.: Cambridge University Press, 1989.

48. Martin Heidegger, "The Thing" in *Poetry, Language, Thought*. A. Hofstadter (trans.), New York: Harper and Row, 1971, p. 170. Emphasis in the original.

49. Martin Heidegger, "Science and Reflection" in *The Question Concerning Technology and Other Essays*. W. Lovitt (trans.), New York: Harper Torchbooks, 1977, pp. 173–4.

50. It helps to remember Wittgenstein's point in his critique of Fraser's *The Golden Bough*, that we should understand a rain dance which is normally performed just before the rainy season, not as a mistaken attempt to cause rain in our sense of cause, but as a celebration in advance of the hoped for rain. As Wittgenstein points out: "[T]oward morning, when the sun is about to rise, rites of daybreak are celebrated by the people, but not during the night, when they simply burn lamps." Ludwig Wittgenstein, *Philosophical Occasions – 1912–1951*. James C. Klagge and Alfred Nordmann (eds.), Indianapolis and Cambridge, U.K.: Hackett Publishing Company, 1993, p. 137.

51. There are also privileged perspectives on reality that don't purport to be a view from nowhere but purport to supersede all other views. They range from Plato's claim that the philosopher has such a perspective once he or she emerges from the cave, to religions such as later Judaism, Buddhism, and Christianity, that each claims to have a true and universally valid perspective, but has no notion of a view from nowhere.

# The Self and the Good
## Taylor's Moral Ontology

**FERGUS KERR**

Since the early work of Elizabeth Anscombe, Philippa Foot, and Iris Murdoch in Oxford in the 1950s, moral philosophers in the analytic tradition have discussed the viability of reconstructing something like ancient Greek ethics (Plato for Murdoch, Aristotle for the other two) in order to avoid versions of Kantian deontology or of utilitarianism, which then seemed the only choice on the agenda. Now that the latter predominates, the challenge, as Charles Taylor puts it, is to get beyond treating "all goods which are not anchored in human powers or fulfilments as illusions from a bygone age."[1] That is to say, he wants to open up a nonanthropocentric perspective on the good, to allow us to see the "sovereignty of good" over the moral agent. *Sources of the Self*, Taylor's major contribution to moral philosophy, is explicitly a "retrieval"[2] of this nonanthropocentric perspective which, as he believes, philosophy since the Enlightenment has been motivated to occlude.

From the beginning of his philosophical career, Taylor has sought to relieve us of philosophical theorising that seems misguided or blinkered. He detected behaviourism at work in influential psychological theories (section 1). He sees modern moral philosophy concerned only with doing right at the expense of considering what the good for human beings actually is (sections 2 and 3). He contends that the ancient belief in the objectivity of the good is still at work in everyday moral behaviour, however confusing and undermining modern philosophical theories are of this idea (sections 4 and 5). Although the moral source external to human persons which Taylor aims to disclose may be something like Nature (section 6), it remains unsettlingly unclear how independent his moral philosophy ultimately is of Christian religion (section 7).

## 1. BEHAVIOURIST PSYCHOLOGY

Much of Taylor's work is concerned with philosophical psychology, and particularly with expounding and opposing naturalistic theories of mind.

The implications of such theories for ethics both as theory and practice are never far from his attention.

Taylor's later work, and most obviously *Sources of the Self*, has at its centre the ambition to expound and defend an "ontology of the human," in which the identity of the self is related (as he says on the first page, referring us to Murdoch) to the "sovereignty of the good." Yet already in *The Explanation of Behaviour* (1964), Taylor showed his interest in moral philosophy, albeit this concern was visible at that stage only between the lines. In a review at the time, hailing it as a "vehemently interesting book," Anscombe noted that the first half, the "philosophical part," as she called it, "displays the most remarkable grasp of the contemporary philosophical situation and its historical roots." It pleased her also to note "a satisfactory absence of the tones and attitudes of any particular philosophical school."[3] The only major philosopher named by Taylor is Maurice Merleau-Ponty, who is referred to in three footnotes. He was surely inspired by the example of Merleau-Ponty's attempts, in *La Structure du comportement* (1942) and *Phénoménologie de la perception* (1945), translated into English as *The Structure of Behaviour* (1963) and *Phenomenology of Perception* (1962) respectively, to steer between Cartesian dualism and reductionist naturalism, in detailed critique of then fashionable behaviourist theories in experimental psychology.

In *The Explanation of Behaviour*, however, as elsewhere, Taylor makes his own what he has learnt from philosophers outside the analytic tradition: his "tones and attitudes" are, as Anscombe says, completely free of standard phenomenological terminology. Paradoxically, his "tones and attitudes" sound very much in tune with Anscombe's own famous declaration, originally published in the journal *Philosophy* (1958), that moral philosophy should be laid aside "at any rate until we have an adequate philosophy of psychology, in which we are conspicuously lacking."[4] Some indication of Anscombe's influence on Taylor's thinking comes indirectly when he records his indebtedness to Anthony Kenny's Oxford doctoral thesis (completed in 1961, it was revised to appear as *Action, Emotion and Will*, 1963). This key work, explicitly rejecting both Cartesianism and behaviourism in philosophical psychology, was much indebted to Anscombe's *Intention* (1957) and to Wittgenstein's *Philosophical Investigations* (1953). In short, although we may see his work as in line with that of the French phenomenologist Merleau-Ponty, Taylor's attack on behaviourist views of will, intention, and action is entirely consonant with post-Wittgensteinian developments in philosophy of mind.

After outlining his critique of Cartesian and empiricist theories of action and intention, Taylor devotes the greater part of the book to detailed analysis of the behaviourism he finds rampant in a crop of experimental psychologists much more recent than those examined by Merleau-Ponty. In order to undermine the influence of such supposedly scientific attempts to explain human behaviour in purely naturalistic terms, Taylor reminds us of the ways of accounting for behaviour in terms of purpose, action, and desire that are implicit in ordinary language. The aim of these naturalistic theories, he contends, is above all to describe human behaviour in language free of "teleological explanation." This might seem "scientific;" but it is a project fraught with moral and political implications. He says that

> The principal ground of interest . . . [is *often* that] the area in which we can attribute responsibility, deal out praise or blame, or mete out reward or punishment, will steadily diminish – until in the limiting case, nothing will be left; the courts will be closed or become institutes of human engineering, moral discourse will be relegated to the lumber-room of history, and so on.[5]

That is perhaps a little overstated. The view that Taylor is out to oppose is that of "many students of the sciences of human behaviour": They hold that "there is no difference in principle between the behaviour of animate organisms and any other processes in nature." More specifically, they contend that "the former can be accounted for in the same way as the latter, by laws relating physical events, and that the introduction of such notions as 'purpose' and 'mind' can only serve to obscure and confuse."[6] The issue here, "of fundamental and perennial importance for what is often called philosophical anthropology" is (he advises us from the outset) a question "*also* central to ethics."[7]

By philosophical anthropology (a phrase that has made little headway since the 1960s) Taylor means "the study of the basic categories in which man and his behaviour is to be described and explained."[8] Taylor immediately reminds us that, "there is a type of ethical reflection, exemplified for instance in the work of Aristotle, which attempts to discover what men should do and how they should behave by a study of human nature and its fundamental goals." He clearly wants to defend this "humanism," as he calls it, in an intellectual environment in which he sees it as under threat. The underlying premise of his reflection – a reflection, he insists, "which is by no means confined to philosophers" – is "that there is a form of life which is higher or more properly human than others, and that the dim intuition of the ordinary man to this effect can be vindicated in its substance or else corrected in its content by a deeper understanding of human nature."[9]

If people in everyday life are prevented by philosophical theories from thinking of human behaviour as guided or prompted (say) by the natural desire for fulfilling certain goals or purposes, then the very idea of "a way of life more consonant with the purposes of human nature" becomes unintelligible. Taylor notes, in a polemical sideswipe at the Continental philosophy of the day, "even the existentialist notion that our basic goals are chosen by ourselves"[10] would collapse. Thus, neither teleological ethics nor Sartrean voluntarism survives if the reductionist naturalism in behaviourist philosophical psychology is allowed to go through. Although Taylor does not allude to ethical matters in the rest of *The Explanation of Behaviour*, it is not difficult to see that the critique of "mechanistic," "non-teleological" explanations of human (and animal) behaviour with which the book is centrally engaged, is motivated by his concern for the effects on moral philosophy, not to mention on moral ideals and practices, of unchallenged and unchecked behaviourist psychology.

Taylor's book is not so much a contribution to providing "an adequate philosophy of psychology" (whatever that might be), as he promises, as a model contribution to the negative task of elimination[11]: namely, of eliminating some of the behaviourist theories that propagate (as he thinks) misconceptions about how we humans really are and which thus, down the line, block the way to the kind of ethics that goes with the ideals of humanism in practical politics and civil society with which Taylor has been concerned all along. *The Explanation of Behaviour* was, after all, written by one of the founding editors of *Universities and Left Review*.

Reminding us of the evident "naturalness" and unavoidability of teleological explanation in human behaviour, whatever the nonteleological philosophical theories maintain, verges on an invitation to retrieve something like the basic concepts in Aristotle's *Nicomachean Ethics*. But, as Anscombe insisted, the first task is to eliminate the philosophical theories that occlude and subvert our everyday concepts of action and purpose.

## 2. ATOMISM

Philosophy of mind, theory of knowledge, and moral philosophy are for Taylor interwoven with social and political theory. In turn, social and political policies and practices are affected by philosophical theories, even if the theories may often be justifications after the event. Reductionist accounts of human behaviour foster inhumane policies in society.

In his work in political theory, Taylor strives to uncover the implications and effects of social contract theories, so foundational in modern liberal-democratic polities. These theories trade on "a vision of society as in some sense constituted by individuals for the fulfilment of ends which were primarily individual."[12] Hobbes and Locke, representatives of such views, "have left us a legacy of political thinking in which the notion of rights plays a central part in the justification of political structures and action."[13] Such theorists insist so strongly on the primacy of individual interests that they encourage us to overlook our obligations to sustain the community to which we belong and owe our identity. What makes this modern liberal individualism plausible, Taylor maintains here, is the hold exerted on our culture by what he calls "atomism" – his term for the Enlightenment doctrine of the *de jure* autonomy and self-sufficiency of the individual. This atomistic perspective on human life involves the postulation of "an extensionless subject, epistemologically a *tabula rasa* and politically a presuppositionless bearer of rights."[14] Atomistic views thus see society as composed of disconnected individuals, each with inalienable and privileged rights, which it is the society's sole function to protect. That is to say, the picture of society as existing solely to protect the bearer of rights is inextricable from the idea of knowledge as grounded only in the experience of the individual subject of consciousness.

In *The Explanation of Behaviour*, as he unravelled the background assumptions that allow behaviourist accounts of human conduct to seem plausible, Taylor attacked "atomism": It was "part of the tradition of empiricism," and "ultimately founded on epistemological grounds."[15] In the essay dedicated to this topic, Taylor wonders if he has got hold of the right label but he is absolutely clear about the central issue he wants to highlight: the assumption in much political theory, as well as in social and political policies and practices, that takes as fundamental and unchallengeable the primacy of the individual's interests and rights, while simultaneously overlooking and even denying premodern assumptions about the primacy of our obligation as human beings to society. In earlier eras of Western society, not to mention other civilizations, primacy-of-individual-rights theories would have no foothold. Taylor appeals to Aristotle's conception of human beings as social and political animals, to the extent that we are not self-sufficient outside a polis – in the sense, then, that free and autonomous moral agents achieve and maintain their identity (insofar as they do) only in subjecting themselves willingly to the common good within a certain kind of shared culture.

The difficulty with this view – the main reason that Locke and others challenged it – is that it expresses and reinforces forms of conventionalism, according to which what passes for knowledge, truth, and so forth, as well as what counts as ethical norms, appears to be no more than the agreed beliefs of a particular restricted community. Even if it is assumed, as by Aristotle, that the goods are somehow grounded in human nature (whatever that may be), the result (one might fear) can only be a homogeneous society, easily tending towards being closed and exclusivist. At worst, it collapses into intimidated conformism in societies that thwart all dissent, in effect totalitarianism.

On one side, Taylor wants to distance himself from the liberal-empiricist tradition which finds foundations for knowledge, truth, and so forth in individual experience, insisting on individual rights and personal autonomy as what matters most in politics. He calls this "the ultra-liberal view."[16] On the other hand, he refuses to endorse neo-Nietzschean views as he finds them in the work of Michel Foucault, according to which all judgements, whether moral, epistemological, or political, are grounded on the interplay of power: "There is no order of human life, or way we are, or human nature, that one can appeal to in order to judge or evaluate between ways of life."[17] In the ordinary everyday sense of the word, Taylor is a liberal – deeply and irrevocably attached to the liberties that liberal societies at least aspire to embody. He wants simply to remind us that "the identity of the autonomous, self-determining individual requires a social matrix."[18] Although the contemporary political theorists he is taking aim at in his critique of atomism "are not at all keen to open these wider issues," his essay concludes with the thought that, if we are to discuss the nature of freedom, and so of rights and obligations, we have to open up "questions about the nature of man."[19]

## 3. THE SOVEREIGNTY OF GOOD

As his philosophical work unfolds, from the attack on nonteleological theories of human behaviour in *The Explanation of Behaviour* through the rejection of doctrines that emphasise individual self-sufficiency (atomism) in social and political theory, Taylor touches on ethics all the time; but it is above all in *Sources of the Self* that he deals with the issue centrally and most extensively.

Taylor starts by noting that modern moral philosophy has tended to focus on what it is right to do rather than what it is good to be, thus on defining the content of obligation rather than the nature of the good life. There is no place in this family of ethical doctrines for a notion of the good as the object of our love or allegiance or, as Iris Murdoch portrayed it, as the privileged focus of attention or will.[20] The reference is to *The Sovereignty of*

*Good* (1970). Like Murdoch, Taylor argues there that we need not assume, as so many do, that emotivism, prescriptivism, projectivism, and other forms of nonrealism offer the only viable way for us now in moral philosophy.

Yet one reason why nonrealism will continue to flourish is that philosophical positions are seldom if ever abandoned: Philosophers will always want to probe the weaknesses of doctrines that affirm the reality of objectivity in ethics. More important, however, to put it crudely, in an intellectual environment in which many have lost belief in a divinely created world with divinely instituted moral law, and in which we seem to be left with nothing but our own minds and wills to generate and judge our ethical ideals and moral practices, we are always going to be prompted, tempted, or compelled to experiment with nonrealist accounts of ethics. For Taylor, all such moral philosophies are unavoidably subjectivist and radically anthropocentric, in the sense that they allow no resources for morality outside ourselves. His purpose in *Sources of the Self* is, as the title signals, precisely to locate "moral sources outside the subject" – but to do so, not in terms of a person's submission to some cosmic order of meanings, but "through languages which resonate *within* him or her, the grasping of an order which is inseparably indexed to a personal vision."[21] Although not engaging with nonrealist accounts directly or in great detail, Taylor alludes (with respect) to the work of such contemporaries as J. L. Mackie, Bernard Williams, and Simon Blackburn. Instead of trying to refute such nonrealist theorists by analysis and argument, he concentrates on telling the long story of how the conception of the good for human beings has developed, particularly since the end of the Middle Ages, in Western culture.

At one level, this is the history of the construction of the modern Western understanding of what it is to be a moral agent, a person, a self, with less and less certainty or agreement about what the good we might desire or do actually is. On another level, however, Taylor is not just telling us a story; he wants the story to persuade us to consider whether we know who we are, or what we are to do in this or that situation or with our lives as a whole, unless we have some overall conception of the nature of the good life, however inchoate and unsophisticated. Moreover, the good life for a human being, in this nonanthropocentric perspective, requires acknowledgement on the moral agent's part, however tacitly, of the authority and desirability of goods that we regard ourselves as discovering more than inventing.

In short, we need have no embarrassment about regarding moral philosophy as primarily to do with exploring the nature of the good life for a human being. This means, as Taylor puts it, that we have to make room,

or (rather) find the already existing place, in our workaday conceptual system, for the "sovereignty of the concept of the good" – the good, whatever
it may be, that shapes and opens our moral world, thereby disclosing or
establishing our identity as moral agents.

There are two moves here, both of which Taylor generously notes as
being anticipated by Murdoch. The first is the move beyond the question
of what we ought to do, to the question of what it is good for human
beings to be. The second is the move beyond the question of what a good
life for human beings might be, to the consideration of "a good which
would be beyond life, in the sense that its goodness cannot be entirely or
exhaustively explained in terms of its contributing to a fuller, better, richer,
more satisfying human life."[22] Taylor goes on at once to say that it is "a
good that we might sometimes more appropriately respond to in suffering
and death, rather than in fullness and life"– and he allows that this takes us
into "the domain, as usually understood, of religion."[23]

## 4. TOO MUCH THEORIZING

According to Taylor, nonrealist and subjectivist philosophical theories prevent us from seeing how ideals of the good remain sovereign in our lives. As
in his early work on behaviourist psychology, his effort goes into debunking
the philosophical theories which, so he thinks, get in the way of seeing things
as they really are. The understanding of the good as a moral source, he contends, has actually been "deeply suppressed in the mainstream of modern
moral consciousness," whereas it was "perfectly familiar to the ancients."[24]
He claims that if we can suspend respect for recent philosophical theories,
we shall find ourselves just as inclined to acknowledge the sovereignty of
the good as a moral resource which we do not create as our ancestors ever
were, simply by attending to the evidence of our everyday practice. We
have, no doubt, "to fight uphill to rediscover the obvious, to counteract
the layers of suppression";[25] but we can, Taylor promises, break free of
"the cramped formulations of mainstream philosophy," in order "to recognize the goods to which we cannot but hold allegiance in their full range."[26]

Thus Taylor devotes much attention to describing and defending the
ordinariness and indispensability of moral perceptions and ways of moral
thought that philosophical theorizings have made to seem problematic.
Reductive naturalistic philosophies have theorized away so much, he contends, that we are either embarrassed to appeal to what we all know to
be the case, or have actually even forgotten that it is so. Basically, we are

inclined to focus on doing what is right because philosophical theory since the Enlightenment has discouraged us from wanting any longer to identify the good which is the transcendental condition of our moral choices. That sounds like metaphysics. Deciding on the right course of action to take in particular circumstances seems a great deal more manageable than delving into metaphysical questions about the good.

Taylor, however, reminds us of the much richer background to moral argument than philosophical theory often allows. In effect, what he wants to show is that, for all the centuries of philosophical pressure to occlude metaphysical questions about the good, in favour of nonrealist, subjectivist doctrines, we remain stubbornly attached to unreconstructed moral realism. For example, our everyday moral intuitions, he insists, operate perfectly naturally and uncontentiously with assumptions about our nature and predicament that are more than anthropocentric. Our place in the world, our status as moral agents, involve training, endless reorientation, even asceticism, as much as epistemological concerns. Controversial as this no doubt seems to philosophers, Taylor clearly thinks that it is perfectly obvious – or, rather, he is only reminding us of what would be obvious if we were not confused by theory. Over against emotivist theories, for example, he suggests that we need only recall the range of discriminations of right and wrong, better and worse, and so forth, which are not rendered valid solely or principally by our instincts, desires, inclinations, or choices, but which stand independent of these and offer standards by which these discriminations are effected and judged.

For a start, there are the demands we recognize as moral which have to do with respect for the life of other human beings. In this or that society, admittedly, respect may not include all human beings; in some societies it may extend to some nonhuman animals. Of course there is variation. Yet, Taylor thinks, this does not subvert the truth that, for the most part, and cross-culturally, human beings have certain moral intuitions, rooted in our animal nature, as one is inclined to say, which contrast with other moral reactions which are indeed inculcated by upbringing and might be quite different or even absent in a somewhat different environment. For example, reluctance to inflict death or injury on our own kind, and the inclination to come to the help of the injured or endangered, seem to Taylor to cut across all cultural differences. These reactions seem primitive, "natural," and such as we expect in any culture, ancient or modern, religious or secular. We often, or at least sometimes, "pass by on the other side," but not without a twinge of shame at refusing to get involved, or some self-justifying excuse. There is a deep-rooted reluctance to kill our conspecifics: Men – sane men – need a great deal of special training before they become comfortable with the idea of killing human beings.

Customs and practices differ from one culture to another. One culture might have a grand narrative, even a theory, explaining why we do not kill and eat one another. It may be held, to take Taylor's examples, that human beings have immortal souls, or that they are rational agents with a dignity that transcends that of any other animal, and that that is why we owe such respect to one another. That we don't eat one another, one might say, is explained by a certain theory in this or that culture – as if we might do so but are inhibited by the theory. In contrast, many of us feel free to eat other animals, perhaps justifying this, if we ever really have to, on the grounds that it is "natural" to do so, or that God gave them to us for food, or that it is all right since they are not rational agents. The reasons meat eaters might find themselves forced to adduce, in an argument with a vegetarian, perhaps show how easily a justificatory theory slips into implausible fantasy. Again, how much theory do people have to have at the back of their refusal to eat one another?

Playing with such possibilities, Taylor encourages us to look again at the range and depth of our moral reactions. Some of the reactions which constitute the moral life, he wants to say, are instinctive, physical, and animal, not unlike vomiting with disgust at stinking and rotting things, fainting with fear of falling, and such like. Such primitive reactions can be modified up to a point: People can be trained to deal with nauseatingly distressing deaths; one can develop a taste for well hung game; a young man might be so embarrassed by his mates that he would force himself to go in for bungee jumping; and so on. But there are some reactions at this level that can never be eradicated (leaving aside physical injury that deprives one of the sense of taste or smell or the like). Whatever the cultural and individual differences, some things just smell bad to everyone; some scenes would distress anyone; love making, giving birth, and dying, one would say, are events which evoke reactions of joy, grief, and so on, intelligible to and thus shareable by human beings anywhere and at any period. These reactions may be trained, redirected, and refined, in more elaborate and sophisticated forms of behaviour specific to a certain local culture. Indeed, distinctive customs in such matters can define a culture, partly at least.

Certain moral reactions, one may say, display something fundamental about the nature and status of human beings. Certain of our reactions turn out, as Taylor puts it, to be practical affirmations of an "ontology of the human." Here, Taylor is reaffirming the argument against reductionism in *The Explanation of Behaviour*. True, as he at once allows, this appeal to the naturalness of our basic moral reactions has been built into certain philosophies of human nature which may well be distrusted, for example because of the use some of them have been put to – justifying the exclusion of certain practices and institutions. Claims that this or that sort of conduct is "unnatural" – not in accordance with our "natural" moral reactions – have been and often still are used to justify excluding certain people from society, perhaps sometimes even imprisoning or executing them. Moreover, claims about how "unspoiled human nature respects life by instinct," and the like, are scarcely credible. Conceding all this, Taylor nevertheless insists that there are everyday moral reactions that articulate and display what it is like to be a human being, whatever the cultural and historical differences.

For Taylor, however, the most intractable problem is that the very idea of a moral ontology grounded in our natural moral reactions lies, as he says, under a "great epistemological cloud."[27] All through Western culture, nowadays, educated people, "inspired by the success of modern natural science," follow "empiricist or rationalist theories of knowledge," for the most part quite unwittingly, which tempt us into resting content with the fact that we have such reactions (if and when we do) but considering "the ontology which gives rational articulation to them" to be, as he puts it, "so much froth, nonsense from a bygone age."[28]

In particular, Taylor resists the "error theory" of moral values, espoused by J. L. Mackie, which depends on a form of the fact/value dichotomy, the only occasion in *Sources* in which he tackles a nonrealist account of morality in any detail. According to Mackie, our "gut" reactions whenever we are confronted with moral questions no doubt have survival value from a sociobiological perspective; but the belief that "we are discriminating real properties, with criteria independent of our de facto reactions" is an illusion. We may hold on to these moral reactions, fine tune them, alter them, and so on, to make life more bearable; but there is no place for a view that "certain things and not others, just in virtue of their nature, [are] fit objects of respect."[29] In face of all this, Taylor appeals to "the whole way in which we think, reason, argue, and question ourselves about morality."[30] Whatever the nonrealist philosophers maintain, we continue to think in much less sophisticated ways. It is not just that we happen to have certain visceral reactions, or that the survival of the fittest shows that certain attitudes and virtues are useful. We simply believe that it would be utterly wrong – intrinsically wrong – to draw a line around the people in the human race whose lives we count as more worth respecting.

Whatever was the case once, whatever it may be in societies very different from our own, when people say that some people's existence is less worthy of respect than others, Taylor claims, we immediately ask what criteria they have for this discrimination. This is what we do with racists, for example. We try to persuade racists that skin colour has nothing to do with that in virtue of which human beings command our respect. Racists will no doubt reply that certain defining human characteristics are genetically determined, some human beings, individuals, or ethnic groups, are less intelligent, less capable of moral consciousness, and so forth. That is to say, racists make empirical claims about supposedly innate intellectual and moral differences. They cite statistics, research results, anecdotal evidence at least, to back these claims. All such claims, Taylor says, are "unsustainable in the light of human history,"[31] but the logic of the debate means that the objects of our moral responses – people with different skin colour – have to be described according to criteria which are independent of our de facto reactions. The racists' gut reactions will be rapidly extended or articulated into their own ontology of the human. The claims made about the object of their contempt are not actually about the survival value or usefulness of their gut reactions. Rather, they make assertions about the (alleged) intrinsic properties of the objects of their "moral" reactions.

## 5. FACT/VALUE

There is a deeply misguided conception of practical reasoning according to which the various ontological accounts that attribute predicates to human beings – such as being God's creatures, emanations of divine fire, agents of rational choice, and so forth – are regarded as analogous to theoretical predicates in natural science. This is so in two senses: first, that they are remote from the everyday descriptions by which we deal with ourselves and people around us ("folk psychology," as thinkers in this line say) and, second, they make reference to our conception of the universe and our place in it. It looks as if we develop ontological or metaphysical accounts about ourselves in ways analogous to our physical explanations. We think we have to start from the facts, which we think we identify independently of our reactions and prejudices, and only then try to show that one assessment would be better than others. But, Taylor argues, as soon as we make this distinction between fact and value we have gone wrong: "We have lost from view what we're arguing about. Ontological accounts . . . articulate the claims implicit in our [moral] . . . reactions. We can no longer argue about them at all once we assume a neutral stance and try to describe the facts as they are independent of these reactions as we have done in natural science since the seventeenth century."[32]

Yet there is such a thing as moral objectivity, Taylor insists. Growth in moral insight often requires that we hold back or restrain some of our reactions; but restraining or enlarging our reactions to people is something we do precisely in order that these others may be more transparently identified in their otherness – "unscreened by petty jealousy, egoism, or other unworthy feelings."[33] Moral argument takes place within a world shaped by our deepest moral responses. The ideal in natural science is to get at the world in as impartial a way as possible, inhibiting or eliminating fears, lusts, nausea, desire, and so forth. It is just a mistake to discuss morals as if we had a neutral perspective on ourselves as beings with moral reactions. In contrast to this stance of impartiality, Taylor proposes that "if you want to discriminate more finely what it is about human beings that makes them worthy of respect, you have to call to mind what it is to feel the claim of human suffering, or what is repugnant about injustice, or the awe you feel at the fact of human life."[34] Nothing can take us from the neutral stance towards the world to insight into moral ontology, but that does not mean that moral ontology and its insights are pure fiction, as naturalists in ethics say. Taylor recommends rather that "we should treat our deepest moral instincts, our ineradicable sense that human life is to be respected, as our mode of access to the world in which ontological claims are discernible and can be rationally argued about and sifted."[35]

This moral ontology of the human is what we draw on, and appeal to, when we have to defend or explain our responses, in this or that dilemma, as the "natural," "appropriate," and "right" ones. This is never easy or straightforward. For one thing you may not yourself be the best authority. The moral ontology operating in one's reactions and views is largely implicit. It seldom emerges unless you are challenged: Somebody tells you that your views are racist, sexist, or whatever; worse still, you are mistreated or abused because of your skin colour, social position, or religious affiliation. Most people, most of the time, take it for granted that every human being has the same rights to life and security. This goes also for the perpetrators of violence. As Taylor observes, "The greatest violators [of people's rights] hide behind a smoke screen of lies and special pleading."[36] Racist regimes no doubt believe in something like human dignity, status, and honour, but they also believe in separate but equal development for this or that scientifically or culturally justifiable reason. In the former Soviet Union, for example, some political dissidents were classified as mentally ill. Controversies about abortion, to take another example, involve one side denying not that certain human beings do not have the same rights as the rest of us but that certain beings are not human in the first place. As Taylor suggests, this is a case where the moral ontology, the background picture about our spiritual nature and place in the universe, comes very plainly to the fore.

Usually, however, the background remains unarticulated, unexplored. We react in the same way, morally, to so much of the suffering and challenge, to so many of the opportunities and misfortunes of human life, that our ontology of the human operates silently, seldom needing to be consulted, exposed, or expounded. But, Taylor argues, often there is resistance to exploring it. There is often a gap, a lack of fit, between what people officially and consciously believe and what they need to include in order to make sense of some of their moral reactions. The philosophers who set moral reactions aside as folk psychology, go on arguing like the rest of us about what objects deserve respect, what reactions are appropriate, and so on. The idea that the first attitude of all can be – ought to be – directed towards a possible disillusion; the idea that we have to begin by being taught a false certainty, are exactly the ideas that there "must be" some neutral stance. Yet this is what Taylor wants to dislodge from moral philosophy.

As mentioned, Taylor identifies the emphasis we put on avoiding human suffering as one of the great characteristics of our moral ontology of the human. This does not mean that we have ceased to inflict pain on one another in everyday life, let alone at the level of the state: Prisoners are tortured and people are degraded in order to punish their rulers. Such horrors are now far more widely regarded as aberrations. In societies like ours we could no longer have executions in public. Part of the reason for this change in sensibility is negative, in the sense that we no longer believe in avenging a terrible crime by an equally terrible punishment. The whole notion of a cosmic moral order which was outraged and had to be compensated for has faded. As that kind of belief has declined, especially with the utilitarian Enlightenment, we protest against unnecessary suffering. Executions take place but they have to be as painless as possible. On the positive side, Taylor thinks, this emphasis on minimizing human suffering has a source in the New Testament, indeed is one of the themes of "Christian spirituality."[37]

Yet not all Christians, let alone non-Christians, would unhesitatingly endorse the suggestion that the stress on relieving suffering is a particularly Christian theme. Of course, Taylor is not, as he acknowledges, neutral on this issue.[38] As we have seen, a central claim in his work is that we cannot have some "naturalist" viewpoint on the moral life which does not lose sight of the realities. But he means more than this: He accepts certain "extra-human" claims. The intention of *Sources* as a "retrieval" of "buried

goods" is "to make these sources again empower, to bring the air back again
into the half-collapsed lungs of the spirit."[39] In the end we are right, he says,
to suspect that his "'hunch' lies towards regarding "naturalist humanism"
as ultimately defective – "or, perhaps better put, that great as the power of
naturalist sources might be, the potential of a certain theistic perspective
is incomparably greater."[40] With typical candour, he allows that he has re-
frained from highlighting this theistic perspective "partly out of delicacy,
but largely out of lack of arguments";[41] and he refers us to Dostoevsky,
"who has framed this perspective better than I ever could here."[42] References to Dostoevsky are in fact scattered throughout *Sources*: his famous
thesis, "If God does not exist, then everything is permitted";[43] his attack
on "utilitarian utopian engineering";[44] the description in *A Raw Youth* of
the mutual tenderness and care which human beings will feel when they
realize that they are utterly alone in the universe, with no God;[45] while of
*The Devils* Taylor remarks that "no one . . . has given us deeper insight into
the *spiritual* sources of modern terrorism."[46]

At the end of *Sources* Taylor refers to the entire project in the book
of describing the modern identity as helping to "shape our view of the
moral predicament of our time." It would take another book to explain
what he means, he says, but he hopes, though he "can't do it here (or, to
be honest, anywhere at this point)" that "our greatest spiritual challenge"
can be resolved: "It is a hope that I see implicit in Judaeo-Christian theism
(however terrible the record of its adherents in history), and in its central
promise of a divine affirmation of the human, more total than humans can
ever attain unaided."[47]

## 6. DEEP ECOLOGY

Throughout *Sources of the Self* Taylor's personal commitment to Christianity
keeps surfacing, yet he is even more explicit about wanting to develop
an account of the authority of goodness in the moral and spiritual life
which is not necessarily theistic in the ordinary sense. Although he clearly
respects Murdoch's attempt to retrieve a conception of the sovereignty of
the good which dispenses with Plato's metaphysical beliefs while retaining
the image of the Good as the sun, in the light of which we can see things with
lucidity, diminishingly self-centred attention, and a kind of compassionate
love, Taylor seems inclined to think that she yields too much to Plato. After
all, "no one today can accept the Platonic metaphysic of the Ideas as the
crucial explanation of the shape of the cosmos."[48] In the end, he hints,

even this allegedly nonmetaphysical notion of the good as the object of the empowering love which shapes a person's identity, belongs to the remote past.[49] The advantage for Christians, at least those of a Platonist inclination, is that God takes the place of Plato's idea of the good, with the difference, obviously, that the love of the good which empowers and indeed confers our identity is not just human love for God but initially God's love for us. The problem, as Taylor rightly says, is to say what happens in this retrieval of objectivity in ethics, when, as for many in our culture at least, there is nothing like any such person-shaping good external to human beings.

Those acquainted with Heideggerian themes can detect variations on them in much of Taylor's apparently standard Anglo-American analytical philosophy. In particular, he writes very sympathetically about what might be called Heidegger's philosophy of ecology. Heidegger's philosophy is opposed to subjectivism, humanism, and nonrealism, in the sense that he holds that there is no future for human beings unless we understand that nature makes demands on us – at any rate, that something beyond the human makes demands on us. Mostly Taylor works this out in terms of Heidegger's conception of language, but the upshot is to challenge the metaphysical idealism, the anthropocentric humanism, that is there (Heidegger thinks) in the founding figures of modern philosophy such as Descartes and Locke and which culminates in Nietzschean claims to the effect that reality is simply what we human beings make of, or project onto it. On the contrary: through language a world is disclosed – a world in which objects matter, as Taylor says, threatening us, attracting us, and so on. Some attract us in ways that prompt the variety of enterprises we now call science. Others provoke or evoke other kinds of responses, other kinds of discourses, including in their own way stories and mythologies, as well as music, painting, and so forth. According to Heidegger, we tend to see language as our instrument and the space of meaning, the world as an order of intelligibility, as something that happens in us that we generate – something that simply reflects our goals and purposes. But what we are – and here Taylor is happy to accept talk of our nature, our essence – is to be found in the ways in which we are attentive to how language opens up a space of meaning, which is not something that we arrange or impose. It is not there without us, but it is there as the context for our entire making and acting. Taylor takes up Heidegger's talk about the space of meaning, the "clearing," as something that happens, that keeps happening, in and as we let certain things be, those things which appear not simply as objects (although there is nothing wrong about their doing that in the appropriate circumstances) or even less as raw material subject entirely to human will. Rather, as the jug, the decanter, the chalice, fulfills its role in our life, in our community, it is heavy with the human activities in which it plays a part – the pouring of wine at the common table, for instance. "The jug is a point at which this rich web of practices can be sensed, made visible in the very shape of the jug and its handle, which offers itself for this use."[50]

Taylor takes up this Heideggerian theme to cast light on the way that some things make a claim on us. They are what he calls strong goods, matters of intrinsic worth. Heidegger envisages this dimension, this connection, Taylor says, as arising from the ritual of pouring wine from a jug in certain circumstances. The modes of conviviality that the decanter discloses are shot through with religious and moral meaning. The jug is something shaped and fashioned for human use, always already emerging from a field of potential further meaning, including our future life together, open-ended, unforeseeable. But it also has a history – a past. Ultimately it depends on the clay, thus on the earth. The whole round of relationships, dependencies, that the jug gathers into itself and extends to all who participate in using it, is "open to greater cosmic forces which are beyond the domain of the formable, and which can either permit them [our activities] to flourish or sweep them away."[51]

Here Taylor is recapitulating Heidegger very sympathetically: "Heidegger is on to something very important"[52] he concludes. Heidegger's understanding of what it is to be human as ultimately the gift of something nonhuman offers the basis for an ecological politics. We have to think of the claims that things put on us to let them be what they are, to let them disclose themselves in a certain way. It is a manner of letting things be, which in crucial cases (Taylor says) is quite incompatible with the approach of will to power over everything. Take for example any region of wilderness. If the rain forests are simply "a standing reserve for timber production," we treat them in a purely self-interested, radically anthropocentric, and instrumentalist fashion. There is exploration as well as exploitation, Taylor immediately agrees. We can, for example, identify species and geological forms, a way of carving up the natural world for our information and convenience. This is all right, Taylor says, "as long as we retain a sense of the necessary inexhaustibility of the wilderness surroundings."[53] In short, he sums up: "Our goals here are fixed by something which we should properly see ourselves as serving."[54] This means that a proper understanding of our ways of dealing with the natural world has to take us "beyond ourselves."[55] Properly understood, the "shepherd of Being," Heidegger's description of the role of the human being in the world, can never be "an adept of triumphalist instrumental reason ... At this moment, when we need all the insight we can muster into our relation to the cosmos in order to deflect our disastrous course, Heidegger may have opened a vitally important new line of thinking."[56]

Plainly Taylor's thinking here is quite exploratory and tentative. Published three years later, this paper on Heidegger is a good deal more explicit than the allusions in *Sources of the Self*. Taylor would be the first to say that we do not need to turn to Heidegger for this notion of ecological politics; there are no doubt many other sources. And although he certainly mentions Heidegger's failure to grasp the significance of what happened in his native land between 1933 and 1945, vigorously criticizing his stance,[57] we might want to hear much more about the ambiguities inherent in this version of a "moral ontology of the human." It appeals to a relationship to something nonhuman as the defining feature of how we should live if we are to flourish; but it is perhaps somewhat more paradoxical than Taylor acknowledges when he connects human flourishing with responsibility for the environment (as he is absolutely right to do) by invoking Heidegger. Heidegger, for all his concern with the environment, showed, some would think, a somewhat diminished sense of human flourishing. But the main point for Taylor is that we human beings need to be in touch with – have to be receptive and open to – the nonhuman creatures in this world of ours, this world of theirs, if we are to hold on to our own identity as humankind.

## 7. PROBLEMS

The intention of *Sources of the Self* was, as noted, "retrieval." As Taylor knows, this is bound to sound to many readers and not only nonrealist, emotivist moral philosophers, like nostalgia for something which either never existed, or, if it did, we must be glad to be rid of. In the end, seeking some nonanthropocentric ethic to correct, supplement, or displace prevailing conceptions of ethics which exclude belief in "sources" of morality that are nonhuman, will seem likely to threaten the achievements of the secular humanism so characteristic of Western society, and so isolated in the world at large and threatened even within the West itself. Time and again Taylor insists in *Sources* on the terrible record of Christianity and other religions. On the other hand, he notes, atheistic regimes such as those of Stalin, Pol Pot, and many others, perpetrate great crimes against humanity in their attempts to "realize the most lofty ideals of human perfection." As he allows, "the highest spiritual ideals and aspirations also threaten to lay the most crushing burdens on humankind."[58] Yet, the fact that traditional metaphysical and religious ethics have often proved oppressive does not mean, he insists, that a high ideal must be invalid if it leads to suffering. He grants that, if cultivating the highest ideals involves so much that is potentially destructive, the prudent course might be to scale down our spiritual aspirations. At any rate, "we shouldn't unconditionally rejoice at the indiscriminate retrieval of empowering goods."[59]

By this point in *Sources*, Taylor is clearly speaking in the first person. Citing the careers of Jean Vanier and Mother Teresa, highly controversial as she at least is for agnostic humanist readers (and many Christian believers), he contends that, as regards extending help to "the mentally handicapped, those dying without dignity, fetuses with genetic defects," the prevailing naturalist humanism is less than satisfactory.[60] On the one hand, the kind of personal recognition of some good for human beings which springs from some other than purely human source, for which Taylor has been arguing all along, has to be spelled out in instances of ordinary everyday discriminations. So much of Taylor's effort goes into showing how philosophical preconceptions seductively prevent us from seeing how much our moral reactions are prompted, commanded, or inspired by something "objectively" good that he does not get around to discussing moral dilemmas in any detail. On the other hand, the instances which he does discuss, like those just cited, are so much the agenda of the version of the Christian religion to which he never conceals his allegiance, that one is bound to wonder what other "source" there is external to the human person than something like the Christian God. Clearly, in the reflections on Heidegger, Taylor offers an account of something external to human beings which might, and indeed for many people already does, shape and sustain a way of being in the world, respecting natural resources, combating small scale and global abuses that threaten human life as a whole, and so on; a "moral ontology of the human"; a "deep ecology" which transcends all anthropocentric subjectivism yet without buying into the supernaturalism of biblical religion.

Charles Taylor's work continues to develop. It cannot surprise readers that, after his exposure of reductionist behaviourism in psychology, his defence of everyday moral reactions against nonrealist philosophical theories, and his narrative of the moral agent's dependence on the "sovereignty of the good," the next stage is to discuss *The Varieties of Religion Today*.

### Notes

1. Charles Taylor, *Sources of the Self: The Making of the Modern Identity*, Cambridge, MA: Harvard University Press, 1989, p. 506.
2. Ibid., pp. 10, 520.

3. G. E. M Anscombe, "Mechanism and Ideology," *New Statesman*, Feb. 5 1965, p. 206.

4. "Modern moral philosophy" in *The Collected Philosophical Papers of G. E. M. Anscombe. Volume 3: Ethics, Religion and Politics*, Oxford: Blackwell, p. 26.

5. *The Explanation of Behavior*, London: Routledge and Kegan Paul, 1964, pp. 42–3. Emphasis added.

6. Ibid., p. 3.

7. Ibid., p. 4. Emphasis added.

8. Ibid., p. 4.

9. Ibid., p. 4.

10. Ibid., p. 4.

11. Ibid., p. 103.

12. "Atomism" in *Philosophy and the Human Sciences. Philosophical Papers 2*. Cambridge, U.K.: Cambridge University Press, 1985, p. 187.

13. Ibid., p. 187.

14. Ibid., p. 210.

15. *The Explanation of Behavior*, London: Routledge and Kegan Paul, 1964, p. 11.

16. "Atomism" in *Philosophy and the Human Sciences. Philosophical Papers 2*. Cambridge, U.K.: Cambridge University Press, 1985, p. 196.

17. "Foucault on Freedom and Truth" in Ibid., p. 177.

18. "Atomism" in Ibid., p. 209.

19. Ibid., p. 210.

20. *Sources of the Self: the Making of the Modern Identity*, Cambridge, MA: Harvard University Press, 1989, p. 3.

21. Ibid., p. 510. Emphasis in the original.

22. "Iris Murdoch and Moral Philosophy" in *Iris Murdoch and the Search for Human Goodness*. Maria Antonaccio and William Schweiker (eds.), Chicago and London: University of Chicago Press 1996, p. 5.

23. Ibid.

24. *Sources of the Self: The Making of the Modern Identity*. Cambridge, MA: Harvard University Press, 1989, p. 92.

25. Ibid., p. 90.

26. Ibid., p. 107.

27. Ibid., p. 5.

28. Ibid., p. 5.

29. Ibid., p. 6.

30. Ibid., p. 7.

31. Ibid., p. 7.

32. Ibid., p. 8.

33. Ibid., p. 8.

34. Ibid., p. 8.

35. Ibid., p. 8.
36. Ibid., p. 9.
37. Ibid., p. 13.
38. Ibid., pp. 102, 517.
39. Ibid., p. 520.
40. Ibid., p. 518.
41. Ibid., p. 517.
42. Ibid., p. 518.
43. Ibid., p. 10.
44. Ibid., p. 24.
45. Ibid., p. 411.
46. Ibid., p. 451.
47. Ibid., p. 521.
48. Ibid., p. 96.
49. Ibid., p. 93.
50. "Heidegger, Language, Ecology" in *Philosophical Arguments*, Cambridge, MA: Harvard University Press, 1995, p. 122.
51. Ibid., p. 123.
52. Ibid., p. 125.
53. Ibid., p. 125.
54. Ibid., p. 126.
55. Ibid., p. 126.
56. Ibid., p. 126.
57. Ibid., p. 125.
58. *Sources of the Self: The Making of the Modern Identity*, Cambridge, MA: Harvard University Press, 1989, p. 519.
59. Ibid., p. 520
60. Ibid., p. 517

# 4

## Articulating the Horizons of Liberalism
### Taylor's Political Philosophy

*STEPHEN MULHALL*

In *Sources of the Self*, his epic historical recounting of the making of our modern moral identity, Charles Taylor attempts to articulate the broader background or horizon (what he there calls the moral ontology) of the specific arrays of moral judgement characteristic of modernity in the West. Without such an ontology, he argues, those judgements can neither secure their distinctive content nor receive a truly rational assessment of their strengths and limitations; and yet many forces fundamental to that same modernity (certain pervasive metaphysical, epistemological and moral assumptions) nevertheless encourage us to ignore or positively repress it. In other words, Taylor sees his overarching project in that book as one of opposing an ethics of inarticulacy. The intuition that guides my necessarily selective consideration of Taylor's wide-ranging and extraordinarily influential contributions to political philosophy is that they can be seen as a contribution to that broader project. Where *Sources of the Self* aims at nothing less than an articulation of the moral sources of the modern conception of selfhood, the essays and lectures in political philosophy that I examine can fruitfully be conceived as attempts to articulate the horizons of a single, but fundamental, strand in the weave of that modern self-identity – the political theory and practice of liberalism.

My discussion falls into three parts. In the first, I examine Taylor's critiques of Isaiah Berlin on negative freedom and Robert Nozick on the primacy of individual rights. In the second, I consider his complex relation to communitarian critiques of liberalism, and his concern with the politics of recognition. In both cases, I argue that his writings are intended to show that those whose work he criticises have an unduly narrow or decontextualized, an insufficiently articulated, conception of their own enterprise. They fail to appreciate the deeper presuppositions and consequences of their own specific political principles, the full complexity of the vision of society to which they cleave (as well as those to which they appear implacably opposed). As a consequence, they fail to appreciate the variety of ways in which their own deepest convictions might be re-articulated – either

**105**

to enhance their plausibility in the face of rival contentions, or even to be rendered compatible with convictions that had previously seemed to be essentially in conflict with their own. In the third and final part of my discussion, I touch briefly on certain conditioning contexts or horizons for Taylor's own work in political philosophy, in order to clarify our sense of the underlying orientation and goals (what Taylor himself might call the narrative unity) of his internal critical engagements with liberalism.

## LIBERAL CONCEPTIONS OF FREEDOM

The distinction between positive and negative freedom has been central to modern liberalism's attempts at self-definition, and one of the most influential attempts to clarify that distinction, and to encourage liberals to identify themselves with negative freedom, was that of Isaiah Berlin.[1] According to Berlin, on a negative conception of freedom an individual is free insofar as she is free from interference or constraint by outside sources; negative freedom is secured when nothing is done to individuals against their will (although if their actions harm others, then society is justified in constraining them). The positive conception of freedom focuses on enabling or empowering individuals to achieve goals or to realize purposes – on the achievement of self-mastery or self-direction. Hence, negative freedom does not guarantee positive freedom (lack of interference by others in one's life is consistent with lacking proper control over its direction oneself), and the search for positive freedom might provide grounds for violating negative freedom (if, for example, one believes that an individual's subjection to a damaging social ideology can be overcome only by preventing her from acting on her present conception of what is in her best interests, and indeed by attempting to alter that conception). Berlin, plainly struck by the ways in which totalitarian political regimes have exploited positive conceptions of freedom, argues that liberals should have no truck with them, and commit themselves instead to a conception of liberty that focuses on maintaining individual spheres of noninterference.

Taylor's critique of Berlin characteristically avoids basing itself exclusively or even primarily on a contrary normative endorsement of positive over negative freedom (although it is true that Taylor is plainly inclined to make such an endorsement).[2] He argues, rather, that Berlin's own narrative stance is based on an inadequate conception of the background distinction it presupposes. More precisely, he suggests that on Berlin's account of the difference between positive and negative conceptions of freedom, negative conceptions appear to rely exclusively on an opportunity concept of freedom (where freedom is a matter of what it is open to us to do, regardless of whether or not we do it), whereas positive conceptions are exclusively exercise concepts (freedom exists only when we exercise control over our lives). On Taylor's view, however, this misrepresents the real complexity of the idea of negative freedom; for although one can articulate the notion in the form of an opportunity concept, one can also articulate it in terms which require the invocation of an exercise concept. If, for example, one's ground for defending a sphere of individual independence or noninterference is that it is essential for the individual to achieve self-realization (since each person's form of self-realization is original to him or her, and can only be worked out independently – as John Stuart Mill argues), then we have a version of negative freedom that cannot deny the significance of internal as well as external obstacles to self-realization (such as inner fears or false consciousness). Hence we cannot rest content with a simple opportunity concept of freedom (since people paralysed by fear of failure from realizing their deepest nature could not be seen as genuinely free).

Contra Berlin, then, negative conceptions of freedom can be articulated in terms of exercise as well as opportunity; and this broadening of the realm of possibilities here matters because on Taylor's view no simple opportunity concept of freedom is defensible. For such conceptions of freedom refuse to draw distinctions between types of action and hence types of constraint on action – what matters is not that people be free to pursue some particular goals or ideals, but that they be free to pursue whatever they themselves take to be a worthwhile goal or ideal. Hence, this aspect of their inarticulacy presents itself as a refusal to rush to judgement, a form of respect for individual autonomy. But in reality, such an across-the-board abstention from qualitative discrimination is impossible. No meaningful notion of freedom can avoid distinguishing some constraints on action as more significant than others. The repression of the right to political expression and the implementation of a system of traffic lights are not equally significant ways of restraining our actions. The former kind of interference matters more because the purpose with which it interferes matters more. Our judgements of the relative significance of human purposes themselves presuppose a certain background or horizon of what Taylor calls strong evaluation.

Human beings have not only (first-order) desires, goals, and purposes, but (second-order) desires about those first-order desires. We qualitatively discriminate between our desires, experiencing some as intrinsically more significant than others. We do so, moreover, in a manner that is entirely independent of their intensity or strength at a given time, and on Taylor's view, we could cease to do so only on pain of entirely losing any sense of who we are (by losing any sense of what truly matters to us, any grip on those moral frameworks on which our awareness of our place and orientation in moral space, and hence any sense of our moral identity, depend). Suppose, then, that we find ourselves carried away by a desire we evaluate as insignificant and acting in a way that overrides the satisfaction of a desire we judge to be intrinsically superior to it; in continuing to identify myself with the overridden desire, I am committed to thinking of my success in satisfying the overriding desire not as an achievement of my freedom but as its subversion – as a failure of self-realization. It is not the satisfaction of this desire but its elimination that would contribute to my self-fulfillment; hence I am committed to acknowledging the possibility of internal as well as external obstacles to my freedom.

Taylor's point is not that these second-order strong evaluations are beyond contestation. On the contrary, others can criticise us for making them (indeed, they are very often in a better position to identify patterns of misperception and self-deception in our thinking than we are); and the acquisition of moral wisdom familiarly takes the form of coming, on detailed reflection, to judge that we were wrong in identifying ourselves with a particular second-order desire. But if the subject of strong evaluation is in no sense incorrigible about those evaluations, it must be acknowledged that individuals are not always and necessarily the best judge of their own interests; so by restricting our concern with their freedom to the non-judgemental defence of a sphere of noninterference with the exercise of their own judgement, we might simply be allowing them to entrench their unfreedom.

Taylor is thus concerned to make three points about Berlin's way of conceptualizing the liberal conception of freedom. First, Berlin fails to see the way in which even a purportedly nonjudgemental conception of negative freedom must in fact operate within a broader background of attributions of significance and strong evaluation; in short, he decontextualizes his own favoured conception of freedom. Second, Berlin presents an oversimplified and misleadingly monolithic conception of the distinction between positive and negative conceptions of freedom. When rearticulated in terms of exercise concepts as opposed to opportunity concepts of freedom, the distinction turns out to be far from absolute, since any defensible conception of negative freedom turns out already to incorporate the step from pure opportunity concept to exercise concept that Berlin's own characterisation of the positive/negative distinction was designed to present as the truly fateful one in this domain. In other words, Berlin's definition generates a misleading appearance, and exaggerates the depth and necessity of conflict in this area. Hence, third, Berlin fails to identify and clarify the true source of dispute between liberals, and between liberals and nonliberals, with respect to freedom. The key issue is not whether to adopt a conception of freedom as the ability to fulfill those purposes that are truly mine; it is whether the form of self-realization that any defensible liberalism must seek to advance can be fully achieved only in certain forms of society, and in a way that avoids totalitarian excesses of the kind that so exercised Berlin. In effect, then, Taylor's rearticulation of the issue of positive and negative freedom is not meant to determine a particular answer to the normative question on which Berlin focusses, but rather to provide a framework within which such answers might be more profitably pursued.

A related set of questions about liberal conceptualizations of freedom is addressed in Taylor's equally famous critique of Robert Nozick's variant of liberal individualism.[3] Here, in the process of identifying and criticising what he calls the atomist tradition in modern political thought (incorporating a vision of society as constituted by individuals for the fulfillment of ends which are in some sense primarily individual), Taylor presents Nozick's notorious version of liberal individualism as an inheritor of this atomist vision. For Nozick makes individual rights a fundamental principle in politics, but denies the same status to a principle of belonging or obligation. Whereas individual rights are unconditionally binding on all of us, any obligation to support, obey, or sustain society is conditional or derivative, dependent on either consent or calculation of our individual advantage. Taylor argues that, given the truth of certain ontological claims about the priority of society over the individual, Nozick's position is incoherent.

Taylor begins by asking why theorists such as Nozick ascribe rights to human beings; what is the point or purpose of so doing? His answer follows the general lines of his notion of strong evaluation: They do so because they regard human beings as possessed of certain potentialities or capacities that are valuable and hence worthy of respect, and it is the nature of these capacities that determines the shape of their proposed schedule of rights. The idea that all human beings have the right to life, freedom, the profession of convictions, and so on, reflects a belief that the capacities involved in the exercise of such rights (the capacities for rationality, self-determination, the free development of one's mind and character) are of special significance; without them, the specifically human potential of the human animal would be crippled or remain dormant.

If, however, we acknowledge the intrinsic worth of these capacities, then we are committed not only to acknowledging people's rights to them (and so to the negative injunction that we avoid interfering with or suppressing them) but also to furthering and fostering them. For if the capacities are good in themselves, then their development and realization (both in others and in ourselves) are also good, and so the task of aiding their development (at least in some circumstances and insofar as we can) is something in which we ought to engage.

In the case of libertarian thinkers such as Nozick, the capacity that is given supreme importance is autonomy – the freedom to choose one's own mode of life. If it could be shown that this capacity, together with any others with which it is connected, could only be developed and maintained in society, or in a society of a particular kind, an assertion of the primacy of rights could not be combined with the assignment of secondary or derivative status to the principle of belonging or obligation. For if, as Taylor believes, the capacity to develop independent moral convictions is impossible outside a political culture sustained by institutions of political participation and guarantees of personal independence, then any failure to sustain those institutions would undermine the very capacities whose preservation is the implicit goal of our commitment to a schedule of rights. The moral conviction that grounds our ascription of rights also commits us to whatever actions are necessary to sustain a society that protects rights. The two commitments are equally unconditional, and stand or fall together.

It should be clear even from this brief summary that Taylor's primary goal with respect to Nozick is to contest his inarticulacy; he wants to demonstrate that even the most determined theoretically minimal form of liberal individualism will draw on a far broader horizon of value judgements and strong evaluations than it is willing to acknowledge. Eliciting that acknowledgement is, however, not the end of the argument, but rather the beginning of a more properly oriented version of it; for liberal individualists who wish to defend a Nozickian position whilst acknowledging Taylor's point will have at least two options open to them. The first would be to reduce their schedule of rights by pruning the list of human capacities that they consider worthy of respect; the second would be to contest Taylor's thesis about the essential socialness of the autonomous liberal self. We could hardly therefore conclude (and Taylor plainly does not so conclude) that this critique could definitively silence Taylor's interlocutor.

What must follow is more argument, the inevitable result of further articulating the presuppositions and consequences of the dialectical moves open to the Nozickian. For example, with respect to the first move, the Nozickian might eschew citing the human capacities for autonomous moral thought, and instead talk solely of sentience. Since the capacity to feel pleasure or pain is widely thought to be part of the endowment of any living creature, and not to stand in need of development or realisation, its creation and preservation will not presuppose any particular social context. For Taylor, however, the costs of such a move are high. For the schedule of rights that respect for such a capacity would support would be minimal indeed: It would include only the right to life, to desire fulfillment, and to freedom from pain – any other rights would have to be means to those ends. We would therefore have no reason for thinking that nonhuman animal life-forms were of any less value or significance than human ones; and we would have no grounds for objecting to a practice of transforming autonomous human agents into childlike lotus-eaters by means of drugs or (Nozick's own example, this) the use of experience machines. What such a schedule leaves out is precisely freedom as a precondition for self-development and self-realisation.

With respect to the second move, matters would be rather more complicated. The Nozickian is unlikely to contest the view that a human child entirely lacking in human company might develop the capacities needed to justify its full schedule of rights, but she might more plausibly argue that the necessary context is not that of society as a whole but the rather more restricted one of the family. Taylor disagrees with this claim: Recall that the kind of freedom that the liberal individualist values is one by which human beings are capable of conceiving alternatives and arriving at a definition of what they really want, as well as discerning what commands their adherence or allegiance, with respect to the most basic issues of life. It may well be that such a capacity is first acquired from those closest to us; but it is transmitted to us through our families from the broader civilization that surrounds them. For Taylor, this specific and complex ideal of autonomy could not have arisen and been sustained without a multitude of interacting and mutually supportive elements in the development of art, philosophy, theology, science, politics, and social organization (to the recounting of which he later devotes *Sources of the Self* ). Without a certain type of political community (with constitutional government and democratic voting practices and methods of representation) and a web of economic and cultural institutions (trade union activity, wage bargaining and business contracts, unarranged marriages, artistic and philosophical representations of the significance of individual autonomy), freedom of the kind so highly valued by Nozick simply could not have arisen and been maintained as a human possibility. Hence those who value such freedom cannot avoid an obligation to support and sustain its social preconditions.

Taylor freely admits that at this level, his argument with Nozick becomes far more wide-ranging and difficult to assess. Ultimately, it will turn on how one assesses the merits of Taylor's famous Heideggerian and Hegelian conception of human beings as self-interpreting animals – his belief that the interwoven vocabulary in terms of which a person understands herself, her responses to her world, and the worldly situations in which she finds herself partly constitutes who and what she is. But the crucial point is that the Nozickian cannot simply avoid engaging with such deep metaphysical issues; specific political commitments are not entirely self-contained or self-sustaining, but are rather rooted in broadly ramifying evaluative judgements about human capacities and human selfhood. Their true content and their rational claims on us ultimately turn on our capacity to articulate and rearticulate them powerfully and convincingly in these broader and deeper regions.

Two other points are worth noting about Taylor's critique of Nozick. The first is that it exemplifies Taylor's deliberately ad hominem – more precisely, his highly contextual – critical style. Even his most general and wide-ranging political and philosophical claims are motivated by close readings of specific authors, and by a responsiveness to the details of their individual claims and perspectives. This in turn exemplifies his belief that practical reasoning of any kind is essentially a matter of reasoning in transitions: Its concern is with comparative rather than absolute propositions, its aim is to establish that one specific position is better than another specific position by demonstrating the epistemic gain conferred by the transition from one to the other (its resolution of a specific contradiction or confusion, its acknowledgement of a factor previously screened out) – in short, by presenting the transition as error-reducing, and by responding concretely to specific criticisms of that presentation. Practical reasoning on this account is one aspect of the essentially interlocutory and narrative structure of human life as Taylor characterises it in *Sources of the Self*, a matter of one person engaging with a specific other or others about how best to understand the unfolding story of a specific intellectual trajectory.

Second, the particular transition that Taylor is aiming to effect in his critique of Nozick is not a rejection of liberal individualism, or of the typical schedule of individual rights advocated by many contemporary liberal theorists. What he wants to demonstrate is that a commitment to any such schedule of rights is not only not essentially in conflict with those who advocate a concern for obligations to and modes of participation in the community, but in fact presupposes exactly such a concern; hence, the transition he advocates is one internal to liberalism rather than one designed to move us beyond that tradition. What Taylor wants to show, in other words, is that any properly thought-through liberal individualism must have an ineliminable concern with the community. His favoured perspective is that of a communitarian liberal. But for many contemporary political theorists, such a perspective could only be a contradiction in terms; so what exactly might such a position amount to?

## LIBERALISM, COMMUNITARIANISM, AND RECOGNITION

It follows from the point just made that Taylor's relation to the debate between communitarians and liberals is a rather more complex one than has often been recognised. Although he is often categorized as a communitarian critic of liberalism, his own most extended commentary on that debate suggests that he finds prevailing characterisations of the participants to these disputes to be multiply misleading.[4] The central reason for this confusion is that commentators fail to distinguish between what Taylor calls ontological issues and advocacy issues. The first set of issues concerns what one recognizes as the factors that account for, the terms one accepts as ultimate in explaining, social life. Here the great division is between atomists and holists, with the former asserting and the latter denying that social actions and structures must be accounted for in terms of the properties of individuals, and social goods in terms of concatenations of individual goods. Advocacy issues concern one's specific moral and political policies, and the relevant spectrum of positions runs from those who give primacy to individual rights and freedom and those who give priority to community life and the goods of collectivities. On Taylor's view, the two sets of issues are distinct, in that taking a position on one set doesn't force one's hand on the other; but they are not entirely independent either, because the stand one takes on the ontological level can be part of the essential background of the policies one advocates.

Taylor's critique of Nozick exemplifies the combination of distinctness and connection between levels that Taylor is here asserting. For that critique claims that if a certain set of ontological claims is true, a specific normative position can be advanced only at a (normative) price that was not at first obvious. This is one way in which an ontological thesis can structure the field of normative possibilities in a more perspicuous way. But the ontological thesis can itself be contested; and even if accepted, it still leaves us with choices which can be resolved only by reference to further normative arguments (for example, should we respond by pruning the schedule of rights we advocate?).

More generally, it follows from Taylor's characterisation of these two interlocking fields of dispute that we should not think of the terms "liberal" and "communitarian" as delineating opposed positions on a single issue or set of issues. Taylor's rearticulation allows for four possible complex positions: atomist individualists (such as Nozick), holist individualists (such as Humboldt), atomist collectivists (such as B. F. Skinner) and holist collectivists (such as Marx). Taylor places himself alongside Humboldt, as part of a trend of thought internal to liberalism that is fully aware of the social embedding of the human agents whose individual liberty it values so highly. And by giving himself a rather more illuminating way to characterise his own perspective, this mapping also allows Taylor to deny the relevance of many lines of criticism of his own position – to argue, for example, that normative criticisms of holist collectivists are no more properly directed at holist individualists than are ontological criticisms of atomist individualists. Perhaps most important, however, it allows him to develop further his early criticisms of Nozickian liberal individualism by identifying what he thinks of as grave problems with the currently dominant procedural model of liberal political theory, problems that flow from its blindness to ontological issues of community and identity.

Procedural liberalism sees society as an association of individuals, each of whom has a conception of the good and a corresponding plan for their lives which it is society's function to facilitate as much as possible, without regard to the specific content of the plan, except insofar as it affects the equal right of others to pursue their own life plans. Procedural liberals believe that this principle of neutrality or nondiscrimination would be breached if society itself espoused one or another conception of the good life; for in a modern pluralist society, in which citizens can reasonably disagree about how best to lead their lives, a society which endorsed one such view would not be treating with equal respect those of its citizens who did not espouse it. Hence a procedural liberal society will give priority to the right over the good. It must evolve basic principles concerning how it should arbitrate between the competing demands of individuals, procedures of decision making that will include respect for individual rights, as well as the principle of maximal and equal facilitation, but without either directly defining what goods that society will further or defending its procedures in ways that make indirect reference to such goods.

Taylor contrasts this with the tradition of civic humanism, according to which a genuinely free society must inculcate in its citizens a willing identification with the polis, a sense that the political institutions in which they live are expressions of themselves, that their laws reflect and entrench their dignity as citizens, embodying a genuinely common good that is the goal of a particular common enterprise and that grounds a bond of solidarity with my fellow citizens understood as fellow participants in this enterprise. Such a notion of a common good is not reducible without remainder to a concatenation of individual goods; its being for us, for the community of fellow citizens who establish and maintain it, enters into and constitutes its value for us. In this respect, it contrasts with what Taylor calls convergent goods, such as the security provided by a police force, which are and could only be produced collectively, but whose value to us is reducible to the aggregate of its value for each individual citizen.

According to Taylor, this republican idea of a common good is far stronger than atomist or procedural liberalism can accommodate. His point is not that the procedural liberal must view political action purely as collective action with an individual point, a way of obtaining essentially individual benefits that could not be achieved through individual action. Although many procedural liberals do take this view, others – for example, Rawls in his more recent work – acknowledge that their view of society embodies and requires a societally endorsed common understanding of what is of value in political community.[5] But that common understanding is of the right, not of the good. It is the genuinely common good of the rule of law, of respect for one another's rights as citizens, and it can form the basis of a powerful notion of patriotism. But such forms of procedural liberalism continue to eschew any form of citizen identification that is based on a broader common conception of the good life for human beings embodied in political institutions and actions, for any such common good would violate citizens' rights to equal respect under the law.

Taylor's view is that even such sophisticated forms of procedural liberalism face difficulties. To begin with, they must recognise that one of the reasons their own vision of a free society can be regarded as viable in the long run is that its conception of respect for the right can form the basis of a strong, spontaneous allegiance from its members – so they will resist any tendencies for that regime to decline into various forms of despotism or anarchy, and manifest a willingness to make the sacrifices needed to ensure its survival. But such patriotism is not just a convergent respect for the rule of right; it is a common allegiance to a particular historical community and its institutions, a willingness to cherish the particular achievements, institutions, and individuals that made this political community what it now is. But if a procedural republic's very survival depends on its capacity to elicit such patriotism, then its avowed neutrality between competing conceptions of the good cannot extend to antipatriots – to those who lack or reject that allegiance to the community's history and heroes, whilst being ready to abide by the rules of the republic. Thus, a certain impurity or limitation in the procedural neutrality of such a republic, a refusal to tolerate what its own self-conception suggests it should tolerate, is in fact essential to its viability.

Perhaps more significantly, even the sophisticated procedural liberal tends to pass over the importance of what civic humanists called participatory self-rule. At best, procedural liberalism might endorse it as instrumental to the rule of law and equality; but the civic humanist tradition thinks of it as essential to a life of dignity, even as itself the highest political good. And Taylor's concern is that the patriotism essential to the viability of free societies might be importantly weakened by the marginalisation of participatory self-rule. If no value is placed on participation for its own sake, on ruling and being ruled in turn, then the governors of this society and its citizens may well become locked in an essentially adversarial relationship, in which the structures of political decision making are the object of manipulation rather than identification. On the other hand, it may be that, in certain circumstances, respected procedures of judicial review and litigation will empower people against the despotic tendencies of bureaucratic government structures, and actually enhance their sense of their shared constitution as a common bulwark of citizen dignity. It is not easy to determine a clear answer to this question, particularly when it is relativised to the tradition and culture of particular societies; what might enhance the viability of one historical community might irreparably damage another. But the difficulties and the dangers are real, and deserve careful consideration.

Taylor's final concern is related to this last point, and concerns the ethnocentricity of procedural liberalism. For it is more than possible that contemporary political theory's fixation on procedural liberalism depends in large part on taking the political tradition of the United States as its sole test case and example. It may well be the case that the procedural model best fits that country's traditions (although even that is disputed[6]), but it will plainly be ill suited to other political communities where patriotism centres on a national culture, defined in part by reference to free institutions but also by reference to history and language. (Taylor cites Quebec, but France, Belgium, and the Netherlands would also serve to illustrate this point.) In such contexts, neutrality between competing conceptions of the good life is a nonstarter, because cultural-linguistic orientation cannot be held to be a matter of political indifference. But then it becomes problematic to identify liberalism with the procedural model; for if the real world of liberal democracies includes a variety of different ways in which free institutions are embedded in social and cultural traditions, then the political theory of liberalism needs to broaden its horizons beyond the borders of the United States.

Taylor develops some of the implications of this charge of ethnocentricity in more detail when he examines one of the more pressing contemporary political issues with which the communitarian critique of liberalism became associated, that of multiculturalism and nationalism, and hence the politics of recognition.[7] The underlying thesis here is that identity is partly shaped by recognition and misrecognition, and so individuals and groups can suffer serious damage if the people or society around them mirror back a confining or demeaning or contemptible picture of themselves. Taylor traces the roots of this species of politics to the development in early modernity of the idea that each individual was capable of authenticity, of being true to her own originality, and hence needed to achieve self-realization. This ideal of authenticity became conjoined with the view that human self-development is an essentially dialogical matter – dependent not only for its genesis but also for its continuance on the acquisition and elaboration of vocabularies of expression that are conveyed through interaction with others. Taylor has great sympathy with the picture of human identity that is at work here, and hence he is concerned to determine how far the liberal political tradition with which he identifies himself can accommodate the demands that these links between identity and recognition have generated.

Taylor argues that the politics of equal recognition has produced two rather different, and apparently contradictory, political strategies. First, there is a politics of universalism, which emphasizes the equal dignity of all citizens and hence the equalization of rights and entitlements. According to this approach, all human beings are equally worthy of respect because they each manifest a universal human potential – the capacity for rational self-direction or self-realisation; and this fact about them is best acknowledged or recognised in a political order that is blind to any differences in the way they develop or actualise that potential. Second, however, there is a politics of difference, according to which what we are asked to recognise is the unique identity of any given individual or group, their distinctness from one another. Once again, proponents of this approach are giving political articulation to a perception that all human beings have a certain capacity or potential – that of forming and defining their own identity, but what they take to require equal respect or recognition is the value of what they have in fact made of this potential.

Hence, whereas the liberalism of equal dignity takes itself to be recognising the equal worth of all its citizens, the politics of difference charges that in reality its blindness to difference amounts to a failure to acknowledge the equal value of the achieved identity of some of its citizens, and argues further that this difference-blindness is not itself value-neutral but rather the expression of a specific, hegemonic culture – a particularism masquerading as the universal.

Taylor is willing to acknowledge that certain forms of liberal politics merit this kind of criticism. He cites Rousseau's interweaving of freedom (nondomination), the absence of differentiated political roles, and a very constraining common good or purpose (the general will) as a blueprint for terrible forms of homogenizing tyranny. But he argues that the full variety of resources available in the liberal tradition should not be reduced to Rousseau's specific articulation of them. After all, Kantian versions of the politics of equal dignity make no commitment to the nondifferentiation of roles in the political community; must they, too, be damned as intrinsically incapable of giving due acknowledgement to difference?

Taylor believes that it is perfectly legitimate for liberals to articulate their familiar schedule of rights in such a way as to be sensitive to the cultural contexts in which they are to be deployed, and thereby to take account of different collective goals, without losing any claim to be genuinely liberal. A procedural liberal will of course be inclined to regard any deviation from political neutrality with respect to specific conceptions of the good life as a failure to respect the equal right of all its citizens freely to choose and pursue whatever such conception they prefer. Taylor, by contrast, argues that when certain goods which must be sought in common are valued highly by a majority of the political community, the threat to equal respect for dissenting minorities that is apparently posed by political actions designed to sustain that good can be neutralized by the way in which that community constrains its actions by means of the rights it accords all its members. The key is to distinguish between fundamental rights, to be respected without exception, and other important privileges and immunities that can be restricted or revoked – but only with very good reason. If, for example, a political community acts in various nonneutral ways that are necessary to ensure the survival and reproduction of the specific culture it embodies (perhaps by legislating to ensure that a certain language is the primary language in schools and business, on public signage, and so on), but does so in ways that never violate fundamental liberal rights (the right to life, liberty, due process, free speech, and so on), then it can, on Taylor's view, legitimately claim to have acknowledged difference without violating the equal dignity of its citizens. The horizons of procedural liberalism may be too restricted to allow for this possibility, but a properly holistic liberalism is well placed to broaden our sense of the real options here, and to get down to the most important business of articulating at the appropriate level of detail exactly when and how such compromises are best made in the context of specific cultures at particular moments in their history.

It must be acknowledged that even this variant of holistic liberalism cannot claim to be providing a neutral ground on which people of all cultures can meet and coexist; but then any such conception of liberalism is a self-deluding fantasy. Liberalism is and always has been a fighting creed; any liberal will have to set limits to the degree to which she can compromise her commitment to the rule of right, and hence must reject any suggestion that she is obliged to regard all forms of human culture as being of equal worth. There may be good grounds to begin from the presumption that any cultural formation that has animated whole societies over a long period of time will have something of value to offer all human beings; but this is very different from the demand that the equality of all human beings can be properly respected only by actually judging every aspect of every existing human culture to have just as much worth as any other. Any favourable judgement of another culture can be a genuine expression of respect for it only if it is grounded in a considered and rational assessment of its actual characteristics; an a priori declaration of equal worth is simply a form of condescension, and a highly homogenizing one at that. Since such a strategy enforces a systematic blindness to difference, no form of liberalism that rejects it can properly be accused of failing to respect the identity of others.

## TAYLOR'S HORIZONS: CANADIAN, CONTINENTAL, THEOLOGICAL

I have tried to provide an accessible account of some of the more important of Taylor's specific interventions into the mainstream of contemporary political philosophy, as well as sketching in some of the recurring features – of content, of method, of style – that give these individual critical and constructive essays a certain kind of unity or family resemblance. But we can, I believe, further sharpen our sense of what is distinctive about Taylor's contribution to political philosophy by directing to his own writings the basic questions that he has consistently applied to the liberal political tradition. What, then, are the background assumptions, the (at least relatively) unarticulated horizons, of Taylor's own holistic liberalism? What are the conditions, and hence the strengths and weaknesses, of his highly individual perspective on liberalism in particular, and political philosophy in general? I conclude by mentioning three interlocking or nested contexts in which Taylor's thought has developed over the years.

The first is his membership in a specific political community, that of the province of Quebec in the federation of Canada; to be more precise, it is his participation in that community's political life. From 1961 to 1971, Taylor helped the New Democratic Party establish itself in Quebec, and was its federal vice-president from 1966 until 1971; he was also a candidate in the federal elections in the province four times between 1962 and 1968 (without success). In 1979, he returned to the political fray in Montreal, to participate in the referendum campaign. A significant proportion of his work thereafter was devoted to analysing the consequences of Canada's adoption of the Charter of Rights and Freedoms, and the subsequent failure of the Meech Lake accord – after which he was one of the experts consulted by the parliamentary commission set up to determine Quebec's constitutional and political future.[8] In short, his work in political philosophy has been effected in tandem with a persistent and detailed attentiveness to, and participation in, the political vicissitudes of a highly complex, specific, and troubled political community.

The influence of this particular practical political horizon on Taylor's more theoretical work cannot be overestimated. It is not just that Taylor's way of understanding the highly charged history and the possible future development of Quebec's relations with the other members of the Canadian Federation is indebted to his critical engagement with the intellectual traditions of liberalism; it is equally the case that that critical engagement has been fuelled and illuminated by his understanding of the ongoing Quebec-Canada crisis. Taylor's attempts to articulate a holistic rather than an atomist liberalism, in which freedom is understood as an exercise concept, the state is justified in acting in order to maintain the necessary conditions for the continued pursuit of a common good, and the political priority assigned to a schedule of rights must be made to accommodate the recognition of cultural difference and particularity, are inseparable from his attempts to find a genuinely fruitful way out of the apparently insoluble antagonisms generated by recent and current attempts to render Canadian and Quebecois understandings of the Quebecois and Canadian political communities mutually compatible.

Taylor's interpretation of the story of the Canadian Charter and the collapse of the Meech Lake accord exemplifies this symbiosis. According to his account, the 1982 adoption of the Charter of Rights and Freedoms aligned Canada's political system with the American one in establishing a schedule of rights to serve as a basis for judicial review of legislation at all levels of government. But this difference-blind procedural liberalism appeared to be in conflict with Quebec's claim to distinctness as a political community in the Canadian Federation. In order to secure the survival of its distinctively Francophone culture, Quebec has regulated who can send their children to English-language schools, required that businesses of a certain size must be run in French, and outlawed commercial signs in any language other than French – legislation that might easily be disallowed by judicial review under the Charter. The Meech Lake accord was an attempt to construct a constitutional amendment that would justify such Quebecois exceptionalism, by proposing to recognise Quebec as a "distinct society" within the federation and to make this recognition one of the bases under which judicial review under the Charter would be conducted. This would have licensed in principle a degree of variation in the application of the Charter in different parts of Canada, and was deemed unacceptable by many, on the grounds that it would amount to licensing unequal treatment of some Canadian citizens as against others, and allow the Quebec government to violate the rights of its Anglophone minority. The accord was rendered defunct by the failure of two of the ten Canadian provincial legislatures to ratify it within the established timetable.

On Taylor's view of the matter, only a holistic liberalism capable of accommodating the pursuit of collective goals in a liberal society by distinguishing the fundamental rights of citizens from less vital provision and privileges could make sense of the Quebecois vision of politics. And only a liberal vision of the Canadian Federation which could conceive of general allegiance to a federal liberal system within which different visions of the good of political community might flourish at the provincial level could provide any way of getting beyond the deep political and ontological disagreements exemplified in the collapse of the Meech Lake accord. So Taylor's suspicion of the restricted and ethnocentric horizons of procedural liberalism derives not just from a long-standing Canadian suspicion of the imperial tendencies of its powerful neighbour to the south; it is rooted in a deep familiarity with a highly specific form of liberal polity whose richness and flexibility is in grave and immediate danger from the apparently unstoppable spread of the procedural model of liberalism from its American heartland.

The second determining context of Taylor's work also has a geographical aspect, but it is more specifically methodological – it is his immersion in, and respect for, what is still commonly known as Continental philosophy. This kind of familiarity with nonanalytical forms of philosophy was almost unheard of in the Anglo-American philosophical community at the beginning of Taylor's career; and although this situation of more or less willful ignorance has been much alleviated in the last decade or so, the degree of Taylor's willingness to draw on nonanalytical writings in his work on predominantly Anglophone political theory continues to make it stand out from that of his peers. More specifically, as well as his famous and highly influential work on Hegel, Taylor is extremely well versed in the Heideggerian phenomenological tradition, and this Heideggerian inheritance has marked his contribution to political philosophy in a number of ways. To begin with, it is the proximate source of his fundamental conception of human beings as self-interpreting animals. As we have already seen, this is the ultimate ontological or metaphysical ground of Taylor's hostility to atomist forms of liberalism such as Nozick's; but it is also at work in his understanding of the distinctive Quebeçois version of liberal democracy, as well as the vision of identity that generates his politics of equal recognition. It is also a central component of the general methodological vision for moral and political philosophy that he outlines in Part One of *Sources of the Self*.

What I want to stress here, however, is another aspect of that Heideggerian inheritance – the idea of philosophical exploration as a process of articulating horizons. It is central to Heidegger's conception of human understanding from *Being and Time* onwards that it is an essentially conditioned or situated phenomenon. For Heidegger, there is no such thing as an essentially self-sufficient or self-contained mode of human understanding; even the simplest and most basic claim about any given phenomenon is itself oriented by a pre-understanding of its subject, will form part of a broader vision of that subject – standing in a relationship of mutual support to a number of other claims about it – and will likely decompose on careful examination into a number of interrelated subclaims. Moreover, any given articulation of this broader totality of interrelated claims, presuppositions, and entailments will reveal a broader context or horizon of unthematised assumptions and commitments in which it is embedded, and that will themselves require articulation if a deeper understanding of what is under investigation is to be attained (and certain possible internal tensions or contradictions avoided). Hence any given attempt to grasp a particular perspective or orientation on the world will be as contextualized or situated as the essentially worldly, temporal, and hence historical beings whose perspective it is; each attempt to articulate it in its full depth and breadth will open up further vistas whose articulation will further illuminate its object, and perhaps prompt a rearticulation of the elements of that perspective that have already been revealed – a more fruitful and penetrating conceptualisation of its underlying strengths and weaknesses.

In my view, this is Heidegger's most consequential legacy for Taylor. Quite apart from his endorsement and elaboration of certain of Heidegger's claims about human modes of being, Taylor's attempts to comprehend specific moral and political views and theories are pervasively imbued with the methodological assumption that such comprehension requires the identification, articulation, and willingness to rearticulate the broader horizon or context within which alone their human significance can become properly manifest. In other words, Taylor's way of engaging critically with liberalism is conditioned by his Heideggerian conception of what is involved in any genuinely fruitful attempt to understand a product of human understanding, to interpret a self-interpretation.

The third and final determining context of Taylor's work that I want to emphasise is that of theology. Taylor is an ecumenically minded Catholic, a Christian who finds greatness in some aspects of Judaism, Islam, and Buddhism; but it is only in recent years, and more systematically in the wake of *Sources of the Self*, that his theism has begun to assume a more explicit role in his writings.[9] Hence, there are few if any explicit traces of this theism in the influential interventions in political philosophy discussed in this essay – although his more recent reflections on the politics of recognition do raise the question of whether a theistic perspective might provide a fruitful grounding for the presumption that all human cultures are of real worth. But the interwoven methodological vision and historical narrative of *Sources of the Self* not only suggest that Taylor's future work will be pervasively inflected by his theism;[10] their perspicuous representation of what must be involved in any accounting or articulation of human values also permits his earlier work (in the realm of political values as well as elsewhere) to appear in a rather different light.

My question is: which aspects of Taylor's portrait of modernity in *Sources of the Self* actually contribute to his concluding claim in that book that our best self-interpretation might well involve reference to God as a moral source? Given his understanding of practical reasoning as essentially transitional or situated, any such contribution must take the form of showing that making a transition to a theistic grounding for the values of modernity from any of its secular rivals would be an error-reducing one. Taylor carries the argument forward on several interrelated fronts.

The first concerns the processes of secularisation after the Enlightenment. This involved the emergence of two new frontiers of moral exploration (the dignity of self-responsible reason and the goodness of nature), which then became available as secular alternatives to the theistic perspective from which they originated. Taylor argues that this mutation of the theistic variants of these values was perceived to be an error-reducing one, but that this appearance was in fact misleading. Certainly, on Taylor's account, every element of modern secular understandings of the self and of moral sources is not only perfectly compatible with but potentially central to a theistic perspective on human reality. The Cartesian turn towards the subject was prefigured in Augustine, down to a version of the *cogito* argument; the powers underlying the dignity of free, self-responsible agents were originally articulated as God-made and as part of the divine plan for the cosmos; modernity's distinctive affirmation of ordinary life is rooted not in a revolt against Christianity but in a Protestant revolt against a specific aberrant form of Catholic Christianity; and the secular vision of the natural world as a self-contained system of interlocking beings is mirrored in a theistic notion of nature as providentially ordered.

But Taylor also utilises this genealogical story to raise the question of whether secular variants of these theistic values might not still be parasitic on their theistic predecessors. He stresses the unparalleled demandingness of the commitments to universal justice and benevolence that pervade post-Enlightenment humanism. He reiterates his claim that the pervasive tendency of secular naturalism to deny the reality of evaluative frameworks will inevitably deprive its proponents of the resources needed properly to motivate and empower their own moral commitments; but he further claims that even if such reductive naturalisms are avoided, secular ways of envisioning the good may not be powerful enough to sustain our commitments. Taylor believes, in other words, that nontheistic sources, unlike theistic ones, are inherently contestable not only with respect to their truth but also with respect to their adequacy. No one doubts that those who embrace theism will find a fully adequate moral source in it; but can the same be said of a belief in the dignity of disengaged reason or the goodness of nature?

The writings of Schopenhauer, Dostoevsky, Nietzsche, and Freud have, in Taylor's view, given us a number of penetrating reasons to doubt the naive Enlightenment vision of nature as unproblematically empowering benevolence, or as moving us to help those who lack the full health and strength of normal human creatures, or in its vision of our acts of benevolence themselves as unproblematically loving and selfless. Hence, if we take these momentous (and mostly secular) internal critiques of modernity seriously, we face a choice that is strikingly parallel to the choice Taylor posed much earlier for Nozick. Either we stick with our contestable secular moral sources, and prune the depth and reach of our commitments to justice and benevolence to match their diminishing vitality, or we maintain our demanding moral standards by beginning to reverse the cultural transition away from the theistic sources that first generated and sustained them.

We will not be able simply to return to theism in the forms in which it was originally rejected; and since contemporary theism constitutes a family of positions, a frontier of moral exploration within which there is much synchronic and diachronic divergence, our turn towards it will not provide us with a single, ready-made articulation of the necessary moral sources. But we will at least have begun to orient ourselves in the right direction if we are to sustain our best moral self-understandings.

The relevance of this line of argument to any assessment of Taylor's political philosophy is, I trust, evident. For liberalism is surely one of the central cultural forms in which we have given expression to our commitment to universal justice and benevolence, our sense of the dignity of the rational, autonomous self in relation to nature. Hence, if Taylor's argument is plausible, it implies that any viable form of liberalism must not only be holistic and open to the politics of difference; it must also be prepared to take seriously the possibility that its underlying ontology will be most fruitfully formulable in theistic terms. This will not be an easy thought for most resolutely secular, Anglo-American political philosophers to take seriously. It will certainly have come rather more easily to a political philosopher who grew up in Francophone Canada, and found his intellectual footing from an early stage in Continental philosophical traditions within which the mutual acknowledgement of religious belief and philosophical endeavour (even in the form of radical mutual critique) is not unfamiliar. But it seems increasingly clear that, in the absence of a more detailed articulation of this particular horizon of Taylor's thinking, the full significance of his contribution to political philosophy is bound to elude our grasp.

## Notes

1. "Two Concepts of Liberty" in *Four Essays on Liberty*, Oxford: Oxford University Press, 1969.
2. "What's Wrong with Negative Liberty" in *Philosophy and the Human Sciences. Philosophical Papers 2*, Cambridge, U.K.: Cambridge University Press, 1985.
3. "Atomism" in ibid.
4. "Cross-Purposes: The Liberal-Communitarian Debate," *Philosophical Arguments*, Cambridge, MA: Harvard University Press, 1995.
5. John Rawls, *Political Liberalism*, New York: Columbia University Press, 1993, especially Lecture V.
6. Michael Sandel, *Democracy's Discontent: American in Search of a Public Philosophy*, Cambridge MA: Belknap Press, 1998.

7. Charles Taylor, "The Politics of Recognition" in *Multiculturalism: Examining the Politics of Recognition*. Amy Gutmann (ed.), Princeton: Princeton University Press, 1994.

8. The main elements of Taylor's writings on this topic have been collected, together with an illuminating introduction, by Guy Laforest, in *Reconciling the Solitudes*. Montreal: McGill-Queen's University Press, 1993.

9. See, for example, J. L. Heft (ed), *A Catholic Modernity?* New York: Oxford University Press, 1999.

10. The concluding chapter of Ruth Abbey's book on Taylor provides a sketch of Taylor's most recent large work-in-progress, based on his 1999 Gifford Lectures, which offers a theistically inflected account of the nature and significance of modern secularity. See Ruth Abbey, *Charles Taylor*, Princeton: Princeton University Press; Teddington, U.K.: Acumen Publishing, 2000.

# 5 Toleration, Proselytizing, and the Politics of Recognition
## The Self Contested

*JEAN BETHKE ELSHTAIN*

Charles Taylor first became known to many through his important essays challenging the regime of behavioralism in the human sciences. For those like myself who were clinging to the hope that there would be room for scholars who were not committed to a positivist epistemology and to the behavioralist outcropping in departments of Political Science, Taylor was a lifeline. He helped many whose training was not in philosophy proper but in its political theory variant to appreciate the distinctive quality of the *Geisteswissenschaften* and to fight back when we were told that the only way to do things was to abandon the ground of meaning and values; to embrace a narrow science of verification; to ignore ontological or anthropological questions altogether; and to hold epistemological debates at arm's length. Taylor's resounding claim, backed up with richly elaborate and elegant argument, was that the human sciences cannot be *wertfrei* because "they are moral sciences" whose subject matter is that "self-interpreting animal," the human person.[1] Taylor's monumental *Sources of the Self* added much needed richness and nuance to the question of identity, displaying in full his historic acumen and knowledge. This volume signaled Taylor's move toward that phase of his career associated with "the politics of recognition," very much linked to questions of identity and current, often heated, debates about multiculturalism.

It is the Taylor of the politics of recognition I hope to engage in dialogue around the problematic of toleration and proselytization and what this says about regnant understandings of the self. Taylor's politics of recognition raises questions about the liberal regime of toleration and about the dynamics of proselytization. Proselytization takes place when I knowingly and determinedly set out to change someone else's mind about something basic to his or her identity and self-definition, like religious belief. Toleration requires that I learn to live with deep differences even though I may disagree profoundly with another's beliefs and identity. Here are the key questions to engage within a broad framework of Taylor's politics of recognition: Is toleration pallid and inadequate stacked up against the politics of recognition?

**127**

Is proselytization fully compatible with the politics of recognition or a challenge to it? I take up these matters because, (a) they are intrinsically interesting and (b) they are in need of clarification given certain current forms of identity politics at odds with Taylor's own understanding. A Taylorian politics of recognition, in other words, can, and should, be brought to bear against that form of identity and recognition politics that pushes either in strongly essentialist or strongly deconstructionist directions. The heart of the matter is our understanding of the human person and in what the dignity of persons consists.

For Taylor, the self cannot exist absent his or her immersion in an inescapable framework. It is within such frameworks that we establish our orientation to the good; that our moral intuitions are engaged and formed to become solid habits; and that these moral instincts go on to become our mode of access to a world in which certain ontological claims serve as a "background picture" against which our own understandings and intuitions are articulated. Taylor argues that such background frameworks may be implicit or explicit, but we can never escape them; we can never step outside them or shed them.[2] Without these frameworks, we would plunge into a kind of abyss, described by Taylor in dire terms: "a kind of vertigo," "terrifying emptiness," anomie, lack of purpose, and the like.[3]

One such framework, for citizens of liberal societies, has been a political ethic of toleration. Selves oriented to this ethic learn to live and let live, even if they do not approve of deep commitments different from their own. Being formed in this framework means being taught that, if one is part of the majority religious or political orientation, ethnic group, or race, one must imagine what it would be like to belong to a minority. This, in turn, spurs appreciation of the necessity of a regime of toleration. Although in the majority now, one might find oneself in a minority position one day. Because selves are, to a greater or lesser extent, self-interested, many argue that prudence alone suffices to buttress a regime of toleration. The Golden Rule is likely to be evoked here, or a secular variant of it. In its classical form, the regime of toleration did not require suspending judgment as between contrasting beliefs, identities, and ways of being; rather, it required not coercing those whose orientations one might find unintelligible, even distasteful, so long as these orientations posed no threat to public safety, nor undermined the overarching orienting framework of toleration itself. Because human beings are, on Taylor's understanding, "strong evaluators," to call for persons to suspend judgment about right and wrong or better and worse, is to call for them to suspend a constitutive feature of their moral personality.

There is a story behind the classical liberal regime of toleration and it is one that speaks to dangers that are assumed to exist *should* selves locate themselves within orienting frameworks that make it impossible, or very difficult, to speak across frameworks. In a sense, the strong evaluations of selves become too strong. What Taylor calls the "qualitative distinctions"[4] push in exclusionary directions. The upshot, so the story goes, is suspicion, fear, if not outright enmity and war. Lost along the way is a humbler epistemological stance, lodged in a recognition of human fallibility. To examine what Taylor's strong politics of recognition does to, or for, standard frameworks of toleration, a more complete unpacking of the received story of toleration is necessary.

## THE STANDARD NARRATIVE

The standard version of the story goes something like this: Mandated liberal toleration saved religion from its own excesses and absolutist demands. By forcing a regime of toleration on religion, liberalism in its constitutional forms demanded that religion act more tolerantly. And so it came to pass that both "sectarian" groups (meaning religious groups) and nonsectarian groups (all others organized along the lines of the liberal mandate) would learn to live happily or if not that, at least peacefully, with and among one another. This truce is insistently represented as a fragile one by contemporary civil libertarians and the most ardent secularists. If religion threatens to get out of hand, it must be beaten back. Often the Spanish Inquisition is trotted out in argument as if this were a serious historic possibility in twenty-first century Western societies.

This is the regnant story. There are other ways to tell the tale. One would take note of the fact that were one to do something as unseemly as a body count of victims, the antireligious ideologies of the twentieth century would win that contest hands down. Murderous intolerance leading to a quest to silence, or worse, to eliminate those who challenge one's own views, is no exclusive purview of those with religious convictions. To this would be added details of the many ways that the regime of liberal tolerance has imposed real hardships on the free exercise of religion. These restrictions on free exercise derive from the suspicion that religious intolerance is more to be feared than anything else and that such intolerance is to be found lurking in the interstices of even the most benign forms of religious expression. One way or the other, this rebuttal would hold, religion per se is not the major problem in the late modern Western democracies but, rather, a dogmatic, highly ideological disparagement of religions and their faithful as an *in situ* threat to constitutional order.

If one traces the beginning of liberal toleration from John Locke's classic *Letter Concerning Toleration*, one discovers that in order for religion to be tolerated it must be privatized. There is a realm of private soulcraft and a realm of public statescraft and never the twain shall meet.[5] In the religious domain, one answers God's call. In the civic realm, God doesn't figure directly any more. One's fidelity is pledged to what Locke calls the magistracy. Should the magistracy egregiously overstep its bounds, there is always the "appeal to heaven" and the possibility of revolution. All religious views – save atheism and Roman Catholicism – are to be tolerated. Constitutional scholar Michael McConnell observes that

> Locke's exclusion of atheists and Catholics from toleration cannot be dismissed as a quaint exception to his beneficent liberalism; it follows logically from the ground on which his argument for toleration rested. If religious freedom meant nothing more than that religion should be free so long as it is irrelevant to the state, it does not mean very much.[6]

How so? Because religion has been privatized and its meaning reduced to the subjective spiritual well-being of religious practitioners. This move toward subjectivism is a general, and troubling, feature of modernity (and the constitutive episteme of modern selves, one might say), observed by Taylor over and over in his work. One strong example is the conclusion of his essay, "Language and Human Nature," in which he describes the "rotten" compromise (intellectually speaking), in which crass scientism and "the most subjectivist forms of expressivism" coexist.[7]

Religious faith has not escaped this subjectivist-expressivist juggernaut. If I am right, Locke did his part to put Western selves – Protestant selves initially, as Catholics were omitted from his regime of toleration – on the pathway toward privatizing whatever grates on, or is discordant with reference to, the dominant liberal, eventually market, paradigm. Taylor notes "the struggle between technocracy and the sense of history or community, instrumental reason versus the intrinsic value of certain forms of life, the domination of nature versus the need for the reconciliation with nature."[8] Whether one casts the battle lines this way or not, it is undeniably the case that that which was privatized over time became subjectivized and reducible to private experience. This undermines any robustness in the notion of a community of faith having a form of membership that exerts strong claims on its members.

This privatizing, even subjectifying, of religion feeds into the bad odor currently surrounding any hint of proselytization. Proselytizing seems at its best bad manners, at its worst, trying to force on me something that I do not want, am not interested in, but may be gulled or intimidated into accepting. The general animus against proselytizing flows from a conviction that those driven in a certain direction will, almost invariably, be persons of overly strong religious conviction; those, therefore, who, should they become dominant, would move to end the very toleration that has made their open proselytizing possible. (The association of the word and process with religion doesn't help. Somehow no one speaks of proselytizing when I try to convince you to change your political party. But if I urge you to change your religion, I am engaged in proselytizing and fall under suspicion.) So, in the name of preserving a regime of toleration, we must not tolerate unrestrained proselytization.

A whiff of this intolerance for proselytizing comes through in the comments of one of Alan Wolfe's respondents in his book, *One Nation After All*. One "Jody Fields" is quoted as saying: "If you are a Hindu and you grew up being a Hindu, keep it to yourself. Don't impose your religion, and don't make me feel bad because I do this and you do this."[9] Imbedded in this comment is an intolerance of religious pluralism should that pluralism reveal itself in a robust, public way. Telling a Hindu to hide being Hindu is scarcely a picture of liberal pluralism, or so, at least, one would think. One way or the other, the continuing privatizing of religion – or the view that that is what it is all about – means that when religion shows its face it must not take the form of trying to persuade someone else of the truth of the religious beliefs being displayed. "Keep it to yourself."

## TOLERATION CHALLENGED

As if this weren't enough to mull over, let's add a more recent trend to the mix. I have in mind the attack on the very notion of tolerance and toleration emanating from a postmodern direction and from those most tied up in the identity politics tendency. The argument goes roughly like this: Toleration was always a sham, a way to enforce a particular Eurocentric, patriarchal, heterosexist, Christian worldview. It was a cover story for hegemony. (And there is always just enough truth to be found in such blanket charges that one cannot simply dismiss them out of hand.) What atheists, or pagans, or non-Western religious devotees, those with once hidden sexual orientations, those who are "third world," or nonwhite, seek is not toleration but *equal normative acceptance*. This equal acceptance will be attained only when the society – any society – refuses to make any normative distinctions between and among any and all comprehensive understandings of what makes a life good, or worthy, or a belief true, or a way of structuring families better than some other. Laws, public policies, the cultural ethos must practice total nondiscrimination, in the sense of refraining from making any normative distinctions as between modes of belief and ways of life. Thus, for example: Serial sexual sado-masochism between consenting adults is not to be construed as a problematic way of ordering human existence by contrast to a monogamous sexual relationship between adults.

All in all, we are enjoined to abandon orienting frameworks that offer criteria whereby we can, and are obliged to, make qualitative distinctions between alternative orientations. Taylor's insistence that human beings cannot but orient themselves to the good is stoutly denied: we not only can but we should if we are going to move beyond toleration to validation of the "free choices" made by selves; if we are going to resist being "judgmental"; if we are going to affirm and "validate" without distinction any and all (or nearly so) ways of being in the world. Those pressing the antitoleration argument see toleration as negative, a grudging thing. They want "validation" and approval – even as they simultaneously proclaim the radical and dangerous nature of what it is they are saying or doing, as if one could have full societal validation and yet remain a permanent voice of radical dissent – but that is another issue.

Those who defend toleration point out that the alternative to toleration historically has not been a happy pluralism where we are all equally delectable peas in the pod but, instead, very unhappy, unpluralistic orders in which religious minorities and dissenters were exiled or tortured or forced to conform; in which political dissenters often faced similar assaults; in which any inkling of a sexual orientation other than that considered normal is grounds for imprisonment or worse, and so on. The defenders of toleration would argue that it is foolish to the point of suicidal for those who are a minority – in any sense – to undermine support for toleration. Toleration is their best bet as the world of indistinguishable "differences" is a chimera. There never has been such a world and never will be.

This still leaves open the matter of just how tolerant of pluralism the defenders of toleration are. There are some legal thinkers who favor increased government regulation of "sectarian" bodies in order to make them conform to standard liberal modes of representation and legitimation in their internal ordering on the view that all associations in a constitutional order must sprout analogous forms of administration. Authentic tolerance based on a recognition of deep, not superficial, differences here gives way before an attempt to normalize along the lines of forcing Catholic hospitals to perform abortions on pain of punitive measures, or requiring the Catholic and Orthodox communities to ordain women, and so on. This attack on pluralism is mounted in the name of a strong normativity that dictates in what equality between men and women consists, that extends to every dimension of human life. It is a view of equality that is taken as *the* view of equality rather than as one among a number of competing views, including those that do not demand homologous internal structures in all the institutions internal to a democratic society – a position that would destroy plurality in the name of equality.

How does Taylor help to adjudicate this knotty matter? Laying out his position is by no means simple. What he believes human selves simply are lodged within, as constitutive terms of their very existence, are deep and complex anthropological circumstances. Different aspects of our embodied and intrinsically social selves are engaged with particular features of equally complex cultures and orienting frameworks. When Taylor argues that a rightly oriented culture is one that promotes identity recognition, what exactly does that mean? What ethical practices are presupposed or called for? Is respect the same as approval or "validation" for a "life-style choice"? Surely not, but working out the details isn't easy. One may be obliged to recognize another as a being of equal worth even as one repudiates that being's choices as unworthy of one whose worth is given by virtue of his or her humanness.

Those who grew up in Christian households will recall the times a mother or father said we were to "love the sinner but hate the sin," or to "walk around in the other person's shoes for a while" and then our hearts would unlock to pity, not as a sickly attitude of paternalism but as a humble recognition of the humanity of another self. Perhaps something like that is implicated here. We need to recognize the worth of another in order to be motivated to deepen our awareness of human commonalities. This awareness of commonalities, through dialogical possibilities, will highlight particular and individual qualities that we don't want swamped by the commonalities: "I want to be me," and so does he, and she.

In his essay on "Self-Interpreting Animals," Taylor describes the ways in which I can make claims on others and they, in turn, on me. He gives an example of a "felt obligation" in the Good Samaritan story. One is called on to help the other – or so Jesus insisted – simply because this wounded and bleeding person is a child of God, a fellow creature, a moral being. For the Samaritan traveler to move on by, as several others had done in the parable because the man left dead by robbers and lying off the side of the road was an Israelite and Samaritans have nothing to do with Israelites, and vice versa, is a sinful act of cruel negligence that narrows the boundaries of the moral life. Instead, Jesus lays a strong obligation of mercy and active concern on one from a tribe not one's own. Taylor rightly names it an obligation of charity.

One is called on to *act*, not simply to *feel* the right way or think good thoughts. We are called to act because we are creatures of a certain sort as is the one who makes a claim on our help. An ability to respond to the claim of the stranger presupposes moral formation of a certain kind and Taylor stresses that identities can be forged in such a way that we experience felt obligations and act on them. Although Taylor prescinds on the formation question, his entire argument is parasitic on some such notion. No doubt there is some sort of bio-evolutionary template for empathic response or the human species would not have survived. But we know well enough that fellow-feeling can be frozen, rejected, or fail to develop in the first place.

## TOLERATION AND POWER

Those who see toleration as just a puny thing, best exposed as bogus and done away with, construe any attempt to proselytize in negative terms because this is, by definition, an assault on someone else's identity. The issue of toleration and the complexities of proselytization have been heavily psychologized in our time. Whatever makes somebody else uncomfortable is to be eschewed. But any strong articulation of a powerful religious or political position is going to make somebody somewhere uncomfortable. Does this mean we are all reduced to bleating at one another across a vast distance, that any attempt to persuade is cast as proselytizing and that is bad by definition?

Somewhere along the line – certainly in the last thirty years or so – a view of power took hold that disdains distinctions between coercion, manipulation, and persuasion. If I change my mind about something after an encounter with you, or after having spent some time in your religious community, the presupposition is that I have been messed with, gulled or brainwashed or taken for the proverbial walk down the primrose path. When we say, as many do these days, that every encounter involves power, we make it harder to distinguish between instances of real intimidation and those of authentic persuasion.

In instances of intimidation there is an implied threat of harm unless you convert to my point of view. In instances of manipulation, I sneakily get you on my side. Neither of these views respects you as a moral agent who can freely weigh alternatives and make up his or her own mind. Persuasion, by contrast, begins with the presupposition that you are a moral agent, a being whose dignity no one is permitted to deny or to strip from you, and, from that stance of mutual respect, one offers arguments, or invites your participation in a community and its rhythms and rituals. You do not lose something by agreeing. One never simply jettisons what one has believed before. But one may reject it. (And those are not identical.) Even among religious persons, however, proselytizing has come to have an unpleasant ring to it. Evangelizing sounds better. The picture of the proselytizer is of some latter-day Savonarola, severe and intimidating, or an Elmer Gantry type of huckster.

The upshot seems to be that both toleration and proselytizing are badly battered as concepts and as practices. Is there any way to redeem one, or the other, or both? I think there is. My example of redeeming both toleration and proselytization comes from Pope John Paul II's pastoral visit to Kazakhstan in September, 2001. Speaking in the capital city, Astana, on September 23, the pontiff, in his greeting to "Dear Young People!" said,

> Allow me to profess before you with humility and pride the faith of Christians: Jesus of Nazareth, the Son of God made man two thousand years ago, came to reveal to us this truth through his person and his teaching. Only in the encounter with him, the Word made flesh, do we find the fullness of self-realization and happiness. Religion itself, without the experience of the wonderful discovery of the Son of God and communion with him who became our brother, becomes a mere set of principles which are increasingly difficult to understand, and rules which are increasingly hard to accept.[10]

I found this moving and I want to explore why briefly. Certainly the combination of pride and humility is a part of it. One places before another, in all humility, one's most profound beliefs, beliefs one holds with pride – not boastful self-pride but with dignity – knowing that these beliefs may well be repudiated or ignored. Also powerful is John Paul's recognition that turning God into a metaphysical first principle is not only "increasingly difficult to understand" but "increasingly hard to accept." Here there is a fascinating dimension to his words to the Kazakh young people for he is proselytizing to those who are already Christians, reminding them of what their profession is all about.

Another of John Paul's homilies in Kazakhstan on this remarkable pastoral visit made an eloquent defense of toleration:

> When in a society citizens accept one another [notice that what is being accepted is one another as citizens, in one's civic status] in their respective religious beliefs, it is easier to foster among them the effective recognition of other human rights and an understanding of the values on which a peaceful and productive coexistence is based. In fact, they feel a common bond in the awareness that they are brothers and sisters because they are children of the one God.[11]

This is a reference to toleration among religious believers.

Unbelievers, presumably, have their own resources to draw on to respect human rights, but the pontiff suggests that the bond of coexistence will have a different – and sturdier – valence between believers and believers than between believers and unbelievers. That said, he reminded his listeners that in Kazakhstan today there are "citizens belonging to over 100 nationalities and ethnic groups" and they live – they have no choice but to live – side by side. Coexistence is a necessity. But "bridges of solidarity and cooperation with other peoples, nations, and cultures" is an immanent possibility that should be realized even as the gospel in all its fullness is preached "in all humility and pride."

This is a filling out of what a commitment to authentic toleration means as a baseline that one is invited to move beyond in the direction of equal affirmation. Toleration rightly understood permits more robust ties of civic sisterhood and brotherhood to grow and to flourish, perhaps between religious believers whose comprehensive understandings differ but whose anthropologies overlap. Toleration also permits more distance when for example, I simply cannot affirm your life choices and comprehensive views. I need not validate them at all. In fact, toleration means I may actively loathe them and argue against them. But, unless you threaten the civic order in a central way, I am not permitted to deny you your "free exercise."

Developing what it means to threaten the civic order in a central way is a topic for another essay, but it derives from Justice Jackson's rueful recognition that the Constitution is not a suicide pact. What is one to do with groups that use freedoms, claim tolerance, set about proselytizing for a future order that would immediately destroy all religious tolerance, to abolish constitutional protections, to establish a theocracy or a militant official atheism (as in twentieth-century communist regimes). Minimally, it means that one who supports constitutional guarantees of tolerance is under no obligation to work up any respect for beliefs that deny the dignity of persons, preach hatred, and directly threaten family, faith, and country. Making me uncomfortable is part of the deal, however, in the order I support. The discomfiture attendant on real toleration and pluralism is very different from a serious threat.

## TAYLOR'S POLITICS OF RECOGNITION AS DEEP TOLERATION

Taylor's politics of recognition encompasses in a single frame both proselytization and toleration. And the versions of each he provides for are robust, not anemic. Let's call Taylor's position one of *deep toleration*, a position whose starting point is his insistence on the dialogical character of human life. "One is a self only among other selves" within a language community or "web of interlocution."[12] The dialogic position commits him to the view that all human beings are creatures of value; that relativism is bound to be self-defeating; that equal recognition does not demand that all positions are equal with respect to the distribution, or understanding, of certain goods. One requires what Taylor calls a horizon of significance to sort this all out.[13]

Deep toleration does not require privatizing our deepest convictions. We live in a dialogic community and our very selves are defined and refined within this web. The dialogic nature of selves and communities means one always remains open to the possibility of proselytizing and being proselytized. The dialogic community in which deep differences become occasions for contestation with the ever-present possibility of persuasion, is pluralistic without being fragmented. Taylor has made clear his position against fragmentation of the sort that takes as a starting point incommensurability between positions familiar to us from hard-edged identity politics, hard-edged identity politics of a kind that insists, "You just don't get it," as both the beginning and the end of conversation.

Taylor's position is neither essentialist nor deconstructionist. Each of these positions is at odds with deep toleration. The essentialist position is at odds with toleration because differences are construed as so hardwired, as cutting so deep, as defining us so thoroughly that the dialogic nature of selves is denied. Denying that dialogic dimension of selves means cutting off the possibility of a dialogic community. The irony is that one remains defined in important ways by the very community whose dialogic features one denies. Because deep toleration is open to proselytization and transformation of identity, the essentialist cannot go for it.

What of the deconstructionist? Here, too, deep toleration is opposed because if there is no truth to be found there is nothing to have deep dialogue about and, further, because that which most deeply defines us is thinned out to consist in privatized ironies. If the beliefs that constitute the core of a dialogically understood self and community are privatized, the dialogic moment is cut off. Deconstructionism, for all the talk of multiculturalism associated with it, seeks not toleration, but validation of all positions absent an airing of what holds those positions together and whether each is equally worthy of endorsement. There are no shared standards for evaluation, in any case, on this view. So both essentialism and deconstructionism in their respective ways push in the direction of antidialogic monologism and are not the stuff out of which deep toleration is made. I hope I have said enough to demonstrate that Taylor's view is not only capacious enough to encompass that which we tend to drive apart – proselytization and toleration – but also that his argument helps to define and refine a position of deep toleration.

### Notes

1. The two essays here referenced are "Interpretation and the Sciences of Man" in *Philosophy and the Human Sciences. Philosophical Papers 2*, Cambridge, U.K.: Cambridge University Press, 1985, p. 57 and "Self-Interpreting animals" in *Human Agency and Language. Philosophical Papers 1*. Cambridge: Cambridge University Press, 1985.
2. This is a brief summary of Taylor's opening and framing arguments in *Sources of the Self: The Making of the Modern Identity*, Cambridge, MA: Harvard University Press, 1989, pp. 3–20.
3. Ibid., p. 18.
4. Charles Taylor, "What is Human Agency?" in *Human Agency and Language. Philosophical Papers 1*, Cambridge, U.K.: Cambridge University Press, 1985, p. 23.
5. John Locke, *Letter Concerning Toleration*, Indianapolis: Hackett, 1983. My argument is not that Locke was covertly irreligious, or that he meant to do religion in. Indeed, he was seeking a free space for its exercise. But by shearing soulcraft from statescraft – making what was essentially a separate spheres argument – he helped to alter a basic orienting framework in which *ecclesia* was the heart of existence, not at the margins, and was very much the public expression of a domain of inwardness, but a domain of inwardness that required, in order that it remain robust and faithful, external signs, symbols, rituals, and participation.
6. Michael McConnell, "Believers as Equal Citizens" in *Obligations of Citizenship and Demands of Faith: Religious Accommodation and Pluralist Democracies*. Nancy L. Rosenblum (ed.), Princeton: Princeton University Press, 2000, pp. 90–110.
7. *Human Agency and Language. Philosophical Papers 1*, Cambridge, U.K.: Cambridge University Press, 1985, p. 247.
8. Ibid., p. 246.

9. Alan Wolfe, *One Nation After All*, New York: Viking, 1998, p. 63.

10. Pope John Paul II, "Allow me to profess before you with humility and pride the faith of Christians," *L'Osservatore Romano*. N. 39–26 September, 2001, p. 5.

11. Ibid.

12. *Sources of the Self: The Making of the Modern Identity*, Cambridge, MA: Harvard University Press, 1989, pp. 35–6.

13. See Charles Taylor, *The Malaise of Modernity*, Concord, Ontario: Anansi Press, 1991, p. 52, for a discussion of "horizons of significance." This language recurs throughout Taylor's work of this period.

# 6 | Taylor and Feminism
### From Recognition of Identity to a Politics of the Good

*MELISSA A. ORLIE*

The most obvious point of contact between the work of Charles Taylor and feminism is his reflections on the politics of recognition. Taylor has been a noteworthy advocate of the view that members of distinct cultural and social groups deserve to be recognized for who they interpret themselves to be and allowed to pursue their collective survival as they understand its requirements.[1] To the extent that specifically feminist questions have been posed in and of Taylor's work, they have arisen on the terrain of the politics of recognition. For instance, Taylor includes "some forms of feminism" in his discussion of those groups that seek recognition in today's politics.[2] In their critical engagement of his thinking, both Susan Wolf and Linda Nicholson question Taylor's apparent assumption that his arguments about distinct cultural identities can be applied to women as a social category.[3]

My aim in this essay is not to elaborate the relationship between Taylor's work and feminism using the politics of recognition as a conceptual bridge. To the extent that both Taylor and feminists operate under the rubric of the politics of recognition of identity, I find their formulations to be symptomatic of some of the most questionable aspects of contemporary political thinking and culture. However, I do want to suggest that we can find a promising alternative to Taylor's formulation of the politics of identity within his own corpus, namely, a politics of the good. A politics of the good does not begin and end with questions about "who I am" or "who we are," as the politics of recognition does. Rather, as I develop the notion here, a politics of the good presses us to say what our visions of the good are, to say what we consider it good to do and to become. To say what our vision of the good is, is at the same time to say something about who we are: To say what we believe is good is to say what we stand for, which no doubt is related in some ways to where we stand and, thus, to what we and others have taken our identity to be. According to Taylor's understanding of the evaluative sources of identity as elaborated in *Sources of the Self*, however, where we stand need not determine or exhaust what we stand for. Our social or cultural positions do not necessarily prescribe our judgments about what is good. Our sense of the good may prove to be unexpected or idiosyncratic in relationship to how others interpret the various identities which may be ascribed to us or even in relationship to how we understand our own social identities.

Taylor maintains that modern Western cultures are morally and politically debilitated both by our diminished capacity to articulate the goods we already value and by our reticence to imagine visions of the good that might inspire us to attain and secure what we value. As an aspect of these larger cultures, feminist theory and politics have become increasingly unable to articulate visions of the good. In some recent instances, feminism seems to have become nearly bereft of such visions and this loss of vision has diminished feminism's capacity to inspire action.

I believe that Taylor's work can offer feminist theory a renewed appreciation for the politics of the good. In turn, feminist theory and politics can teach Taylor and admirers of his writings lessons about why the tension in his work between a politics of recognition of identity and a politics of the good is best resolved in favor of a politics based on what we value rather than on who others take us to be or even who we understand ourselves to be. I suspect that before partisans of the politics of recognition can begin to see the desirability of a politics of the good, however, it may be necessary to recast or at least clarify the concept of the good operative in Taylor's thinking. Here, I offer a preliminary sketch of what such an alternative conception of a politics of the good might be.

## A POLITICS OF THE GOOD

As feminist theorists and activists have become more astute about power, they have become less articulate about their visions of the good. If Taylor's reading of modern culture is right, such a failure of expression is not peculiar to feminism. But for those who are committed to feminist principles and aims, such lack of fluency should be especially troubling.

First, like other new social movements, feminism depends on our inspiration to act on our motivation and energy to use our bodies, skills, and resources in ways that can transform our own lives and the lives of those with whom we share the world. Compelling accounts of the wrongs that women suffer which feminists aim to redress are obviously one element of what may motivate us to act. But a rehearsal of wrongs and suffering alone, no matter how rich and detailed, cannot inspire action. When we are preoccupied with our injuries and suffering, we may come to feel afflicted and incapable of constructive action. We may come to think of ourselves as victims rather than as actors, confusing complaint with constructive action. Taylor is right to emphasize how visions of the good not only remind us of what it is good to be, but also empower us to pursue and achieve the good we envision.[4]

Like other social and political movements today, feminist politics and theory need to reclaim an avowedly normative dimension, in my view. This normative project must not be considered antithetical to the analysis of power but must be conjoined with it. Or, at least, the normative must be conjoined to the analysis of power if we want to attend to the power effects and political implications of our orientations toward the good. Although I cannot fully argue the point here, I think that one feature shared by most feminist visions of the good – with the possible exception of certain forms of liberal feminism – is a sense that it is both right and good for us to be responsive to the claims of others, particularly when our exercise of freedom has harmful effects on others.[5] Ironically, I find signs of such a widely held moral and political sense of responsiveness to others in the reluctance of contemporary feminists to offer affirmative articulations of what we see as good. Feminists of all stripes have become more inclined to say what we are against rather than what we are for. In part, no doubt, this reticence in articulating our sense of the good can be attributed to a self-protective defensiveness. But hesitation to affirm a particular vision of the good is also informed by an aversion to doing harm, an aversion to excluding others or doing injury to them. Such reticence bespeaks a normative impulse. I think, however, that this normative aversion to doing harm should be transformed into more explicit, affirmative statements about what we regard as good. We need to make more affirmative statements because in the absence of such affirmative visions and of actions in accordance with them, our politics will always be oriented by the harm that we have already done rather than by the good that we seek.

From one angle, discussion of the good seems antithetical to modern cultures characterized by multiple and competing goods. In this context, the move to talk about the good is often taken to be antimodern and dogmatic. Perhaps theorists of the good have found relatively little audience among feminist theorists because feminists have presumed that discourses about the good are inherently conservative. Have feminists not been right to make this assumption? But questions of the good are especially important to feminism because many of the sorts of wrongs and forms of conduct that concern feminists are matters of the good that cannot be legislated without violating valuable political principles.[6] Questions of what it is good to be are absolutely crucial in regimes alive with multiple and competing goods. In such political cultures, many persons have a relatively wide berth of freedom in their exercise of power.[7] Many of the harms that threaten residents of such regimes, and the constructive developments that can redress those harms, are not matters that can be legislated without unduly compromising freedom, which is to say, without imposing one conception of the good and foreclosing others. Whether we extend respect to others, and whether we receive respect in turn, often involves forms of conduct and motivation that cannot be legislated as a matter of right, but involve and require our concern about what it is good to be.

According to Taylor's understanding, the modern notion of respect involves acknowledging others' autonomy and valuing our own autonomy.[8] This peculiarly modern sense of what respect involves "gives salient place to freedom and self-control, places high priority on avoiding suffering, and sees productive activity and family life as central to our well-being."[9] These are the very arenas of life that are of paramount concern to many feminist and queer theorists and activists. In these arenas, what is authorized as legally right is of crucial importance, including matters of sexual harassment, domestic violence, reproductive and parental rights, freedom from discrimination in employment and other civil rights touching on matters such as housing, health care, and death benefits. But these matters of right are certainly not exhaustive politically speaking. Matters of human dignity, even of discrimination, cannot be touched by issues of right alone, but also involve questions of how it is good for us to treat one another. Respect for human dignity entails not only respecting basic rights but also matters of what Taylor calls attitudinal respect, or all that is involved in commanding the respect of others and granting respect to them.[10] In short, there are ethical dimensions that undergird political right: There is the letter of the law and then there is its spirit.

Obviously, to make political issues of "what it is good to be" and "what kind of life is worth living" is a double-edged sword. Claims about the good are often invoked to deny not only respect to women, ethnic, racial, and sexual minorities, but also concrete rights and opportunities to act. But in politics everything is dangerous and there are no guarantees. Taylor does not always seem to fully acknowledge or do justice to the threat and dangers involved in deliberations about the good.[11] For instance, he claims that for us moderns the fear of condemnation has given way to the danger of meaninglessness.[12] But there are social groups that still suffer the realities of social condemnation and the scars of abjection. And, in the main, the headway these groups have made against social abjection has flowed from a politics of the right and not from a politics of the good. Still, I think that Taylor is right in his judgment that avoiding questions of the good will not protect us and only denies us resources that can inspire us, resources we need to defend and sustain our lives.

Discourses of obligatory action are insufficient once we are dealing with actions and consequences that cannot be explained by the outright violation of another's rights. Once we are faced with questions about which forms of power are conducive to freedom, then what Taylor calls constitutive and life goods must become our concern. Many post-Nietzscheans share Taylor's sense that discourses of what is right and obligatory do not exhaust, and may even obscure, the most vital issues of our time.[13] Post-Nietzscheans and Taylor share a sense of the vital importance of our very capacity to say and transform what we want. But I think Taylor is right that we post-Nietzscheans by and large have been far too reticent about articulating the evaluative distinctions that inspire and direct our thinking and action. Our reticence to say what we value is ironic to say the least, given Nietzsche's conviction that one of the greatest dangers of our time is our unwillingness or inability to feel and say what we value. As Nietzsche says in the course of elaborating what he means by the phrase beyond good and evil, "At least this does *not* mean 'Beyond Good and Bad'."[14]

If Taylor's influence on feminism has been limited to this point, perhaps this is due to certain prejudices about the good in contemporary cultures, prejudgments that Taylor himself diagnoses. But these prejudices against a politics of the good are not without warrant, and Taylor's own formulation of the politics of the good at times may reinforce these prejudices against the good rather than provide a viable alternative. I find two veins in Taylor's thinking about evaluative sources and identity. One vein of thinking locates reflections on the good squarely within the tradition of modern skepticism about ultimate claims, whereas another vein still longs to transcend such skepticism and to *substantialize* the good, especially in the form of group identities.[15] By substantialize I mean quite literally to turn into a substance and to embody as something firm and real. In contemporary parlance, I suppose one might say that in this vein of his thinking Taylor veers toward being a cultural essentialist on matters of identity. As I have said, however, I am less concerned about the politics of identity and more interested in the political and ethical implications of how we conceptualize the good.

In the first case, I have found in Taylor a most promising line of thinking that takes us beyond a politics of identity premised on claims about "who

I am" as a matter of social position and, instead, conceives our identity to be oriented by evaluative sources and aims that unsettle and transform any claim, once and for all, to know or secure the good that inspires our action. This line of Taylor's thinking resonates with Wendy Brown's noteworthy suggestion that we might "incite a shift in the character of political expressions and claims," supplanting "the language of 'I am' – with its defensive closure on identity, its insistence on the fixity of position, its equation of social with moral positioning – with the language of 'I want this for us'."[16] As Brown notes, the reference point of "for us" orients this politics of desire beyond the expression of "I want" in terms of liberal self-interest, and looks instead to the collective or political good as the aim of my desire. It seems obvious that Brown's goal is that we develop a politics of desire "for us" that does not constitute the political too narrowly and thereby reinstate in a more collective form the very fixed and closed social identities that she criticizes. But what can forestall this process of closure? Preventing or interrupting such closure in discourses of identity is especially difficult given the apparent inevitability of moments of identification within desire. As counterintuitive as it may sound, my sense is that only a politics that seeks to articulate its vision of what it is good to be, alongside its claims about what it is right to do, can counteract our human (all–too–human) tendency to seek the closure of personal and collective identity.

The reason my claim about the desirable character of the politics of the good is likely to seem counterintuitive is illustrated by the second line of Taylor's thinking, namely, his willingness to approve the substantialization of collective identities and their good. Claims to be and do good tend dogmatically to fix the boundaries of identity, and it is this tendency, I think, that is behind the wariness of so many feminists, among others, to engage in a politics of the good. What I try to suggest below is that a politics of the good need not take this dogmatic form. If the good is conceived as finally indeterminate and undefinable, as never once and for all in our sights or within our grasp, our visions of the good can supply us with the energy to transform the self-serving fixity of our identities.[17] I celebrate the unsettling and transformative potential within evaluative sources not because I regard mobility as good in itself. I think Taylor rightly criticizes many post-Nietzscheans for the valorization of mobility as an end in itself. Rather, I emphasize the way our concern for the good may unsettle and transform us because I think that such movement is part and parcel of our concern for the good. This movement of a perpetual effort to grasp what is good, while recognizing that one cannot altogether hold or fully know what is good, I take to be a sign of the fact that the good has become a problem for us. The meaning of our whole being, Nietzsche maintains, may be summed up in the fact that the will to truth has become a problem for us, has become something that we acknowledge and engage as problematic.[18] According to Nietzsche's understanding, the only way to do justice to the truth is to experience it as a problem. I think the same can be said about what is good. According to my understanding, one vein of Taylor's thinking teaches that the meaning of our being is that we have become conscious of the good as a problem. That is to say, we cannot avoid avowing what we believe to be good, but neither can we ever be certain that we know what we value or the value of what we believe we value.

Our concept of the good, and more generally our conception of the concept, is of real political importance. Below I suggest how the highly abstract and apparently narrowly philosophical question of how we conceive of the Hegelian concept of universality and of the good – which I think ultimately divides feminist thinkers like Seyla Benhabib and Judith Butler – is of the utmost political significance. Still, it is true that theoretical debates about our conception of the concept are not politics per se. Feminist theoretical debates over the character of the concept of universality and normative principles have political ramifications, and the arguments we make and the stances we take in these debates usually say a great deal about our vision of the good. But political contests are fought and often won or lost by the evocative power of our visions of the good. We must regain the courage to articulate our visions of the good. Luckily, as Taylor shows us, the very articulation of our vision of the good can empower us to act.

## IDENTITY AND THE GOOD

In *Sources of the Self*, Taylor argues that there is an intrinsic relationship "between senses of the self and moral visions, between identity and the good."[19] In his view, to say "who I am" is to say where I stand on matters of the good: "My identity is defined by the commitments and identifications which provide the frame or horizon within which I can try to determine from case to case what is good or valuable, or what ought to be done, or what I endorse or oppose."[20] We cannot act without some orientation toward the good: Orientation toward the good is a crucial feature of human action.[21] Taylor characterizes our stance toward the good as part of the "transcendental conditions of human agency"[22] because without such evaluative orientations we simply cannot make sense of our lives. That is to say, in the course of living our lives, we make qualitative discriminations:

In fact, we cannot help but make such "strong evaluations." Taylor claims that the moral orientation toward the good which is constitutive of identity requires that we each make "discriminations of right or wrong, better or worse, higher or lower, which are not rendered valid by our own desires, inclinations, or choices, but rather stand independent of these and offer standards by which they can be judged."[23] Who we are is constituted through the accumulation of these strong evaluations, evaluations that taken together could be said to comprise our orientation toward the good.[24]

Taylor's argument that there is an ineluctable relationship between identity and a vision of the good is an important resource for feminism and other new social movements. But few feminist theorists have explicitly drawn on Taylor's work as they have on the writings of Foucault, Habermas, Derrida, Rorty, or even Gadamer. As of yet, Taylor's writings have had little obvious impact on feminist theory, even as his diagnosis of the reserve that modern cultures assume toward the good affords important insights into the current condition of feminist theory and activism. Many feminists may resist my claim that Taylor's work has much to offer feminism, and in some cases this resistance will be for good reasons.[25] Taylor's framework is amenable, however, to transformations that will enable it to respond to feminists' current preoccupation with relationships of power.

In my view, one of the most theoretically troubling and politically debilitating features of contemporary discourse is the stark antithesis between rich normative reflection such as Taylor's and astute analyses of power such as those which have increasingly come to characterize feminist discourse. But in the sum total of Taylor's writings we find both a strong normative and an incisive critical orientation. On the one hand, in *Sources of the Self*, Taylor resuscitates contemporary moral reflection on the good in the face of paradigmatic preoccupation with questions of right. On the other hand, in his widely discussed essay on "The Politics of Recognition," he explores how "Nonrecognition or misrecognition can inflict harm, can be a form of oppression, imprisoning someone in a false, distorted, and reduced mode of being."[26] Taylor is one of the few philosophers who at once is highly attentive to the good and offers trenchant analyses of power. Still, his framework must undergo certain changes in order to respond to the variety of concerns that feminists might raise about it, while at the same time sustaining his basic insight about the importance of regaining our powers of expression in relation to the good.

When Taylor speaks of morality and of moral sources, he uses the terms more broadly than most contemporary moral philosophers. He wants to expand our consideration of morality beyond the right to include the good, beyond questions of what it is right to do, to include questions of what it is good to be.[27] Throughout this essay, I speak instead of *evaluative* sources and orientations, although Taylor himself might very well resist this shift in terminology. I adopt this broader language for two reasons. First, I think it underscores Taylor's more expansive understanding of morality, an understanding that takes us beyond the neo-Kantian preoccupation with offering basic reasons for a course of action to include articulation of the visions of the good that inform action.[28] If we speak of evaluative sources and orientations, rather than moral ones, we can sustain Taylor's emphasis on qualitative distinctions and the strong forms of evaluation they require. At the same time, the Nietzschean notion of evaluation works rhetorically to highlight both our lack of certainty about our visions of the good and the absence of transcendental guarantees – even provisional and revisable ones – for the judgments that follow from our visions of the good.[29]

Second, by drawing a contrast between *moral* sources and orientations on the one hand, and *evaluative* sources and orientations on the other hand, I want to call attention to a tension and ambiguity in Taylor's thinking. One of the most important achievements of his work is that he returns us to questions of the good, and does so in a manner that acknowledges how the problem of skepticism arises out of our existential condition.[30] The fact that we cannot be certain about the good, the fact that we exist in a cultural time in which it is widely acknowledged that there are multiple and competing conceptions of the good, has resulted in the suppression of talk about the good. As Taylor amply demonstrates, however, silence about our visions of the good does not mean that claims about the good are absent – only that they are unavowed. When we do not attend to the visions of the good that animate our arguments and actions, we do not accept responsibility for those visions and their effects on others, and this inattention is not only philosophically significant but also has political and ethical consequences.[31] In a context where both our conceptions of the good and the power effects of our commitments tend to remain unavowed, to call for and to become more articulate about the good, as Taylor does, is to take an important step toward joining rich normative reflection with acute sensitivity to power.

Taylor, then, is one of a diverse group of philosophers, among whom I would include Iris Murdoch and Stanley Cavell, who have sought to return us to discussion of the good while fully acknowledging our skeptical condition. In this vein, Taylor emphasizes our always contestable answers to inescapable questions[32] and the tentative, searching, uncertain character of many of our moral beliefs.[33] But Taylor's acknowledgment of our skeptical circumstances sometimes falters. In another vein, Taylor seems to return to the conventional association of the good with absolute claims. More specifically, he says that, as he uses the term, the good refers to "whatever is picked out as incomparably higher in a qualitative distinction."[34] Because evaluative statements are always made by finite human agents, and because he speaks often of the diversity of goods, perhaps we can presume that Taylor would be willing to follow Nietzsche's lead and add "incomparable for me" to each articulation of the good.[35] At some moments, it seems as if Taylor associates being oriented toward the good with an experience of its incomparability. At such moments, he seems to think that to be authentically oriented toward the good I must feel that it is not only good for me but good, even incomparable, for others as well, even as I recognize that they may not agree. In short, at times Taylor seems to associate being oriented toward the good with an affective experience of sureness about the good and with a sense that the good is ultimately definable. At moments such as these, Taylor works against his own effort to resuscitate vocabularies of the good by reinforcing the modern assumption and prejudice that talk about the good necessarily trades in moral certitudes about human nature and ends. I do not know how to square those moments when Taylor associates moral sources with an experience of the incomparability of substantively definable goods, with other moments where he endeavors to teach us to be less dogmatic in relationship to particular goods and to acknowledge the diverse goods that we actually affirm and draw on.[36]

When Taylor approvingly speaks of a judgment of the incomparability of the good in such a manner, he falls prey to his tendency to allow the good to be turned into a substance, and more specifically, to his willingness to allow the good to become located in a particular culture or collective identity. In his discussion of the politics of recognition, Taylor seems to consider it legitimate for a group not only to lay claim to a particular conception of the good, but also to claim that their conception of the good and, thus also their group identity, is incomparable.[37] I must emphasize that whenever Taylor speaks of a good being distinctive to a particular group, or of how different groups may come to share a conception of the good even amid their differences, he always does so with the highest degree of nuance. As I have already said, Taylor has a remarkably keen sense of the dynamics of power, especially of the oppressive consequences of attempting to establish "unity-through-identity" rather than "unity-through-difference," as well as of the deleterious consequences of denying how one's own group has learned from and been influenced by other groups or cultures.[38] As a consequence of Taylor's subtlety as a thinker, the usual criticisms of "liberals" for presuming that their culturally specific norms are universal or of "communitarians" for ignoring the mutual influence and historical transformation of the communities they extol, do not really get at what may be most worth critically engaging in his work. The more fundamental matter at hand is the different ways of conceptualizing the good that can be drawn from his work and the various moral and political implications that follow from those different concepts.

If we compare Taylor's concept of the good with that of Iris Murdoch, whom he cites often and approvingly, we can see more clearly what is at stake in the tension between different conceptions of the good within Taylor's thought.[39] For Murdoch, there is something profoundly delusional about the claim to the incomparability of one's good or group. Such claims are delusional precisely because the good is not finally definable.[40] If I read him correctly, sometimes Taylor's understanding of the good accords with Murdoch's and, like her, he stresses the ways the good is always beyond us, is something that we can never fully articulate. This sense of the undefinable good is especially strong in Taylor's discussion of personal identity and the good in the early sections of *Sources of the Self*, in his discussions of the arts and, more recently, in his work *A Catholic Modernity?* At other moments, however, Taylor treats the good as something common, as the sort of thing to which a group can lay claim in saying who they are. This more substantial sense of the good appears especially when he reflects on group identity in "The Politics of Recognition," but also at some moments in *Sources of the Self*.[41] For Murdoch, I think, when you are actually seeking the good – rather than deluding yourself and serving your ego – the good unsettles and potentially transforms who you are. Conversely, for Murdoch, the good is betrayed or lost from sight when we transform it into a substance to which a particular group or identity can lay claim. In contrast to Murdoch, and perhaps building on his early formative work on Hegel, Taylor at times seems inclined to grant the good a collective and substantial character. There are different ways of reading Hegel and the status of the concept in his corpus; this is an issue to which I return below.

For now I simply want to call attention to a basic tension between Taylor's claim that our identity is constituted by our orientation toward the good and his substantialization of group identity. I find two competing conceptions of the relationship between identity and the good in Taylor's writing. On the one hand, he suggests that who I am can be expressed in terms of evaluative sources and an orientation toward the good that can never be fully articulated and is likely to be inexhaustible because the good is as infinite and elusive as reality itself.[42] I associate this view with a *politics of the good*. On the other hand, Taylor apparently acknowledges approvingly the fact that groups of people presume that the vision of the good which their experience yields is definitive of their collective identity, whether that group identity is a cultural, ethnic, or a so-called gender, sexual, or racial identity.[43] I associate this formulation of the relationship between identity and the good with the *politics of recognition*.

Drawing on what distinguishes Murdoch's and Taylor's thinking, I would like to suggest that the problem with the formulation of the relationship between identity and the good associated with Taylor's understanding of the politics of recognition is that it vitiates the power that evaluative sources and distinctions have to unsettle and transform our sense of identity. These unsettling and transformative aspects of moral and evaluative sources are important for the ways they enliven and sustain our orientation toward the good.[44] When the good is conceived as undefinable, the good toward which we keep striving can more readily challenge our tendency to fix and fixate on our identity or a particular experience of the good. In this way, the good is kept alive and not confused with some delusion of the self.[45] In contrast, when the good is conceived as a substance in the form of a group identity, our delusional claims to know the good, to be and do good, are protected – and often enough at exactly those moments when we least deserve to claim that we are being and doing good.

## FEMINIST THEORY AND POLITICS

According to Taylor, contemporary moral philosophy tends to obscure the relationship between identity and the good, so it is hardly surprising to find that the same can be said of contemporary feminist theory and activism. But my guess is that feminists, and a whole range of their contemporary fellow travelers, will be reluctant to follow me in affirming Taylor's diagnosis of the condition and consequences of our modern reticence to talk about the good. I think they would be reluctant even bearing in mind the reservations and qualifications I introduced above. As Taylor himself acknowledges, one of the great achievements of post-Nietzschean thinking is to show us how visions of the good are connected to certain forms of domination.[46] The insight into the relationship between claims about the good and the exercise of power is most popularly associated with the work of Michel Foucault, but it has become ubiquitous. One of the great diagnostic achievements of *Sources of the Self* is to show the specifically moral sources – which is to say the visions of the good – behind various contemporary forms of reluctance to discuss the good. Taylor points out that empirical naturalists and utilitarians reject qualitative distinctions. He explains that liberals and neo-Kantians believe that social peace and justice demand a discourse of right that adopts a stance of impartiality relative to competing senses of the good. Taylor also points out that for post-Nietzscheans, every invocation of the good is an act of power that asserts one form of life and seeks to foreclose others. In each case, Taylor reveals the unavowed conception of the good at work in each position. I am sympathetic to the resistance that all these positions are likely to offer to Taylor's demand that we avow and become articulate about our visions of what is good. Still, I want to press Taylor's case. More specifically, I want to use Taylor's framework to set out on what I take to be a useful path for understanding certain transformations that feminist theory and politics have undergone in the last two decades.

I want to sketch and elaborate the following general picture. In the 1970s and early 1980s, there were distinct forms of feminist discourse – call them liberal, radical, and socialist – each of which was relatively explicit about its evaluative sources and affirmative visions, as well as quite decided about the limitations and failings of its competitors' sources and visions. As these forms of feminist theory and activism have become increasingly sophisticated in their analyses of power, however, they have also become increasingly reticent about their evaluative sources and affirmative visions. Virtually all forms of liberal, radical, and socialist feminist theory and activism have felt compelled to respond to critiques of their initial analyses of oppression and affirmative visions which have pointed to their failure to come to terms with crucial forms of power. More specifically, proponents of each of these various political theoretical positions have had to respond to charges that their theory and activism, while challenging certain forms of power and privilege, at the same time drew on other forms of power and privilege, leaving them unseen and unchallenged. Liberal, radical, and socialist feminists alike have been called to account for structural inequalities related to racial, sexual, and class differences. In a sense, feminists have been called to recognize the distinctness of racial, class, sexual, and gender identities.

One way to gain a sense of the transformation in feminist discourse that I have in mind is simply to contrast representative texts from the 1980s and 1990s. My claim is not that one set of texts is politically good and the other set bad. Rather, my suggestion is that with greater nuance in the analysis of power has come a suppression of the "strong evaluations" and affirmative visions that implicitly inform the critiques of power in question.

Although it was a long time coming, increased acknowledgment of the current and historical realities of racial injustice was one of the marked achievements within dominant feminist discourses of the 1980s. This achievement is best exemplified in the United States by the appearance and reception of *This Bridge Called My Back. Writings by Radical Women of Color*, edited by Cherrie Moraga and Gloria Anzaldua.[47] In the 1990s, the rise of postcolonial discourse has represented a more global and an even more historical and contextual perspective on issues of racism and imperialism. Examples of postcolonial discourse are collections such as *Third World Women and the Politics of Feminism*, edited by Mohanty, Russo, and Torres[48] and *Feminist Genealogies, Colonial Legacies, and Democratic Futures*, edited by Alexander and Mohanty.[49] As a text of the 1980s, *This Bridge* is characterized by broad statements about the injustices suffered by women of color, coupled with impassioned statements about what the writers take to be just and unjust, good and bad. By contrast, the 1990s postcolonialism texts are characterized by increasingly local, historically particular, and thick descriptions of the dynamics of power. In a sense, the latter offer more precise and variegated analyses of power, but these have been achieved at the cost of more explicit critiques and normative declarations, at least by comparison to *This Bridge*. In these later works, there are few general normative statements about the wrongs under study and even fewer articulations of the alternative goods sought. These normative and affirmative statements are in short supply for fear of mirroring or perpetuating the very structures of power that are the focus of the analyses. In her preface to the second edition of *This Bridge*, Cherrie Moraga appears to second this more chastened normative expression and politics when she reports on the difficulty of organizing a Third World feminist movement in the United States and on the need for a more international perspective.

Survey texts that might have been assigned in feminist theory courses to capture the state of current theoretical debates and political challenges also changed over the course of the 1980s and 1990s. Allison Jagger's *Feminist Politics and Human Nature*[50] and Rosemarie Tong's *Feminist Thought: A Comprehensive Introduction*[51] were published in the 1980s. Each text articulates the basic assumptions that inform liberal, Marxist, and radical feminisms, the forms of political analysis and concern they typically pursue, and the criticisms they commonly face. Tong's text was published in 1989 and also includes references to "psychoanalytic," "existentialist," and "postmodern" feminisms. In the 1990s, *Feminist Contentions. A Philosophical Exchange* between Seyla Benhabib, Judith Butler, Drucilla Cornell, and Nancy Fraser was an often cited feminist text and served as a springboard for many critical discussions.[52] The book arose from a symposium ostensibly on the theme of feminism and postmodernism held in Philadelphia in September 1990.

What is notable about the text, besides the acrimony which sometimes characterizes the exchanges within and beyond its pages, is that debate about the philosophical foundations of feminist politics has displaced explicit debate about what the goods of feminism could and should be. I say "explicit debate" because I think different conceptions of the good are at stake in these debates about feminism's philosophical foundations. I will develop this claim in a moment.

Some might characterize the changes in feminist discourse over the course of the 1980s and 1990s as a move from the political to the highly theoretical, from the activist to the academic. Although such antiintellectualism is always fashionable, even in the academy and especially in the United States, I think that such a characterization of the development of feminist discourse obscures and thus overlooks a crucial problem that reading Taylor brings to light. Contemporary feminist theory offers us increasingly theoretically sophisticated analyses of power and its working, and ever more astute reflections on the philosophical foundations of feminism. Against these theoretical developments, some feminists have formulated a pragmatist reaction and call for concrete policy initiatives and political action.[53] But those who declare themselves more pragmatic than theoretical, more activist than academic, are rarely any more explicit in their articulations of the good or inspiring in their affirmative visions. In other words, both the most highly developed theoretical formulations and the most pragmatic calls to action lack an explicit statement of the vision of the good animating their politics.

The finer articulations of the workings of power that have come to characterize feminist discourse, especially in the last decade, are genuine theoretical achievements that correlate with real political gains. For every feminist who has doubted the political efficacy of calling into question the fixity or inclusiveness of gender as an identity category, there is no doubt another feminist whose existence has become more livable. Judith Butler states the matter simply and well when she says that "One might wonder what use 'opening up possibilities' finally is, but no one who has understood what it is to live in the social world as what is 'impossible,' illegible, unrealizable, unreal and illegitimate is likely to pose that question."[54] At the same time, I think, this greater understanding of the complex workings of power has led to a retreat from our normative frameworks, normative frameworks that, following Taylor, I believe we unavoidably have and draw on. These normative frameworks provide the evaluative resources that afford us our vision for political critique. In other words, there are affirmative visions within these contemporary feminist critiques but they remain insufficiently articulated. It seems that our heightened awareness of how power relations infuse and inform the very articulation and formulation of the categories and ideas central to politics has led to a reticence to say what we are for, or an inability to say anything more than what we are against. As a consequence, feminist discourse seems to be plagued by the same sort of apparent value neutralism that Taylor identifies and criticizes in modern Western cultures generally. When feminists of all stripes say, for instance, that they are against racism – without moving on to say what they think it is right to do, not to mention what they think it is good to be or become – the political and moral differences between various feminist discourses become difficult to discern and our evaluative sources and affirmative visions are suppressed.

At first blush my claim that differences between feminists are muted and difficult to discern may seem ill-informed, perhaps even preposterous. We need only consider the pitch of dispute among the feminist theorists in *Feminist Contentions* to wonder at my characterization of feminist discourse in terms of an apparent, if deceptive, value neutralism. But my claim is not that there are not actual differences among various feminist theoretical and political positions. Rather, my claim is that it has become increasingly difficult to make out the qualitative political and moral distinctions that animate those different positions. What are the distinct affirmative visions animating these debates and controversies? What is politically and ethically at stake in the goods to which these political theoretical positions are, even if only implicitly, committed?

I take debates about the philosophical foundations of feminism, such as those found in *Feminist Contentions*, to be genuine, if not yet fully successful, efforts to reformulate answers to questions about what we value and affirm in light of the new insights into the operations of power, insights that have preoccupied feminist theory and discourses of the left more generally over the last three decades. More specifically, I understand the debate between Seyla Benhabib and Judith Butler in *Feminist Contentions* to be a dispute about the *concept* of universality. Benhabib might not agree, for she characterizes the dispute as a debate about whether or not we are willing to make reference to and orient ourselves according to the universal. The absence of such commitment and orientation toward Enlightenment universality, says Benhabib, "may eliminate not only the specificity of feminist theory but place in question the very emancipatory ideals of the women's movement altogether."[55] What Benhabib calls "postmodernism," which she associates with the rejection of Enlightenment regulative principles of agency, autonomy, and selfhood, threatens to "undermine the very possibility of feminism as the theoretical articulation of the emancipatory aspirations of women."[56]

What makes Benhabib's argument plausible to some, I suggest, is the reticence of post-Nietzscheans like Butler to offer sufficiently explicit articulations of their visions of what they think it is good to be or become.[57] But as Butler first suggested in her response to Benhabib and Nancy Fraser in *Feminist Contentions*, and makes even clearer in her recent articulations of the specifically Hegelian cast of her own thinking, to claim, as she does, "that the universal has not yet been articulated is to insist that the 'not yet' is proper to an understanding of the universal itself: that which remains unrealized by the universal constitutes it essentially."[58] Like those of Charles Taylor, one of Butler's chief preoccupations has been to develop Hegel's critique of Kantian formalism for failing to address the ways in which the abstract is always dependent on the concrete, the formal on the substantive and, Taylor would add, the right on conceptions of what is good. Butler argues that Benhabib, and more recently Susan Okin and Martha Nussbaum, ignore the ways in which the reasons and principles for which they claim universality carry within them particular cultural content that limits their claim to the universal.[59] Such unavowed foreclosures pose a problem for theorists whose discourse aspires to universality. Such foreclosure limits what we can regard as viable ways of living, and it delimits what is livable without acknowledging either its power to do so or the contestability of its claim to do so.

Since Benhabib understands her own contextualized universalism to be a response to Hegel's critique of Kant, the differences between Butler and Benhabib cannot be fully clarified, let alone resolved, simply by reference to a contest between Hegelian and Kantian concepts of universality.[60] As Taylor might suggest, to understand what is politically and morally at stake in debates like that between Butler and Benhabib, we need more explicit statements about what they each want for us politically, about what good and goods they would have us value and seek.

Both Taylor's and Butler's thinking may be characterized as significantly inflected by their encounters with Hegel, but they offer quite different renderings of the logic of the Hegelian concept. More precisely, I expect that Butler would judge the logic of Taylor's thinking to be too identitarian and substantialist and, in this way, a failed attempt to realize the significance of Hegel's critique of Kantian formalism.[61] But rather than ascend to this level of theoretical debate, in this context I turn to the implications of Taylor's philosophical background as they appear in his formulation of the politics of recognition. Rather than measure and contest Taylor's debt to Hegel, I leave these philosophical issues in the background and focus instead on Kwame Anthony Appiah's important critique of Taylor's formulation of the politics of recognition.

## CONCEIVING THE GOOD

On my understanding, Appiah's reservations about Taylor's formulation of the politics of recognition turn on what he discloses as Taylor's substantialization of the good in the form of group identities.[62] Like the majority of students of contemporary philosophy, Appiah follows Taylor in insisting on a dialogical and nonessentialist understanding of identity: There is no self prior to social relations and the self comes into existence in dialogue with others. Beyond this point, Appiah has serious reservations about Taylor's formulation of a politics oriented around group demands for recognition of identity. Appiah objects to the fact that Taylor grants greater weight to the collective than to the personal dimensions of identity. As a matter of intellectual history, Appiah argues, Taylor neglects the oppositional aspects of the ethics of authenticity. That is to say, the demand for the recognition of one's true self often occurs in the name of the individual against society and against one's particular social group or groups. Appiah suggests that, like many contemporary theorists of the politics of recognition, Taylor attends only to those cases when a claim is made in the name of a minority social group against the majority. According to Appiah, Taylor tends to conflate the collective and personal dimensions of identity and, as a consequence, he does not acknowledge the threat that social groups can pose to the personal dimensions of identity and individual autonomy. Recognition of group identity becomes a source of personal injury when the individual is pressed to comply with positive life-scripts about her or his racial, gender, or sexual identity in order to aid that social group in its battle against the negative life-scripts about the group that have reigned in the larger society. As Appiah says, "The politics of recognition requires that one's skin color, one's sexual body, should be acknowledged politically in ways that make it hard for those who want to treat their skin and their sexual body as personal dimensions of the self. And personal means not secret, but not too tightly scripted."[63]

I want to press Appiah's point against Taylor, but I think his criticism must be recast slightly if the value of his objection is to be fully appreciated. As I see it, Appiah's criticism would be even more forcefully made if recast in terms of competing ways of conceptualizing the good rather than as a matter of whether one places primary emphasis on the personal or collective dimensions of identity. Appiah suggests that Taylor overlooks things of profound value and misses important aspects of the dynamics of power. But as formulated, Appiah's objection seems to ignore the very dynamics of power that concern Taylor, dynamics of power that Taylor seeks to address by way of the politics of recognition. As Appiah would surely acknowledge, whether one can even experience and explore the personal dimensions of one's identity may depend on the recognition of, and granting of respect to, one's racial, sexual, or gender group. Taylor might very well reply to Appiah's criticism by noting that to explore the personal dimension of one's identity is all well and good, but the precondition of such exploration is the survival and protection of one's social group. The tone of Appiah's remarks throughout his essay leave little doubt that he would not disagree with the speculative reply I attribute to Taylor. If I am right about Taylor's and Appiah's basic agreement on this ground, it seems that the contrast between the personal and collective dimensions of identity does not really get to the heart of Appiah's critique of Taylor's formulation of the politics of recognition.

But a closing, if not fully explained, comment by Appiah does go to the heart of the matter: "It is a familiar thought that the bureaucratic categories of identity must come up short before the vagaries of actual people's lives. But it is equally important to bear in mind that a politics of identity can be counted on to transform the identities on whose behalf it ostensibly labors."[64] Appiah does not explain how and why it is that identities are transformed by the politics undertaken on their behalf. Identities certainly are not necessarily or always so transformed, for Appiah is right to acknowledge the way the politicization of identity governs the possibilities of identity. Indeed, as we saw in the *Feminist Contentions* dispute between Benhabib and Butler, the relationship between normative claims on behalf of the rights of particular identities and the normalizing effects of such claims has been a major point of contention in feminist discourse in relationship to identity politics and in debates between critical theorists and poststructuralists.

As I suggested at the outset, however, at least one vein of Taylor's thinking about the relationship between our evaluative sources and our identities gives us a viable account of what transforms identity. The crucial issue is not whether we are more or less wedded to the individual or collective dimensions of our self-identity but rather how we conceive the normative sources and good that we affirm and toward which we aspire. Our identities change not because they are prescribed by social position or because individuals acquire a space free of power from which they can arrive at the personal meaning of who they are and what they value. Who we are is shaped and infused by the evaluative sources and aims that animate our lives. It is our concern for the good, and our effort to articulate what we believe it is good to be, that can change who we are by deepening our sense of what we believe to be good. Such engagement with the question of what it is good to be or become may open up forms of life and political possibilities that a politics of recognizing given identities feels compelled to refuse. But whether or not a politics of the good has this transformative effect on who we are and what we value depends on the concept of the good toward which we aspire.

## CONCLUSION

Given the predominance of disputes between "liberals" and "communitarians" in recent decades, it is not unusual to characterize primary political differences in the way Appiah does his main difference from Taylor, namely, in terms of their contrasting emphasis on personal or collective identity. Disagreements between liberals and communitarians are one axis of the politics of recognition of identity; the disputes between "poststructuralists" and "communicative ethicists" are another. Taylor's main contributions and challenges to contemporary political theory can be represented in terms of the politics of the recognition of identity. I have argued, however, that this is not Taylor's most important contribution to contemporary political theoretical reflection. The most timely contribution of Taylor's work is to enable a transition from a politics of the recognition of identity to a politics of the good. In contrast to a politics of recognition, a politics of the good does not begin and end with questions about "who I am" or "who we are." Rather, a politics of the good presses us to say what our visions of the good are, to say what we consider it good and right to do and to become. The politics of the good has become submerged and unavowed in our time for reasons that the writings of Taylor help us better understand. As Taylor has deepened our understanding of this loss, he has worked to make us more aware of and articulate about the good. More specifically, Taylor has made us more aware of how we abide by notions of the good that we fail to avow explicitly with the deleterious consequence of unknowingly placing limits on what we can or will affirm in our own lives and in the lives of others. Taylor has worked to make us more articulate about what we believe to be good so that we might become more inspired to take action for its sake.

A politics of the good is of vital ethical and political importance because it encourages us to see better what we value and thereby fires our imagination and cultivates our energy to take action on behalf of what we believe to be good and right. No amount of attention to harm and injury can inspire and sustain constructive action without some corresponding sense of the good that is violated or deprived by harm and injury. And there are pervasive forms of harm and injury in contemporary societies that simply cannot be addressed by a politics of legislation without violating freedoms that we take to be fundamental. Whether we respect one another, whether we use our freedom in a manner that allows others to live in peace, or whether we allow one another to survive and thrive to pursue our own good are not issues that can be legislated wholly as a matter of right. Rather, they entail forms of conduct and motivation that involve and require our concern about what it is good to be.

But whether or not a politics of the good actually possesses these advantages, and whether or not it is amenable to feminist and queer political theoretical concerns, depends on the concept of the good at work in our politics. As recent feminist theoretical debates such as that between Judith Butler and Seyla Benhabib make abundantly clear, how we conceive of normative sources and principles of universal significance is of vital political and ethical importance. Some have judged such debates about abstract theoretical concepts to be beside the point politically. Others have represented such disputes as occurring between those who affirm the normative and universal and those who reject such notions altogether. A careful reading of Taylor's work teaches us that the possibilities for conceiving normative sources and the good are far richer and more varied than can be captured by the question of whether one is for or against the Enlightenment. Once we acknowledge, finally, that the issue is not whether we should rely on normative sources and principles, but rather whether or not we think through the political and ethical implications of different normative sources and concepts, then perhaps we can become more articulate about the good, then perhaps we can get down to the more explicitly political and ethical work of saying what we think it is right and good to do and to become.

### Notes

Thanks to Jonathan Allen and Sam Frost for their comments on an earlier draft of this essay.

1. Obviously Taylor's engagement with these matters is informed by his participation in decades of debates about Quebec and the fate of its distinctive culture.

2. Charles Taylor, "The Politics of Recognition" in *Multiculturalism: Examining the Politics of Recognition*. Amy Gutmann (ed.), Princeton: Princeton University Press, 1994, p. 25.

3. See Susan Wolf, "Comment" in *Multiculturalism: Examining the Politics of Recognition*. Amy Gutmann (ed.), Princeton: Princeton University Press, 1994, p. 75; Linda Nicholson, "To Be or Not to Be: Charles Taylor and the Politics of Recognition" in *The Play of Reason: From the Modern to the Postmodern*, Ithaca: Cornell University Press, 1999, pp. 129–43.

4. *Sources of the Self: The Making of the Modern Identity*, Cambridge, MA: Harvard University Press, 1989, pp. 92–5.

5. I think we need to articulate more fully the various ontological commitments and visions of the good informing this manifest sense of what we owe to others. The writings of Drucilla Cornell have done more than most to articulate these principled commitments and to articulate their truly radical potential and demands on us.

6. Where we draw the line between right and good is an object of political contest that depends on our vision of the good. Taylor associates discourses of the good with moral philosophy and generally does not speak of the good in relationship to political theory, unless in relationship to the good of a particular community. My discussion in this and succeeding paragraphs should make clear why I cannot separate the good from politics or restrict conceptualizations of the good to the claims of particular communities.

7. See Melissa A. Orlie, *Living Ethically, Acting Politically*, Ithaca: Cornell University Press, 1997.

8. *Sources of the Self: The Making of the Modern Identity*. Cambridge, MA: Harvard University Press, 1989, pp. 12–13.

9. Ibid., p. 14.

10. Ibid., p. 15.

11. Taylor might rightly criticize me for transposing questions of the good, which belong to the domain of moral philosophy, into the political realm as he endeavors to maintain a distinction between the two. I have already said why I think this slide is unavoidable. The key issue then becomes how we attend to the dangers that accompany political contest among divergent views of the good.

12. *Sources of the Self: The Making of the Modern Identity*, Cambridge, MA: Harvard University Press, 1989, p. 18.

13. There is much to be learned from the work of William E. Connolly and Jane Bennett on this theme.

14. Friedrich Nietzsche, *On the Genealogy of Morals*. Walter Kaufmann (ed., trans.), New York: Vintage Books, 1967, p. 55.

15. For an introduction to Taylor's thinking about the good, see Ruth Abbey, *Charles Taylor*, Princeton: Princeton University Press; Teddington, U.K.: Acumen Publishing, 2000, pp. 9–53. I understand my reservations about certain of Taylor's articulations of the good to cut across his formulations of "hypergoods" and "constitutive and life goods." That is to say, I do not think my reservations are

based on Taylor's avowed theism or his view that most moral frameworks make reference to a hypergood or that all moral frameworks make contrastive and hierarchical judgments about the good. It is more accurate to say that I am calling attention to different attitudes toward or ways of experiencing the good that are evident in Taylor's writings. For example, at some moments his discussion of hypergoods appears to resonate with the first vein of his thinking I identify here, whereas at other moments his formulation seems to draw freely on the second, more substantializing vein of his thinking that I criticize here. In short, there are at least two ways of conceptualizing the good (or two different conceptions of the concept) in Taylor's writings and I find one far more amenable to feminist theoretical concerns, especially those that have been influenced by poststructuralism.

16. See Wendy Brown, *States of Injury*, Princeton: Princeton University Press, 1995, p. 75.

17. In *A Catholic Modernity?* Taylor discusses how a concept of the good (or, in this case, God) that is sufficiently transcendent as to be perpetually beyond our grasp and finally unknowable and undefinable requires "opening yourself to a change in identity," New York: Oxford University Press, 1999, p. 21.

18. Friedrich Nietzsche, *On the Genealogy of Morals*, Walter Kaufmann (ed., trans.), New York: Vintage Books, 1967, p. 161.

19. Charles Taylor, *Sources of the Self: The Making of the Modern Identity*. Cambridge, MA: Harvard University Press, 1989, p. x.

20. Ibid., p. 27.

21. Ibid., p. 33.

22. Ibid., p. 33.

23. Ibid., p. 4.

24. For a more detailed discussion of Taylor's understanding of selfhood, see Ruth Abbey, *Charles Taylor*, Princeton: Princeton University Press; Teddington, U.K.: Acumen Publishing, 2000, pp. 55–100.

25. Annette Baier is a feminist who thinks that Taylor has little or nothing to offer feminists. See her "Critical Notice of *Philosophy and the Human Sciences*," *Canadian Journal of Philosophy*, Vol. 18 (1988), pp. 589–94.

26. Charles Taylor, "The Politics of Recognition" in *Multiculturalism: Examining the Politics of Recognition*. Amy Gutmann (ed.), Princeton: Princeton University Press, 1994, p. 25.

27. Charles Taylor, *Sources of the Self: The Making of the Modern Identity*. Cambridge, MA: Harvard University Press, 1989, p. 3.

28. Ibid., p. 77

29. Taylor is a moral realist. I think he would reject my formulation in this and the preceding sentence as incompatible with any form of moral realism. I would reject such a characterization of my position which I think relies on an unduly constrictive idea of what counts as moral realism (for instance, I think Nietzsche is a kind of moral realist, albeit of a quite different and new sort), but I cannot argue for my claim in the limited space available here.

30. For a resonant formulation of the relationship between the skeptical problematic and our human condition, see Stanley Cavell, *The Claim of Reason*, Oxford: Oxford University Press, 1999. Although Taylor and Cavell are very different thinkers, I see each as seeking to understand the roots of the skeptical problematic and the epistemological deadlocks into which it gets us. Each would also have us turn toward the good, although they have quite distinct understandings of what that entails.

31. See Melissa A. Orlie, *Living Ethically, Acting Politically*. Ithaca: Cornell University Press, 1997.

32. Charles Taylor, *Sources of the Self: The Making of the Modern Identity*. Cambridge, MA: Harvard University Press, 1989, p. 31.

33. Ibid., p. 10.

34. Ibid., p. 93.

35. See Charles Taylor, "The Diversity of Goods" in *Philosophy and the Human Sciences. Philosophical Papers 2*, Cambridge, U.K.: Cambridge University Press, 1985, pp. 231–47.

36. The former more dogmatic conception of the good is related, I think, to Taylor's tendency to substantialize identity. His willingness at times to affirm substantializations of the good is, in turn, rooted I think in his interpretation of Hegel, an interpretation that appears to be constitutive for his thinking. Perhaps I am failing to recognize that Taylor's reflections on the good are yet another occasion for his characteristic effort to "reconcile solitudes." For a discussion of this tendency, see Ruth Abbey, *Charles Taylor*, Princeton: Princeton University Press; Teddington, U.K.: Acumen Publishing, 2000, p. 4. But still I find it politically and ethically constructive to attend to these competing conceptualizations of the good in Taylor's thinking.

37. I take this to be the basic objection in K. Anthony Appiah's important response to Taylor's formulation of the politics of recognition which I discuss later in this chapter.

38. See *A Catholic Modernity?* New York: Oxford University Press, 1999, p. 14.

39. Also see Taylor's discussion of Murdoch and of the resonances and differences between their approaches to the good in his "Iris Murdoch and Moral Philosophy" in *Iris Murdoch and the Search for Human Goodness*. Maria Antonaccio and William Schweiker (eds.), Chicago and London: University of Chicago Press, 1996, pp. 3–28.

40. See Iris Murdoch, "The Idea of Perfection" and "The Sovereignty of the Good and Other Concepts" in *Existentialists and Mystics*, New York: Allen Lane, 1998, pp. 333, 383.

41. Charles Taylor, *Sources of the Self: The Making of the Modern Identity*, Cambridge, MA: Harvard University Press, 1989, pp. 35–8.

42. Iris Murdoch, "The Idea of Perfection" in *Existentialists and Mystics*, New York: Allen Lane, 1998, p. 333.

43. I say "apparently" because Taylor's work on "multiculturalism" might be as much descriptive as prescriptive. I owe the suggestion of this possibility to

Patchen Markell. Ronald Beiner makes the merely descriptive character of Taylor's discussion of the politics of recognition and its lack of normative prescription a central point of his criticism of Taylor; for example, see *Philosophy in a Time of Lost Spirit*, Toronto: University of Toronto Press, 1997, p. 164.

44. Iris Murdoch, "The Idea of Perfection" in *Existentialists and Mystics*, New York: Allen Lane, 1998, pp. 316–36.

45. See Murdoch's discussion of the self as a false sun, "The Sovereignty of the Good and Other Concepts" in *Existentialists and Mystics*, New York: Allen Lane, 1998, p. 383.

46. Charles Taylor, *Sources of the Self: The Making of the Modern Identity*, Cambridge, MA: Harvard University Press, 1989, p. 100.

47. New York: Kitchen Table Press, 1980.

48. Bloomington: Indiana University Press, 1991.

49. London: Routledge, 1997.

50. Lanham, MD: Rowman & Littlefield, 1988.

51. Boulder, CO: Westview Press, 1989.

52. *Feminist Contentions: A Philosophical Exchange*, London: Routledge, 1995.

53. For a reading of this terrain, see Beatrice Hanssen, "Whatever Happened to Feminist Theory?" in *Critique of Violence: Between Poststructuralism and Critical Theory*, London: Routledge, 2000, pp. 232–58.

54. Judith Butler, Preface, *Gender Trouble*. London: Routledge, 1999, p. viii.

55. Seyla Benhabib, "Feminism and Postmodernism: An Uneasy Alliance," *Feminist Contentions: A Philosophical Exchange*, London: Routledge, 1995, p. 20.

56. Ibid., p. 29.

57. In my view, Butler's work has changed of late in this regard. She seems to have found a manner of articulating what she values and why she values it that skirts the problem of normalization of which she is rightly wary. For example, see her emphasis on the value of self-preservation and the living of ordinary life (eating and sleeping) in the Preface to *Gender Trouble*, London: Routledge, 1999, pp. vii–xxvi and in "Ethical Ambivalence" in *The Turn to Ethics*. Marjorie Garber, Beatrice Hanssen, and Rebecca Walkowitz (eds.), London: Routledge, 2000, p. 27.

58. Judith Butler, "Restaging the Universal" in *Contingency, Hegemony, Universality: Contemporary Dialogues on the Left*. Judith Butler, Ernesto Laclau, and Slavoj Zizek (eds.), London: Verso, 2000, p. 39. See also Judith Butler, *Excitable Speech: A Politics of the Performative*, London: Routledge, 1997, and "For a Careful Reading" in *Feminist Contentions: A Philosophical Exchange*, London: Routledge, 1995, pp. 127–43.

59. *Feminist Contentions: A Philosophical Exchange*, London: Routledge, 1995, pp. 127–43 and "Restaging the Universal" in *Contingency, Hegemony, Universality: Contemporary Dialogues on the Left*. Judith Butler, Ernesto Laclau, and Slavoj Zizek (eds.), London: Verso, 2000, pp. 35–6. Butler's criticism of Nussbaum is particularly germane to my argument here since Nussbaum's neo-Aristotelianism might be cast as a form of the politics of the good. Drawing on

Murdoch and Butler to leaven aspects of Taylor's thinking, I mean to suggest a politics of the good that is distinct from Nussbaum's in some crucial ways while resonant in other ways with the theory of justice she is developing. See Martha Nussbaum, *Sex and Social Justice*, New York: Oxford University Press, 1999.

60. For this larger context of Benhabib's work see generally *Situating the Self*, London: Routledge, 1992.

61. One basis for my conjecture is her discussion in "Restaging the Universal" in *Contingency, Hegemony, Universality: Contemporary Dialogues on the Left*. Judith Butler, Ernesto Laclau, and Slavoj Zizek (eds.), London: Verso, 2000. See also her "Preface to the Paperback Edition" in *Subjects of Desire: Hegelian Reflections on Twentieth-Century France*, New York: Columbia University Press, 1999. For a resonant reading of Hegel, see Robert B. Pippin, *Hegel's Idealism: The Satisfactions of Self-Consciousness*, New York: Cambridge University Press, 1989.

62. Although Appiah poses his criticism of Taylor in terms of individual versus group identity, whereas I emphasize the central importance of the concept of the good on which a thinker draws. See K. Anthony Appiah, "Identity, Survival: Multicultural Societies and Social Reproduction" in *Multiculturalism: Examining the Politics of Recognition*. Amy Gutmann (ed.), Princeton: Princeton University Press, 1994, pp. 149–63.

63. Ibid., p. 163.

64. Ibid.

# 7 | Catholicism and Philosophy
A Nontheistic Appreciation

*WILLIAM E. CONNOLLY*

"Occasionally, I laugh."

Charles Taylor

## PHILOSOPHY AND FAITH

Charles Taylor is a thinker of singular importance. He breaks new ground in contemporary thought by refusing to align himself unreservedly with the large options presented to us. He is not easily definable as either a secularist or devotee of a lost Christendom, a defender of modernity or one who seeks to return to an enchanted world, an empiricist or a rationalist, a simple universalist or an obdurate relativist, a defender of philosophy against faith or of faith against philosophy, a tight lipped analytic philosopher or a loose tongued continental thinker. Each time a philosophical or theological faction seeks to etch a division in stone, Taylor surfaces to complicate the picture. He chastens the contending parties and proposes options that command the attention of reflective thinkers.

His work is admirable in another, related respect. Over the last four decades he has displayed a remarkable ability to move across the metaphysical, epistemological, anthropological, political, and ethical registers of thought, showing others through these explorations how each dimension of his work helps to define the others. Showing them, too, how a similar complex of loose implications and interdependencies operates within their own thinking. In this way, Taylor extends the horizon of contemporary thought. He encourages you to check one dimension of your thought against others, even as you test the larger complex against his multidimensional perspective.

I am doubly indebted to Taylor. I am indebted positively to his critiques of rationalism, empiricism, reductionism, and normative neutrality in the nineteen sixties and seventies, drawing sustenance from his elucidations of deep interpretation, the complexity of identity, and reflective normative engagement. I am indebted, second, to the distinctive mix of Christianity and philosophy he has developed. His thinking in this domain has encouraged me to refine my nontheistic orientation to interpretation, ethical cultivation, the politics of identity and difference, and deep pluralism. My relation to Taylor on the first themes is one of indebted engagement; on the second it is that of agonistic respect. "Agonistic respect" may remind Taylor of the "warrior ethic" he opposes because of its opposition to an ethic of "benevolence." To me, however, agonistic respect means a relation of respectful connection across difference and competition, one in which active intellectual competition is chastened by reciprocal appreciation of the deep contestability of the projection each partisan makes into being. Agonistic respect strengthens rather than weakens connections because it does not require a positive fund of commonality as its only base. The connection can also grow out of the shadow of opacity the experience of the other presents to you and you to him.

Exactly what in Taylor's thought invites respect from a nontheistic perspective? It can be brought to light by addressing a key move he makes in *Sources of the Self* with respect to the "sources" of ethical life. Philosophies that focus exclusively on the rational justification of moral rights, basic obligations, or justice, he contends, miss something profoundly important to the ethical life. It is not simply that they fail to pay enough attention to "the good" (although they do); it is that they also fail to come to terms with how people are inspired to respond to ethical responsibility and to marshal the energies to carry out the ideals they endorse. It is because I agree with Taylor on the importance of sources that I find so much to draw from his work. It is because I dissent from his depreciation of sources prospected in some nontheistic traditions that I contest it.

It is the complex relation between words and the fugitive sources they touch that is important here. "Moral sources," Taylor says, "empower":

> To come closer to them, to have a clearer view of them, to come to grasp what they involve, is for those who recognize them to be moved to love or respect them, and through this love/respect to be better enabled to live up to them. And articulation can bring them closer. That is why words can empower; why words can at times have tremendous moral force.[1]

A formulation inspires and energizes an individual or constituency ethically when "it brings the source closer." And "an effective articulation releases this force," thereby investing power in the words through which the articulation proceeds.[2] No articulation, however, makes the source it articulates lucid or transparent in itself. That is indeed one of the reasons some moral philosophies shy away from engaging this dimension of ethical life.

Why is a source unsusceptible to full articulation? Because, first, that which subsists below articulation is moved and altered as it is drawn into a historically specific world of dense contrasts, similarities, identities, and negations. And, second, because the highest source – an infinite, loving God – is unsusceptible in principle to full articulation in human terms. Taylor says the paradoxical character of articulation or manifestation is now appreciated in a variety of modern expressivist philosophies: "to talk of 'making manifest' doesn't imply that what is so revealed was already fully formulated beforehand. Sometimes that can be the case.... But in the case of the novel or play... I am taking something, a vision, a sense of things, which was inchoate and only partly formed, and giving it a specific shape."[3]

Moral articulation thus has a double or, perhaps, duplicitous character. One might think of Augustine's *Confessions* or the music of Mahler in this way. The expression of what was previously inchoate inspires and energizes the words or the score, but that inspiration now is manifested through an uncertain mixture of that which preceded articulation and that which is shaped and moved by it. To articulate is to mix. But Taylor also wants, understandably enough, to speak of better and worse articulations. The best articulations, he contends, are those that draw close to a transcendent source beyond human representation. A transcendent source is the highest source. Taylor uses cautious language in discussing transcendence as a source. He generally invests presumptive priority in it by suggesting that attempts to articulate other sources either implode through performative contradiction or give insufficient recognition to a demand built so deeply into the human being as to locate a ground of morality strong and authoritative enough for the critical role we ask morality to play. So he speaks of articulations that "bring the source closer," that "recognize" something inchoate that precedes them, and that are "attuned" to a fundamental "bent of being." A transcendent source is thought to be the only one that really has the qualities needed. He crafts a language that suggests the possibility of recognizable distortion in articulation while still respecting the impossibility of representing a transcendent source as it is in itself. In another key, he preserves truth as a goal at which to aim while denying that the most fundamental truth can be represented or reduced to knowledge. Taylor walks a fine line.

This is the fugitive juncture, you might say, where faith enters Taylor's philosophy. Some of his secular critics insist that because faith does enter the picture Taylor has left philosophy behind. A compelling philosophy of ethics must avoid faith. But like Taylor, I find that that response evades the crucial role fugitive energies play in life. Philosophy and faith are interwoven, if you take each term in a reasonably broad way: So far no philosophy known to me has established itself authoritatively by argument alone. An element of faith is thus discernible in commitment to a particular philosophy. I slide, then, close to Taylor's reading of the connection between philosophy and faith.

It is just that where he projects or confesses a loving God who transcends articulation, I project a reserve or virtual field below articulation without intrinsic purpose or salvational promise. The contestable source I cultivate exceeds articulation not because its intelligence transcends us but because its energies have a complexity that does not correspond entirely to human capacities for conceptual thought.[4] Whereas Taylor seeks to give greater expression to the God who inspires him, who precedes his subjectivity, and who informs his ethical practices, I seek inspiration from a nontheistic reserve of being that energizes me, that precedes my subjectivity, and that embodies a protean diversity that can help to inspire a positive vision of pluralism. My ethic of cultivation, like his, is not entirely reducible to subjectivity or intersubjectivity. But the slack is not taken up by a designing or loving God; it is taken up by an abundance of being over identity that can exceed and energize us.

Another way to put this is to say that whereas Taylor reworks Plato, Augustine, Hegel, Wittgenstein, and Heidegger to develop a theistically inflected faith capable of governing ethical life, I rework Epicurus, Lucretius, Spinoza, Nietzsche, Thoreau, Deleuze, and Prigogine to develop a nontheistically inflected faith that inspires presumptive appreciation for both already existing diversity and the dicey politics of becoming by which new events, pursuits, and identities are periodically ushered into being. For me obligation, responsibility and agonistic respect do not precede being: They are secondary formations growing out of a presumptive care for the diversity of being that precedes them. Such an ethic of cultivation, you might say, is not juridical in the first instance. The difference between us, despite what Taylor sometimes suggests, is not reducible to that between one party who endorses a positive ideal and another who limits himself to critiques of existing practice. The difference is elsewhere: in the dicey disparity between an appeal to the whisper of transcendence and an inspiration drawn from the fugitive well of immanence.

I think this discrepancy in existential faith is linked to real political and ethical differences, even though there are usually other intervening steps between the former and the latter. It is also unlikely to yield to final resolution by definitive argument. I say that after agreeing in advance that argument can make a real difference in this domain, and even after having heard for two decades how impossible, self-contradictory, cold, negative, or otherwise unwise the nontheistic faith I embrace "must" be. Here we may enter a somatic or spiritual zone where visceral experiences of attachment, identification, and conversion are not entirely amenable to the resources of argument and analysis. This is partly because the latter are looser and more porous in character than their strictest devotees acknowledge and partly because gut commitments formed through diverse experiences of life themselves help to shape our respective responses to the paradoxes and aporia we encounter. Augustine's affirmative response to the paradox of time bears a structural similarity to Nietzsche's affirmative response to the paradox of truth, even though the response of the former deepens his faith in human dependency on a gracious, authoritative, unfathomable God whereas that of the latter strengthens his appreciation of somatic layers that provide food for thought without themselves always taking the form of thought.

In the second tradition, thought itself is layered, with the most refined layers of complexity drawing part of their energy and direction from less complex, affectively imbued layers. The amygdala, for instance, is a fast, crude little brain nodule involved in the activation of fear and anxiety; the subsystem in which it is set both interprets messages processed directly according to its crude capacities and is invested in a series of looping relations with other, slower, more linguistically refined brain subsystems. People whose amygdalae have been damaged are marked by a certain reduction of affect that makes it extremely difficult for them to read cues of danger.

The key ethical question for me is not how to resolve the difference between commitment to immanent and transcendent sources. I agree that critical explorations of comparative tensions, paradoxes, and mysteries in each position are very pertinent to that question. Such dialogues can inform each party and might well spur one or both to modify previous views. They might even propel one or another partisan toward conversion. Nonetheless, since it seems improbable that we are all apt to be converted in the same way at the same time, the key ethical issue is the sort of reflexive relation to negotiate between such different, embodied perspectives, when the parties do not share a common moral source to which to appeal. Put another way, the key meta-ethical question is not how to find a common moral source, but how to negotiate relations between constituencies who honor different ethical sources.

The negotiation between people like Taylor and me, then, may form a microcosm of sorts of a larger set of possible negotiations. How these differences are negotiated might expose larger possibilities for formation of an ethos of engagement between interdependent partisans who address common issues in a setting where no single theistic or nontheistic faith defines the authoritative source to which all the others must subscribe.

I assume, with Taylor, that no operative philosophy or practice of ethics avoids this fugitive juncture between the source on which it draws and the practices it solidifies. The difference between philosophy and faith – which has formed the hallmark of secular thinking – is not recognized by either of us to be a distinction of type. It functions at best as a delineation of components within a religious/philosophical perspective. Every faith has a philosophical component. And every philosophy is invested with faith. The attempt to maintain a sharp line of distinction between the two is one of the things that has placed Catholic philosophy in limbo in academic life. And, I must add, it also encourages many philosophers and theologians to place a minority, nontheistic faith in the West, advanced variously by Epicurus, Lucretius, Spinoza, Nietzsche, Deleuze, and Foucault, in the same position.

Once you come to terms with the element of faith in utilitarianism, Kantianism and Hegelianism, and then re-encounter the philosophical components of Christianity, Judaism, Buddhism, and Islam, the academic marginalization of both Catholicism and Nietzscheanism loses much of its intellectual grounding. The modern, secular line of distinction between philosophy and faith begins to blur. By faith in this context I mean a lived interpretation which so far has not been subjected to definitive demonstration, one that involves both refined reflection and a gut commitment below the threshold of complex intellectualization. The human condition that makes faith unavoidable, plural, and effective is the same condition that makes the key question of ethics less how to resolve issues within a shared moral creed and more how to negotiate relationships between constituencies, within and across state lines, inhabited by different operational faiths.

The critical juncture between a moral source and its articulation that Taylor identifies, and that I have glossed in my way, seems at once ineliminable and indispensable to ethics. Its indispensability is bound up with the crucial role that tactical work at this juncture plays in ethical life. Most practices of ethics involve somewhere in their compass a distinctive set of exercises, tactics, arts, and rituals designed to work on the visceral or spiritual register of being below direct intellectual control. True, many theorists of secular morality purport to bypass this register of being. But neither the theistic tradition Taylor embraces nor the nontheistic tradition I invoke does so. That's why it is disappointing when Taylor occasionally adds his voice to secularists who reduce the arts I endorse to a self-indulgent aestheticization of ethics or politics. Taylor is at his most persuasive in uncovering fugitive moral sources and appreciating the importance of cultivation to the ethical life. But he is not always at his best in addressing nontheistic perspectives to ethics that also embrace those two orientations.

## FAITH AND NIHILISM

In *Sources of the Self* Taylor contends that "high standards need strong sources."[5] Although evincing respect for some alternative orientations, he suggests that the grace of a Christian God is the strongest source to appeal to in western life. This thesis is pursued in *A Catholic Modernity?*, a book in which Taylor writes the lead essay and several Christian intellectuals respond. That essay points in two directions. First, it calls on the Catholic Church to open itself to further diversity inside its faith and to tolerance of diversity outside it. Second, it defends the view that a transcendent source is needed to provide inspiration, guidance, and tenacity in ethical life.

Catholicism, Taylor says, should be taken in the early and encompassing sense expressed in *Katholou*, "universality through wholeness."[6] The idea is to weave "God's life into human life" by coming to terms with variations in culture, understanding, and practice that arise each time a new constituency is brought into the fold. Taylor agrees that the demise of Christendom, whereby the Catholic Church had created the authoritative background in which European governance was set, is a good thing for both freedom and faith. A widening of faith is needed today, freed from the narrowness of Christendom. What is needed, more precisely, is something like a double take on your own faith, in which you first embrace it and then seek to broaden its connections to other faiths that engage transcendence in a positive way. Drawing sustenance from Matteo Ricci, the Catholic missionary who came to terms in the seventeenth century with a Chinese culture disconnected from Christian tradition, Taylor enunciates a principle in which there "is no widening of the faith without an increase in the variety of devotions and spiritualities and liturgical forms and responses to Incarnation."[7] He says that the Catholic Church has too often failed to follow this principle in the past, but it is one that can and should guide it today.

There is not just a need for diversity within the Church, then, but also for appreciation of a diversity that exceeds Christianity itself. What are the terms and limits of the latter? Taylor starts by saying that the historical record of "militantly atheistic regimes" is no better, perhaps even worse, than the historical record of the Catholic Church in Christendom. I concur. Both histories have much to apologize for, and it is admirable that Pope John Paul II has moved in that direction, even if there are crucial omissions in the apologies he has offered to date with respect to the Church's adamant opposition to doctor-assisted suicide for those whose faith allows it, its historic treatment of homosexuality, and its history of relations to "pagan" faiths. I would not want to live in either a militantly atheistic or a militantly Catholic regime.

Taylor goes on to argue that today both secularism and "exclusive humanism" are insufficiently attuned to deep moral sources. I share some of his reservations here, if "exclusive humanism" means, first, that public life must avoid reference to a plurality of theistic and nontheistic faiths, and, second, that ethical life is reducible to an intellectualism governed entirely by argument and belief. For, again, it seems to me that no ritual, theistic, or nontheistic ethical perspective in currency today is in fact entirely reducible to the explicit arguments made on its behalf. It is always invested with a faith that exceeds it and that flows into the arguments made on its behalf. Visceral elements of faith and sensibility, situated below explicit deliberation and belief, not only feed directly into human conduct; they also inflect the arguments we advance and prefigure how the arguments of others are absorbed and weighed. Some humanists acknowledge these points, too. But to the extent that humanism is oriented to the self-sufficiency of intellectualism and delegitimizes any appeal to transcendence, I concur in Taylor's dissent from its claim to exclusivity. To the extent, however, that his protest also implies the need for general endorsement of a transcendent realm, I dissent from it. For, along with a minority of other citizens, I participate in an ethic of cultivation that draws part of its energy and generosity from an immanent register of being. I do not oppose or disparage the pursuit of transcendental illumination by others. Far from it: A culture of deep pluralism is one in which interdependent partisans negotiate a generous ethos of engagement, and in which, therefore, some of the parties to such negotiations draw on transcendent sources of sustenance.

Although endorsing some themes in Taylor's critique of secularism and exclusive humanism then, I remain uncertain about the breadth of his commitment to deep pluralism. Deep pluralism, among other things, involves agonistic respect for a variety of ethical sources operative on the same politically organized territory. Let's probe my concerns by seeing how Taylor comes to terms with those who draw sustenance from a nontheistic source. This is a strategic case, partly because it interests me viscerally but also because the miserable record of Christendom at different junctures with respect to pagans, Indians, Jews, women, homosexuals, Muslims, heretics, Marranos, and Conversos has often been connected to its definition of the "atheist" as a restless, egoistic, narcissistic, blasphemous, amoral, or nihilistic type. A significant shift in Catholic representations of the atheist might consolidate a promise pursued by Taylor and the Church in other domains.

Taylor's first move in the essay in question is both promising and perplexing. He draws Buddhism into the orbit of perspectives that appreciate a transcendent dimension of life. Yes. But as I receive Buddhism, its proponents do not place an intelligent, personal God at the apex of being. And they often emphasize the priority of intensive practices over singular commitments to doctrine. Buddhism, you might say, is situated in between European philosophies of Christian transcendence and an immanent field as the latter has been promulgated by thinkers such as Epicurus, Lucretius, Spinoza, Nietzsche, Foucault, and Deleuze. Along with most of these figures, many proponents of Buddhism resist the strong claims to doctrinal authoritativeness often associated with Christian faith, while pursuing an experience of "nothingness" or "emptiness" from which vital energies of compassion can emerge. Such a version of Buddhism is perhaps closer to Henry Thoreau or William James than to either Catholic Christianity or Nietzschean philosophy.[8] A meeting point for Buddhist, Christian, and immanent perspectives, however, is that all three play up the importance of a register of being below direct intellectual control and emphasize the importance of tactics and practices that cultivate other-regarding virtues defined variously as love, compassion, generosity, the spiritualization of enmity, agonistic respect, and critical responsiveness.

I am at an early stage in engaging Buddhism, but it is already clear why it appealed to Michel Foucault as well as to Charles Taylor.[9] And it is also clear how closer engagement with it might pluralize a dialogue in "the West" too often restricted to those who profess the sufficiency of secular intellectualism and those who confess Christian versions of radiance, mystery, and faith. Does Taylor forget Buddhism when he turns to western modes of nontheism irreducible to secular intellectualism? What, exactly, is the standard that places Buddhism on the trustworthy side of his line and a nontheistic ethics of cultivation on the suspicious side? Is it that proponents of the former reside mostly in territories previously under the province of "Christendom"? Or that nontheistic practices aimed at a reserve below intellectual refinement are further removed from Christian faith in a personal, salvational God than Buddhism? Even if they are, why is it so important at this historical juncture to draw the most definitive line wherever transcendence ends?

Taylor sees how confessors of nontheistic gratitude for the abundance of being support him in checking the claims to self-sufficiency of secular intellectualism. And he sees some value in their resistance to the hegemony of Christendom. But he has a hell of a hard time seeing anything "positive" in nontheistic philosophies located in the former provinces of Christendom. This difficulty may flow in part from the fact that the inspiration nontheists draw on is as unavailable to him experientially as his transcendent faith is to us. It might also be explained by his understandable tendency to treat Nietzsche as the definitive figure here, and a less understandable tendency to focus only on that side of Nietzsche that accuses Christianity and is hostile to the democratization of modern life.

Given the paradoxical relation of ethical sources to articulation, isn't this precisely the site at which modesty and self-hesitancy are most appropriate? And given the history of dismissive accusations and punitive actions against "atheism," is this not a zone of engagement to be particularly reflective about in territories haunted by the ghost of Christendom? I pursue this question by reviewing things Pope John Paul II says about atheistic nihilism, to compare them to representations Taylor makes in the book in question.

In "Faith and Reason," sections of which were reprinted in the *New York Times* in October of 1998,[10] John Paul II asserts that only faith and reason together can support the search for truth. "It is," he says, "the one and the same God who establishes and guarantees the natural order of things upon which scientists confidently depend and reveals himself as the Father of our Lord Jesus Christ." John Paul II goes on to contend that the radicalization of rationalism during the Enlightenment made many think reason could be self-sufficient. So they ended up "espousing a rational knowledge sundered from faith." This sundering eventually secreted a new phenomenon: nihilism. "In the nihilist interpretation, life is no more than an occasion for sensations and experiences in which the ephemeral has pride of place. Nihilism is at the root of the widespread mentality, which claims that a definitive commitment should no longer be made because everything is fleeting and provisional." So nihilism is faithlessness and faithlessness spawns reckless amorality.

I agree that philosophy and faith are interwoven, even while challenging the reading of nihilism advanced by the pope. John Paul II identifies nothing in the history of Catholic Christianity itself that contributed to the nihilism he decries. He acts as if nihilism both emerged externally and finds its most extreme expression in the thought of Nietzsche. His account thus touches and breaks with that of Nietzsche – the philosopher who placed the term "nihilism" into western philosophical discourse – at these two points. To

Nietzsche, it is because Christianity insisted for nineteen centuries on a necessary equation between transcendence and morality that, as confidence in transcendence wavered inside Christendom, confidence in morality was also jeopardized. The history that consolidated the first equation set into motion the second experience of meaninglessness. So nihilism in the largest sense is a product of the historical vicissitudes of Christianity, a claim that begins to make more sense as we encounter faiths in other areas of the world that do not depend so strictly on an equation between morality and transcendental command.

A key historical moment is the challenge posed in the late medieval period by Christian nominalists to the teleological doctrine that had informed Christian faith. These challengers sought to protect an omnipotent God from any restriction to His untrammeled power by eschewing from the Church any reference to a purpose inherent in the world. The historic struggle between nominalism and finalism highlighted a durable dissonance in the Christian idea of transcendence: the conflict between giving priority to intrinsic purpose over the freedom of God or to the freedom of God over purpose. The shape of this struggle within the Church eventually helped open the door to conceptions of science, reason, and secularism neither party anticipated. For, as Hans Blumenberg has argued, the idea of a dangerous, contingent world secreted by the nominalist attempt to preserve an omnipotent God was next to intolerable for most until they invested within humanity itself the capacity to exercise significant control over nature.[11]

Blumenberg draws on Nietzsche to make his historical case, as well he might. Nietzsche, in his characteristic way, condenses Church history to focus the attention of those not heretofore prepared to hear it. He says, in one of his most condensed formulations, "Briefly: the categories 'aim', 'unity' 'being' which we used to project some value into the world – we *pull out* again: so the world looks *valueless*."[12] As a result, "One interpretation has collapsed; but because it was considered *the* interpretation it now seems as if there were no meaning at all in existence, as if everything were in vain."[13]

Pope John Paul II's response to a condition said to be engendered outside the Church is to seek a return to a transcendent unity unnecessarily forsaken. Nietzsche's response to a unity sundered by instabilities engendered by the history of the Church is to proceed through Christianity and the nihilism it engendered to existential affirmation of the protean diversity of being. He does not demand that everyone adopt his new faith. He knows that a majority will not join him on that journey, thereby acknowledging in his uncomplimentary way a powerful bent in most to seek transcendence. But at his most admirable (which is often enough), he and Zarathustra express a love of the protean character of this world in a way that first inspires a minority of devotees to draw sustenance from it and then encourages them to fold generosity, forbearance, modesty, and thoughtfulness into relations with those in other faiths "noble" enough to embrace from their side such a set of relations. That is Nietzsche's highest response to the advent of nihilism. He doubts, again, that most will embrace it. And he disparages them for not doing so. But a "spiritualization of enmity" between bearers of alternative faiths is the highest agenda he would pursue if he could convince himself that many from other faiths would adopt it. These are the spiritual relations he would establish with "the Church" if the Church would come to such a view from its side.

Although Nietzsche has a strong hand to play, I think he overplays it. An account internal to the Church is relevant but insufficient. But by offering that account, he concentrates our attention on a possible response often ignored by Christians and secularists alike: existential affirmation of the protean diversity of being in an undesigned world. I endorse that response while modifying his relation to others. Although bestowing agonistic respect on those who invest or uncover transcendence in the world, I seek nourishment from attachment to a protean diversity of being that informs the presumptions I adopt when particular issues arise. Now another source is placed into contention with those Taylor admires most, even though it does not possess the characteristic of transcendence he sometimes demands. To pluralize in this way the fugitive sources to which people might appeal is to focus awareness on the obdurate element of contestability in each reflective articulation of an ethical source. As another candidate is added to the array of sources, the gate opens wider to reciprocal cultivation by devotees of different types of comparative modesty. The call to pluralize sources is not a call to nihilism, unless you assume that nihilism must result unless all parties accept the authority of the unstable source preceding the advent of pluralism.

Ethical pluralism in a world of multiple sources. On my reading, it is not that participants in every faith must incorporate the experience of uncertainty into their own experience of faith, though I very much admire those who do so. The sixteenth-century Spanish priest, Bartolome de las Casas, after he was compelled to acknowledge the devastating effects conversion to Christianity was having on the indigenous peoples of South America, moved in that direction. And Henri Bergson and William James provide recent examples of such an orientation, within Christianity broadly construed. The latter figure, particularly, embraces the whisper of transcendence while displaying considerable evidence of uncertainty about the faith he embraces.[14] So does Derrida, perhaps, within Judaism. Nietzsche and Foucault do the same outside the religions of the Book, as when Nietzsche accentuates the role that "conjecture" plays in his basic existential faith. This is a reasonable stance to adopt because a dicey question always arises with respect to any source that is both important and fugitive: To what extent do the practices designed to amplify the source augment or produce the experience of it?

Some communities of faith, however, conclude that a confession of uncertainty is at odds with the demands of their faith. If and as that judgment emerges, a second noble step is to emphasize how contestable your faith must appear to those who neither experience it nor participate in the institutional traditions, practices, and beliefs that consolidate it. That is, perhaps, where Matteo Ricci stood.

Too seldom noted is the fact that many devout Christians neither pursue nontheistic gratitude from the inside nor participate in the relevant arts cultivated over the ages by Epicurus, Lucretius, Spinoza, Nietzsche, Foucault, and Deleuze. Thus, devotees of transcendence and immanence respectively not only stand in a relation of partial opacity to the sources they prospect themselves, but each finds the defining experiences of those who confess the alternative to be even more opaque. Out of this reciprocal experience of relational opacity a potential space opens to nurture a public ethos of agonistic respect across lines of difference. This space of difference is all too often filled with recrimination and worse. But the point is that there is another way to go. The pursuit of agonistic respect can be grounded (partly, and for some) on the element of difference in oneself from the faith one embraces and partly in the way the faith of the other is opaque to you. For no individual or constituency has the time or opportunity to experience every credible faith from the inside. Given the large number of possibilities and the relative shortness of life, we all encounter stringent limits to the number of alternatives we can subject to existential test.

In the late-modern world in which, first, the acceleration of tempo compresses distance and intensifies interdependence, second, no more than thirty percent of human beings call themselves Christian, and, third, secular intellectualism provides too thin a gruel to serve as the neutral matrix to regulate relations between faiths, the cultivation of reciprocal self-modesty across a wide range of faiths sets a positive condition for a generous ethos of pluralism.

## PHILOSOPHY AND LAUGHTER

Such an orientation to the plurality of final ethical sources sets the backdrop against which I consider formulations from Taylor in *A Catholic Modernity?* Taylor is talking about the role of love in ethics. Is it possible, he asks, to enlarge its scope to encompass humanity? He says that "it makes a whole lot of difference whether you think this kind of love is possible for us humans. I think it is, but only to the extent that we open ourselves to God, which means, in fact, overstepping the limits set in theory by exclusive humanism."[15]

My response is to appreciate the impetus to love Taylor and many others find in such a faith and then to contest the existential universal suggested by the phrase "only to the extent that we open ourselves to God." One might ask Taylor to consider examples of individuals and constituencies acting in ways he would find decent or noble who do not embrace such a faith, and consider the prospect that it may be possible for many others to do so as well, particularly if they form specific communities of practice. It is, admittedly, a fine line to walk: to affirm theistic or nontheistic faith, to invite others to join it, and to cultivate agonistic respect for those whose experience of being belies that faith. One claim on behalf of walking this line is that it provides more support for the diversity of life than any other rope strung across the contemporary condition.

Given his appreciation of the diceyness of sources, what does Taylor say about the asecular, nontheistic tradition? The record of the book in review is ambiguous. When he mentions Nietzsche or Foucault, for example, he sometimes finds an insight to admire in their thinking. But he often represents these same perspectives in a way that either purges positive ideals from them or reduces them to monological, cruel dispositions at odds with benevolence. I note a few examples:

> [In Nietzsche] there is nothing higher than the movement of life itself (the Will to Power). But it chafes at the benevolence, the universalism, the harmony, the order. It wants to rehabilitate destruction and chaos, the infliction of suffering and exploitation, as part of the life to be affirmed.

Both secular humanists and antihumanists concur in the revolutionary story; that is, they see us as having been liberated from the illusion of a good beyond life and thus enabled to affirm ourselves. This may take the form of an Enlightenment endorsement of benevolence or justice, or may be the charter for the full affirmation of the will to power – or the "free play of the signifier," the aesthetics of the self, or whatever the current version is.

> A Foucaultian influence or at least an affinity [with the negative view of freedom] is evident in important strands of feminist theorizing, gay liberation, and some other calls for the recognition of "difference." . . . The goal seems to be one in which the person or group concerned will have achieved full autonomy and will no longer be controlled or influenced. No place is allowed for another possible telos of this struggle, one in which the agents or the groups, previously related by modes of dominance, might reassociate on a better basis.[16]

There are things in these thinkers that conform to Taylor's representations. But there is much that goes beyond them, too, and these have been glossed by numerous advocates for at least two decades. Nietzsche, for instance, treats the will to power above all as a differential process by which the new surges into being; he often supports an ethical orientation that subtracts the element of resentment from our response to new formations; he advocates a spiritualization of enmity between faiths in which the most noble among the contending parties become "more spiritual, more prudent, much more thoughtful, much more forbearing" in their relations[17]; he confesses how much his basic philosophy (or existential faith) contains a "conjecture" he has not been able to prove; and he charts his attachment to a subterranean process in which "the religious instinct is growing powerfully but is rejecting theistic gratification with deep distrust."[18] Moreover, no Foucaultian I know locates in Foucault the monological ideal of autonomy Taylor attributes to him.[19]

Most pertinently, a large crew of theorists and activists, while drawing selective sustenance from Nietzsche, have reworked the Nietzschean message to (a) democratize its conception of "nobility as multiple nobilities"; (b) develop conceptions of freedom irreducible to negative freedom; (c) pursue a positive ethos of engagement between diverse constituencies to reconstitute classical models of pluralism; (d) explore ethical arts of the self, tactics, and micropolitics that work on the visceral register of subjectivity and intersubjectivity; and (e) cultivate arts of critical responsiveness to the emergence of new constituencies that jostle established patterns of diversity. What these proponents typically do not profess, however, is the quest for transcendence that inspires Taylor, though there is diversity on that issue as well.[20]

Agonistic respect is expressed in the way you engage faiths that bypass the source you honor most fervently; it thereby finds expression in the way you represent the beliefs, practices, and ideals of your adversaries. One set of representations presses you to come to terms with the challenge posed by the alternative faith; another relieves that pressure by defining its adherents to be negative, reckless, or unreliable. On this score, Taylor forges new ground. But he still remains a little too close for my comfort to Vatican reductions of nontheistic faith to nihilistic atheism, negative freedom, warrior ethics, and self-indulgent aestheticism.

That being said, there are openings and breaks that hold considerable promise. That is why Taylor is so pertinent to engage. Let me pursue one opening here, since I have pursued others elsewhere. In a reply to his critics in the book under discussion Taylor distances himself from the "snarling" temper of the Christian Right. Then he says:

> Of course, anti-Christian attack can be provoking. I have to admit my prac-
> tice falls far below that suggested by my serene tone here. When it is sug-
> gested that, by virtue of being a Catholic, I must be working night and day
> for the return of the Inquisition, I usually fly into a rage and throw back
> some (I hope) stinging rebuke. . . . Occasionally, I laugh.[21]

I identify with Taylor here. My conduct often falls below the standard I seek to embody in relations with theistic faiths. I have my excuses, par-ticularly when adherents of such a faith suggest that by virtue of being a post-Nietzschean I must be working day and night on behalf of nihilism. But it is pertinent for me to recall that I too would not want to live in a militantly atheistic culture. That would undermine from another side the deep pluralism I embrace.

It is Taylor's attention to laughter, however, that intrigues me most. Here, it conveys the sense that secular and nontheistic partisans seldom have hands as clean as their wholesale judgments of the history of Christendom imply. Fair enough. Beyond that, I have heard Taylor laugh. It has an in-fectious quality, as it rolls across an entrenched line of difference without dissolving it. Such laughter can expose and augment a line of connection between partisans, without sinking them into a matrix of commonality.

In an interdependent world where multiple faiths are apt to persist, it is important to cultivate connections across differences as well as to identify commonalities where they subsist. On occasion the diastolic rhythms of some will resonate with the systolic rhythms of others, as when the con-fessed theist feels tremors of uncertainty, or the adamant nontheist hears the whisper of possible transcendence. Here a seed of connection across dif-ference is planted, in a situation where the partisans honor different moral sources. Epicurus, for instance, advised his disciples to overcome worries about what might happen after death in order to overcome that resent-ment of human mortality that so often issues in punitive actions against others. He thus acknowledged, before the advent of Christianity, a human tendency to project life forward beyond death. He testified, therefore, to a stubborn propensity inside those who participate in his faith, one to work on in a way at odds with the later Christian drive to salvation but nonetheless connected obliquely to Christian faith. It is not too big a step for a late-modern Epicurean both to work on that tendency as Epicurus advised and to build up a certain admiration for others who cultivate the feeling for transcendence we pass by. Many theists, from their side, testify to similar dissonances in their faiths. Kierkegaard provides an example, exploring incorrigible moments of (atheistic) forgetfulness that punctuate the pursuit of faith. And James, as I already mentioned, is exemplary in this regard.

What if many discern a little atheist or little theist in themselves periodically punctuating their dominant investments of faith? Can such inverted connections across dominant lines of difference provoke laughter on occasion? A laughter that might crystallize into agonistic respect? The chiasmatic structure of such relations *is* amusing, and it can encourage parties to appreciate those who actually run existential experiments they themselves might have run had things broken differently. "One is *fruitful* only at the cost of being rich in contradictions; one remains *young* only on condition the soul does not relax."[22] If and as such a difference from ourselves in ourselves is repressed, it readily becomes translated into an imperious demand to suppress the other. But when expressed through laughter it can also provide the impetus to forge connections to those who invert the condition in which you find yourself. Laughter is contagious, as it conveys an abundance beyond identity. So are the connections forged through it.

Taylor often focuses on the danger of fragmentation, "that is a people less and less capable of forming a common purpose and carrying it out." Fragmentation occurs when citizens see "themselves more and more atomistically."[23] I focus on neither "atomism" nor "a people." My focus is on the cultural promise of a network of connections across multiple dimensions of difference in the domains of religion, ethnicity, moral source, gender practice, and sexual orientation. Assemblages of collective action can grow out of multidimensional pluralism, if and as the assemblage is nourished by a positive ethos of engagement. Such a focus curtails the drive to devise a transcendent matrix in which to locate all specific moral sources; it encourages you to pour the experience of relational self-modesty into the transcendent or immanent source you cultivate, as Taylor himself does on many occasions. And to issue similar invitations to others.

Fragmentation, on my reading, is most apt to emerge from competitive attempts to define the basic moral source everyone must endorse. Such struggles, at their worst, promote religious and nationalist wars; at lower levels of intensity they foster cultural war. They are best surmounted by negotiating a generous ethos across multiple lines of difference, an ethos of engagement grounded in reciprocal self-modesty about the particular faith in transcendence or immanence you embrace. As already indicated, similar sentiments are discernible in Taylor's work, particularly when he engages transcendent faiths outside the tradition of Christianity. It is only when he encounters nontheistic faiths inside the historic territories of Christendom that his generosity sometimes falters. Even here Taylor's tolerances often enough flow over and under the language of transcendence, recognition, commonality, fragmentation, and atomism.[24] Taylor often stretches the reach of connection beyond the pursuit of commonality and the danger of atomism. Follow the line of laughter. As you do the admirable character of Taylor's work surges forth.

### Notes

1. Charles Taylor, *Sources of the Self: The Making of the Modern Identity*, Cambridge, MA: Harvard University Press, 1989, p. 96.
2. Ibid., p. 96.
3. Ibid., p. 374.
4. Besides the group of philosophers whose work I invoke, such a view today finds expression in some philosophies of science. Ilya Prigogine, for instance, the Nobel Prize winning chemist who helped invent complexity theory, speaks of physical systems in disequilibrium that follow irreversible historical trajectories and engender new forms that are unpredictable. See Ilya Prigogine and Isabelle Stengers, *The End of Certainty: Time, Chaos and the New Laws of Nature*, New York: The Free Press, 1997.
5. *Sources of the Self: The Making of the Modern Identity*. Cambridge, MA: Harvard University Press, 1989, p. 516. In a thoughtful study Stephen K. White compares Taylor and me on the role, risks, and possibilities of moral sources. He finds plausibility in Taylor's reading of sources while arguing against his contention that reliance on nontheistic sources leads to an ethic that gives short shrift to benevolence. See *Sustaining Affirmation: The Strengths of Weak Ontology*, Princeton: Princeton University Press, 2001.
6. *A Catholic Modernity?* New York: Oxford University Press, 1999, p. 14.
7. Ibid., p. 15.
8. My encounter with Buddhism was launched in an unexpected way. I find the work of neurologist Francisco Varela to be fascinating in the way it exceeds representational and reductionist models of thinking, and that interest in turn has propelled me into his exploration of points of contact and difference between Buddhism and contemporary neurological research. The first work finds

expression in Varela Evan Thompson and Eleanor Rosch, *The Embodied Mind: Cognitive Science and Human Experience*, Cambridge, MA: MIT Press, 1993, and the second in Francisco Varela (ed.), *Dreaming and Dying: An Exploration of Consciousness with the Dalai Lama*, Boston: Wisdom Publications, 1997. I clearly have more work to do.

9. See, for example, "Michel Foucault and Zen: a Stay in a Zen Temple" in *Religion and Culture: Michel Foucault*. Jeremy R. Carrette (ed.), New York: Routledge, 1999, pp. 110–15. In this conversation between Foucault and a Zen master, Foucault displays great interest in Buddhist arts and techniques, as might be expected of one who makes so much of the relation between tactics of the self and ethical life.

10. *New York Times*, October 11, 1998.

11. Hans Blumenberg, *The Legitimacy of the Modern Age*. Robert M. Wallace (trans.), Cambridge, MA: Harvard University Press, 1983.

12. Friedrich Nietzsche. *The Will to Power*. Walter Kaufmann and R. J. Holingdale (trans.), New York: Vintage Books, 1968, #12, p. 13.

13. Ibid., #55, p. 35,

14. As I was putting the final touches on this essay Taylor's new book appeared, *Varieties of Religion Today: William James Revisited*, Cambridge, MA: Harvard University Press, 2002. At the time of writing, I had not yet read it, though I encountered parts of it in a symposium on secularism involving Taylor and me at Rutgers. It will be fascinating to compare it to the essay by him I examine here. My first engagement with James appears in "Memory Traces, Mystical States and Deep Pluralism," Chapter 5 of *Neuropolitics: Thinking, Culture, Speed*, Minneapolis: University of Minnesota Press, 2002.

15. *A Catholic Modernity?* New York: Oxford University Press, 1999, p. 35.

16. Ibid., pp. 27; 29; 115.

17. Friedrich Nietzsche. *Twilight of the Idols*. R. J. Hollingdale (trans.), Middlesex: Penguin, 1969, p. 44.

18. Friedrich Nietzsche. *Beyond Good and Evil*. Marianne Cowan (trans.), Chicago: Gateway, 1955, p. 60.

19. As Foucault says,

> In the serious play of questions and answers, in the work of reciprocal elucidation, the rights of each person are in some sense immanent in the discussion. . . . As for the person answering the questions, he too exercises a right that does not go beyond the discussion itself; by the logic of his own discourse he is tied to the questioning of the other. . . . The polemicist, on the other hand, proceeds encased in privileges that he possesses in advance and will never agree to question. . . . The polemicist relies on a legitimacy that his adversary is by definition denied.

Michel Foucault, "Polemics, Politics and Problematizations: An Interview" in *Foucault: A Reader*. Paul Rabinow (ed.), New York: Pantheon Books, 1984, pp. 381–2.

20. Exemplary here are studies by Romand Coles, *Rethinking Generosity: Critical Theory and the Politics of Caritas*, Ithaca: Cornell University Press, 1997; Melissa Orlie, *Living Ethically/Acting Politically*. Ithaca: Cornell University Press, 1997;

Jane Bennett, *Thoreau's Nature: Ethics, Politics and the Wild*, London: Sage Press, 1994; Thomas Dumm, *The Politics of the Ordinary*, New York: New York University Press, 1999; Bonnie Honig, *Political Theory and the Displacement of Politics*, Ithaca: Cornell University Press, 1996; and Lawrence Hatab, *A Nietzschean Defense of Democracy*, Chicago: Open Court, 1995. The issues with respect to Nietzsche are thoughtfully explored by several interpreters in *Why Nietzsche Still?* Alan D. Schrift (ed.), Berkeley: University of California Press, 2000. Two symposia on "Left Conservatism" have engaged these issues. The first was published in *Theory & Event* in 1998, http://muse.jhu.edu/journals/theory_&_event/toc/archive.html#2.2. The second was in *Boundary 2* (fall, 1999). In the second symposium Thomas Dumm draws together the work of twenty or so contemporaries whom he calls the new pluralists. An excellent study of the positive dimensions in Gilles Deleuze can be found in Paul Patton, *Deleuze and the Political*, London: Routledge, 2000, a study that crystallizes points he has made about Deleuze for several years now. In 1979, as one indebted to Foucault, I criticized him for his early refusal to adopt a positive vision of society. He dropped such a position – of his own accord – as early as 1981. My thinking about a democratic pluralism that maintains creative tension between existing diversity and new drives to pluralization, a generous ethos of engagement, and the political virtues of agonistic respect and critical responsiveness was launched in a 1987 study and is perhaps best crystallized in *The Ethos of Pluralization*, Minneapolis: University of Minnesota Press, 1995. The people on the list assembled above are indebted significantly to Nietzsche, Derrida, Foucault, or Deleuze, without conforming to Taylor's representations of how these debts play themselves out.

21. *A Catholic Modernity?* New York: Oxford University Press, 1999, p. 124.

22. Friedrich Nietzsche, *Twilight of the Idols*. R. J. Hollingdale (trans.), Middlesex: Penguin, 1969, p. 44.

23. *Philosophical Arguments*, Cambridge, MA: Harvard University Press, 1995, p. 282.

24. These sentiments find expression in Taylor's appreciation of multiculturalism. But even here the language of commonality may limit the reach of connection through diversity. For Taylor is oriented to territorially concentrated constituencies within a state, such as the Quebecois and the Inuit in Canada. But many internally connected minorities are scattered across a territorial regime rather than concentrated in territorial regions. Gays, ethnic minorities, those who claim a right to doctor-assisted suicide, and members of minority religions exemplify constituencies sprinkled across territorial space rather than concentrated regionally. Here the complex connections across differences discussed above come into play. The practice of justice is often not sufficient to these issues either. For first the practices and faiths of the constituencies involved must be lifted from a place below the threshold of justice onto its register. Gay rights is an example. Being gay must be elevated above its previous standing as an objective disorder before issues about discrimination, equity, membership, and so forth can be given adequate play. So, on another register, is the right to die. When those who do not participate in the Christian faith that life must

continue until God has taken it come out of the closet and convince others that they are governed by moral sources worthy of respect, the terms of debate over doctor-assisted suicide may shift. It will then be more vivid how the proponents of one faith compel others who do not accept its terms to forgo self-oriented action profoundly important to them. Many Christians have already moved in this direction, either through modification in their own faith or by cultivation of agonistic respect for that of others. For exploration of such issues in relation to Taylor's theory of multiculturalism, see my "Pluralism, Multiculturalism and the Nation-State: Rethinking the Connections," *Journal of Political Ideologies* (1), 1, (1996); 53–74.

# 8

## Taylor, "History," and the History of Philosophy

*TERRY PINKARD*

Charles Taylor's conception of agency has always worn its relation to history on its sleeve. Even his earliest pieces, such as *The Explanation of Behavior*, which can look like a piece of analytical philosophy of action (or a piece of French inspired phenomenology developing itself into analytical philosophy) was concerned with "retrieving" a teleological model of agency and arguing for its virtues in the context of what was at the time of its writing a widely accepted bias in favor of behavioristic models of explanation. Taylor's more recent books, particularly *Sources of the Self*, bring the historicist elements of his thought front and center. In *Sources*, he explicitly joined other contemporary theorists, such as Alasdair MacIntyre, in arguing for the impossibility of a rational philosophical account of agency without also taking into account the various historical embeddings of our ideas of agency. No mere analysis of agency will give us an adequate understanding of agency, since the concepts that are being analyzed can only be understood in terms of their own complex history.

In his writings, and in *Sources* in particular, Taylor also has a particular point to make about how we are to understand history itself, particularly in terms of the vexing (and perhaps overworked) theme of "modernity." The overarching theme of modernity in the wider culture is that of triumph and optimism: Modernity is identified with progress, which itself tends to be associated with technological improvements and ethical-political gains (rights for women, rights for minorities, decoupling of church and state, and so forth). On the other hand, in the writings of those particularly influenced by Heidegger, there is an ongoing theme of loss in such accounts of modernity – loss of values, community, sense of wholeness. All of this is connected with a kind of pessimism about the modern world (that somehow we are all destined to be the "hollow men"). For the Heideggerians especially it is fruitless to ask for "solutions" to modernity's "problems" since part of the problem of modernity is the misguided faith in the efficacy or importance of the human will to resolve such issues and thereby to think of everything in terms of "problem solving." (Heidegger thus famously remarked to Rudolf

**187**

Augstein in *Der Spiegel* that "only a god can save us now." Earlier he had put his faith in a much lesser figure to rescue Germany.)

Taylor falls into neither of these camps, styling himself as neither a "knocker" nor a "booster" of modernity.[1] On his view, although there are indeed various malaises of the modern world – its excessive individualism flattening the meaning of the world, its granting overarching normative authority to instrumental reason, and its social atomism undoing our deeper connections to our communities and histories – these are still only "malaises," not intrinsic features of modernity, and they arise from a misguided sense of what it means to be modern individuals and communities. There is a potential in modern life that has been distorted and obscured by the very ways in which we have come to express and describe it, distortions which are shared by both the "boosters" and the "knockers" of modernity. Thus those who are pessimistic about modern life see us as fated to be flattened, atomized, rational calculators with no sense for the "higher" or "deeper" things, whereas those more optimistic see our task as the more efficient employment of instrumental reason to fashion technologically more sophisticated solutions to our problems. Both the "boosters" and the "knockers," that is, share a common horizon of understanding about what is possible for us and what can ultimately matter to us, but each tells a different story about how that came about and why it is our only option.

It is that widely shared articulation and expression of modern life that Taylor has been at pains to argue against. For those who are the "boosters," it leads to the view that the only appropriate approach to human reality is naturalistic, that is, the view that human activity is best studied by approaches that model themselves on the methods and styles of the natural sciences, and that the only things that can count as explanations are therefore the kinds of causal schemes used in the natural sciences. For naturalists, human reality is best explored with the tools of, for example, evolutionary theory and rational choice theory. For the "knockers," it seems that the only alternative is to turn to nonscientific – which in the distorted self-descriptions of modernity means "nonrational" or "suprarational" – modes of accounting for or elucidating human reality in terms of its openness to religious or quasireligious sources, or to develop a highly metaphorical, nonnaturalistic vocabulary for "evoking" or "disclosing" those elements of human reality that a naturalistic treatment cannot. Taylor's argument has consistently been that this simply does not exhaust the alternatives: One can be as hard-nosed about the truthclaims of modern science as any hard-bitten naturalist and still not be committed to philosophical naturalism; and one can hold that there are crucial elements of human reality that defy naturalistic accounts without being a dualist or obscurantist or being antireason (to use a necessarily vague covering term for all those who distrust reason while identifying it as leading to naturalism).

The problem in modernity's own account of itself is that by its own terms it has not only failed to come to terms with what is really at stake in it, but it has also actually obscured what is of importance in the modern turn to natural science coupled with its faith in technology. Instead of polishing up the standard self-account of modernity, what is in fact required is an account that both draws out and defends the picture of human agency and human reality which has been submerged by that distorted self-account. It is also necessary to give an account of how it is that we came to share such a widely held distorted picture of ourselves, which at the same time contains within itself the potential for a much richer and potentially satisfying account of agency.

In *Sources*, Taylor offers his version of the history of our self-conceptions that attempts to do just that. He explicitly denies, however, that his own account constitutes a historical explanation of its subject matter. It does not, that is, offer much, if any, answer to the quasi-causal question: What brought about the modern self-identity (the modern self)? The answer to that question would have to include far more than the history of philosophy that obviously takes up the lion's share of the book (for example, economic changes, developments in trade, art history, demographics, chance events, natural catastrophes, and so forth).

Indeed, it might even look as if history (taken seriously) would be at odds with any kind of purely philosophical account of the modern self. In the discipline of modern philosophy, the "history of philosophy" (or at least courses with that title) has typically been taken to consist in a series of canonical books read in chronological order. From the point of view of a typical professor of philosophy, the history of philosophy looks like an autonomous discipline, whose central and most interesting parts develop themselves independently of the social conditions surrounding them. One sees Hume responding to Descartes and Locke, one sees Kant responding to all of them, almost in a timeless fashion, as if they were all colleagues sitting at a conference table sequentially reading papers written on the spot in response to the previous paper. Sometimes that history can be taken to be progressive, so that the last paper read (in other words, the present stage of philosophy) is the truth, since it is responding to and correcting the defects in argumentation in the previous papers. The timelessness of that way of looking at things, however, also allows a nonprogressive reading of the history of philosophy, as we modern interlocutors read our own contributions into that story, arguing, for example, that Kant did not refute Hume, did not understand Hume, or that Aristotle's arguments were unappreciated by Hobbes, and so on.

Almost no historian nowadays would be content to approach the history of anything in that way: The history of philosophy itself would have to be viewed as part of something else, and the ideas developed by British empiricists could not be understood apart from understanding why, say, seventeenth-century Britain had the shape it did (a question which is not going to be answered merely by a closer reading of Locke's text). In fact, the approach to philosophy that looks for good arguments and truth can often be (and usually is) at odds with the more properly historical approach that can only see the development of those ideas as the partial, contingent expression of many other contingent, explicitly nonintellectual developments.

Genuine historical explanation, that is, has to view philosophies as simply one more element in the mix to be explained. It must take an objective stance to philosophy, seeing it as only one more phenomenon among many (like kingship, nonmarket economies, demographic effects of disease, and so forth). Whereas the historian interested in explanation need not deny that such philosophies may themselves play a part in bringing some key events into being – perhaps the Reformation is unintelligible without the input from various theologians egging it on – that kind of historian nonetheless cannot attribute the causation of those events simply to those ideas without assuming a rather implausible thesis about historical causation.

There is a long history of alternative, more "intellectualistic" approaches to history. In the reception of Hegel's philosophy of history, there was a tendency to see Hegelianism as a doctrine holding that the causal force in history is reason itself, that changes in human self-consciousness are in fact the basic explanation for what happens (in politics, economics, and so forth), and that those changes are themselves brought about by purely intellectual factors in the way that failures of certain forms of self-consciousness (somehow or another) logically lead to their successors – and that is surely as problematic a thesis about historical causation as one can get. (That this is not actually Hegel's thesis is another matter, but we need not go into that here.[2])

In distinction from this, Taylor claims that his historical sketch in *Sources* is intended to capture what certain conceptions of agency meant to those people living through crucial transitions and developments in our

conception of selfhood. That question is, as he argues, not causally explanatory but interpretive, and "answering it involves giving an account of the
new identity which makes clear what its appeal was."[3] This interpretive approach is not so much an alternative to the explanatory approach to history
as it is a complement to it, indeed, one that is necessary for a successful historical explanation in the first place.[4] The question remains: What special
appeal does the history of philosophy have for such an interpretive project?
Why not, for example, a history of literary projections of the same thing?

Taylor's approach to the sources of the self as involving an account of
the history of philosophy is part of his longstanding criticisms of all purely
"objectivist" ways of understanding agency. For Taylor, agency can only be
adequately understood from the "inside," from a grasp of what it is to be an
agent, something that cannot adequately be understood from a third person
standpoint. Understanding what it is to be an agent is to grasp how it is
that we (and other agents) lead our lives, how things matter to us. Taylor
clearly thinks that this more phenomenologically oriented approach does
not commit him to any kind of "subjectivism" or mental/physical dualism:
To grasp what it is like to be an agent is not to know what it is like to be
aware of some private set of mental facts. That would repeat the mistake of
the objectivist standpoint in that it assumes that the "inside" view of agency
must consist in a set of "subjective" facts as distinct from "objective" facts;
in both cases, there is supposedly a set of facts on which we report, and the
distinction is that one set is publicly accessible, while the other set is only
accessible from the first person standpoint. Being an agent, however, is not
a matter of reporting on facts at all; it is a way of taking a stance toward
oneself and the world, a way of taking up one's experience (of oneself and
the world) in terms of what matters to oneself, not in terms of reporting
on some set of internal facts. It is, that is to say, a normative matter, not a
factual matter.[5]

We are, in Taylor's well-known formulation, self-interpreting animals.
Animals do not confront this problem; they may display great intelligence,
even complex social arrangements, and perhaps some of them can even
display some kind of grasp of their own mortality, but, even for dolphins
and higher primates, there is no question of what it means to be such a
creature. The dolphin, for all its intelligence and sociality, never has to
ask itself what it means to be a dolphin. For human agents, however, the
question of what it means to be a human being is always an open question,
always open to interpretation. Is it to be the image or servant of God? To
be an agent whose noumenal reality is that of transcendental freedom? A
being whose essence, whose realization presupposes the *polis*? Or an animal

to be understood in terms of evolutionary psychology? As Heidegger put it, we are the being for whom our being is always an issue. Our nature is to be never simply what it is but consists in part in how we take it to be, how we conceive of ourselves, how we interpret our complex embodied social existence.[6]

To grasp agency as a normative matter is to grasp it in terms of its self-relation, a way of assuming a stance toward ourselves, a kind of self-conscious distance from ourselves, which realizes that even in our most straightforward and mindless dealings with things, we are never simply dealing with them in a way that bypasses our interpreting our encounter with them. Our grasp of anything in our encounters with the world is always mediated in terms of what we "take" that experience to mean. To make this point, Taylor draws on two sources of argument: one has to do with Kant and the post-Kantian legacy; the other draws on a line of thought that runs through Heidegger, Wittgenstein, and Merleau-Ponty. The stress on self-relation is part of the Kantian legacy in philosophy. In Kant's well-known formulation, "it must be possible for the 'I think' to accompany all my representations."[7] The Kantian turn in philosophy meant that it was no longer possible to conceive of experience as any kind of direct encounter (or "direct, unmediated awareness") with objects; all experience has its meaning as it is "taken up" by us, and that meaning is at least in part spontaneously constructed by us. As meaningful, all experience is subject to the conditions of reflection on it, on the "I think" being "able to accompany it," on, that is, our ability to achieve a certain kind of self-consciousness about our place in the world. Understanding that self-consciousness is crucial to understanding all our claims to knowledge, spiritual integrity, aesthetic truth, and political rightness.

That Kantian formulation, however, can be somewhat misleading, since it might suggest that we only deal with our representations of objects, not with the objects themselves (even though Kant himself goes a long way toward undermining this very suggestion). That "representationalist" view is another part of the "objectivist" misinterpretation of human agency. The picture with which such a view operates sees human agency as consisting primarily in our being the subject of representations of the world outside of our minds or of various ends that are either desired or feared. This inevitably generates the problem of knowledge of "other minds," since such representations end up ultimately being construed as private "mental entities" of some sort, unavailable to outside observers. This also presupposes, as Taylor phrases it, that our agency is structured by a monological and not a dialogical consciousness.

Taylor draws on the Heidegger/Wittgenstein/Merleau-Ponty line of argument to stress that not only can the objects of experience not fully determine how we are to take them; they cannot function as independent "things" on which we can rely to keep us on the right track independently of any of our own ways of "keeping ourselves" on the right track vis-à-vis those objects. To understand the meaning of the way we talk about ourselves in our encounters with each other and the world, we follow "rules" (or, to phrase it differently, we are norm-guided) and, as Wittgenstein's argument about "rule-following" shows, there is nothing in the world itself that determines what counts as a deviant way to follow the rule. Following the rule cannot be a matter therefore of having a mental representation of the rule in our minds and consulting it to determine what counts as a deviation from it. No further interpretation of the rule could suffice to fix what counts as following it, since that interpretation would itself be subject to the same kinds of worries. Thus, as Wittgenstein concluded, "What this shows is that there is a way of grasping a rule which is not an interpretation, but which is expressed in what we call 'obeying the rule' and 'going against it' in actual cases. . . . And hence also 'obeying a rule' is a practice."[8]

Taylor rejects those interpretations of Wittgenstein's conclusion (such as the well-known and influential reading given by Saul Kripke) which hold that when Wittgenstein says, "I obey the rule blindly" he means that we must therefore be acting without reasons. This is taken to imply that no demand for reasons is appropriate, and that the rules governing our behavior must be conceived as simply imposed by society so that the link between them and our behavior can only be that of brute connection.[9] The other interpretation (which has affinities with some of what Merleau-Ponty says) holds that the "background" against which we determine what counts as a deviant following of the rule really does incorporate understanding, but it is an unarticulated, prereflective grasp of what the rule means. Such an unarticulated, prereflective grasp of the sense of the rule not only does not rule out giving reasons when they are demanded, it is actually the condition that puts us in the position of being able to formulate such reasons in the first place.[10] Not acting for explicit reasons (as representations to be entertained) is not to act without reason; and often the reasons for our action can only emerge when we are challenged to come up with them. Moreover, although meaning cannot be cashed out in terms of internal mental representations, it also cannot be cashed out naturalistically as behavior or dispositions to behave in a certain way.

Here, as elsewhere, Taylor tries to suggest that the traditional dichotomy of "in the mind" or "merely behavioral" does not exhaust our options;

the Heidegger/Merleau-Ponty/Wittgenstein line of thought offers another
option for understanding meaning in terms of an agent's being a participant
in a practice. As these thinkers argue, to be an agent is to be primarily
engaged in practices in which the norms are implicitly taken up, not as
representations, but as a kind of know-how, a way of being able to get
around in one's world. Our activities of constructing representations of
this know-how are themselves only comprehensible against this implicit
background understanding of normativity; they are secondary to it and are
not the primary phenomena out of which such understanding is constructed.
In riding a bicycle, driving a car, solving a mathematical problem, reading
a novel, and understanding even simple sentences, we are always bringing
to bear our implicit, unformulated background understanding of what does
and does not count toward understanding what is at issue and how we are
to go on from there.

A practice in Taylor's terms is any stable configuration of shared activity,
whose shape is defined by a certain pattern of norms (by do's and don'ts,
as Taylor puts it).[11] We can be subject to such norms only insofar as we
take them up, however, that is, only insofar as we are at least implicitly
self-conscious about them. (This might be taken as a linguistic version of
a Kantian conception of the "I think" being able to accompany all the
ways in which I "follow a rule.") As self-conscious agents, we express and
articulate what it is we take ourselves to be doing, and in these activities
of articulation and expression, we give ourselves a sense of where we are
taking the practice. We are proposing an interpretation of what it means
to follow the rule which takes into account both what we understand the
past "interpretations" of that rule to have been and what we also take to be
the correct interpretation of what would count as following the rule in the
future. An interpretation, in that sense, is as much a normative proposal for
future action as it is an explication of what we take the rule's injunctions
to be. We are orienting ourselves, giving ourselves something to hold onto
as we navigate our way through time in the circumscribed social spaces
defined through our embodiment, our history, and our sociality. This does
not rule out our projecting future actions that break with the "rule," that
propose something new and untried.[12] Our always implicit distance from
our practices, no matter how much we may be absorbed in them, means
that when challenged, we can respond with an articulation of what it is that
we took ourselves to be doing, and, in more complex cases, with some kind
of account that would (attempt to) justify it.

What it is like to be that kind of agent "from the inside" thus requires
us to understand how it is that agents normatively orient themselves in

their worlds. This cannot be described in an "objectivist" manner, since the facts at issue are normative facts, and their meaning is always open to interpretation and new and different articulations. For agents, there is always the issue of things mattering to them, and that issue of mattering is not to be construed as simply some kind of brute registering of subjective facts or "representations" but in terms of the agent's being already oriented and continually orienting and reorienting himself to those things that matter to him. As a social enterprise, it is a matter of individuals sustaining a certain type of self-relation (of taking themselves to be a certain way, as self-interpreting animals) in light of holding themselves and others to these kinds of norms and being held by others to those norms. In Taylor's own terms, "Objectifying a given domain involves depriving it of its *normative* force for us."[13]

As Taylor stresses again and again in his works, to be an agent is to be oriented to a basic good or set of goods.[14] The self-relation at work in Taylor's conception of agency has to do with the stance we take to ourselves and what matters to us; to be self-conscious – or self-situating – is to be concerned for our goods and our identities; it is not to have an awareness of internal sensations, that is, is not a matter of "self-awareness" in the Lockean and post-Lockean sense. (For this reason, "self-relation" is probably to be preferred to "self-consciousness" in expressing Taylor's views.) As concerned with what ultimately matters to oneself (which is always a "dialogical," social concern), a person is, in Taylor's well-known terms, a "strong evaluator," taking a stance on what must be an end worthy for its own sake. This in turn confers a kind of value on other subordinate matters (in that they may be means to that end, or components of that end, and so forth). The end that is worthy for its own sake makes a claim on us, demands our allegiance to it, as opposed to our having chosen it. Taylor's rejection of that very modern epistemological worry about matching up internal representations and external facts, or linguistic utterances and that which would make them true, partially underwrites his realism about these goods. The goods toward which we orient ourselves are real, even if they depend on the existence of humans for them to be goods; they are not merely projections that we force onto the world.

The claim that goods make on agents is not itself direct. As self-interpreting animals, we maintain an always implicit reflective distance from those goods that make these claims on us. For an agent to have such an orientation to good requires the agent to be in possession of some language and the various cultural components that, although themselves nonlinguistic (that is, those elements belonging to what Wittgenstein called a practice, not an interpretation) are necessary for mastering the language. For something to be a good for you it must provide you with a reason for action. Agents, however, do not merely have goods and reasons for action; such goods can manifest themselves to those agents (and make their claims on them) only by virtue of the agent's possessing a language and a culture, which gives the agent a distance from those goods. As having both an orientation to those goods and a distance from them, agents must attempt to articulate those goods (give them some kind of linguistic or symbolic expression) before they can integrate them into some ongoing way of living. The goods themselves therefore make their claim on us only as we interpret them and incorporate them via those interpretations into the directions in which we individually and collectively take our lives. To incorporate those goods into our ways of living, moreover, means that we must reason about them. We must see to what else such an incorporation commits us (or to what else it inclines us or for which it offers additional motivation), and we are often thereby called to evaluate and reevaluate that orientation as it is being lived out.

As the product of cultures and languages, these articulations are contingent expressions; as normative, they also call out for, if not demand, justification. The recognition, however, of the contingency of our articulations of norms and the necessity to justify them places a particular type of strain on our conceptions of agency and the good. Justification, if it is to hold, has to be in terms of reasons that are acceptable to others; but the contingency of our norms suggests that what counts as a reason is itself only contingent, that its acceptability is as much a matter of circumstance as it is of its inherent rationality or universalizability. The demand for justification pushes us in the direction of noncontingent rationality. The recognition of the contingency of norms pushes us in the direction of skepticism about whether any such justifications are even possible (and, further, whether the demand for universal justification is not some deeper ploy to disguise the deployment of particular interests and power).

The response to this dilemma has typically been to look for some kind of viewpoint that is external to the norms in question (to look for a foundation or for some set of criteria that all sides must accept).[15] Such external views are not available, however, to the kind of practice-oriented account Taylor gives. They assume that there is some manner of standing outside of all human practices and viewing them from no point of view at all, whereas it is only possible to view and evaluate things from within the standpoint of particular (and seemingly contingent) practices. Taylor's own view is quite self-consciously developed as an argument against and counterweight to the dominance of the foundational or criterial approaches themselves.

Thus, although Taylor argues that his own approach is "interpretive" and not "explanatory," he nonetheless argues that in any adequate historical explanation, one must understand people's self-interpretations and their visions of the good if one is to explain how they arise; that is, historical explanation cannot do without an understanding of what *mattered* to people during the period and the transitions that the historian is explaining. Taking a purely "objectivist" approach to agency necessarily blinds one to the way people are living their lives in this period and therefore to what could be motivating them to do the things they do. The motivations related to the claims that various goods make on those agents cannot appear in any kind of "objectivist" account except in some truncated or distorted form (as brute causes, or as people being "driven" to act the way they did by virtue of their "perception" of these goods).

An "objectivist" historian can perfectly well accept the general way these claims about subjectivity and agency have been made and still hold fast to the view that only "objective" factors count in historical explanation (and in the explanation therefore of the "sources" of the modern "self"). Marriage might have meant such-and-such to people at the time, and people might have acted on that understanding, but the explanation for its having meant such-and-such (or having changed its meaning) is to be taken from, say, changes in the economic conditions of society, in demographic pressures, in new technologies of printing, and so forth. On that view, any genuine history therefore abstracts from the normative; at best it views it as a fact that people held that such-and-such was normative for them, not that it really was (or is) normative. (Something like that view was held by Max Weber in his distinction between the interpretive and explanatory.) Philosophy would be no different; although from the inside, philosophers may be concerned with the arguments being made and the normative force of the claims that different philosophers historically have made, viewed from the outside, the explanation for the transition from, say, Hume to Kant, would be in terms of nonrational, nonphilosophical matters. (The "history of ideas" promulgated by historians would thus inevitably take a different shape from the "history of philosophy" done by philosophers.)

Taylor's interpretive account, however, is intended to do more than merely portray people's motivations as it lays out the developmental story it tells about the modern sense of self, will leaving untouched the realm of historical explanation. It is not as if the "interpretive" account is to take us "inside" the people's sense of themselves, whereas the explanation (the real mover) in the story comes from outside. The view is that we can best understand and therefore articulate for ourselves what matters to us only if we understand how what has come to matter, even unconditionally, for agents is the result of a rational development out of what mattered to their predecessors. For Taylor, what has obscured the discussion about this is the way in which the issue of rational justification has been played off as if it were a choice between universal norms presupposed by all agents in general and shifting, contingent norms that only express the outlook of a particular person or period in history. That view also helps underpin the attractiveness of foundationalist or criterial conceptions of reasoning.

Such views fail to realize, however, the comparative nature of the basic ways in which we practically reason about goods. Our practical reasoning is bound up with the substantive goods we pursue. We become aware, however implicitly, inchoately, or even lucidly, of a good, and we reason about how it would be best to achieve that good or whether that good should be pursued at all if it is in conflict with some other good. In each case, our reasoning takes the form of adjusting our conceptions of what it would take and what it would mean to realize that good and what the meaning of that good really is. It obviously need not be instrumental reasoning, picking the most efficient means to some given end. It may involve specifying an end more precisely, as when one deliberates about what being "holy" might actually mean if it were to be realized. It might in turn involve reasoning about how best to realize a certain end in practice, where the issue of whether the "best" is the most efficient is itself a matter of further specification. (Someone trying to express his or her devotion might not opt for the most "efficient" way of doing that, whatever "efficient" might even mean in that context.) Practical reasoning is part and parcel of expressing and articulating what we take to be our "strong evaluations," the goods that make claims on us.

In all these cases one is choosing among goods, among specifications of goods, or among different articulations of goods. In such cases, there is no need for an absolute judgment of goodness, merely a comparative judgment that, for example, this specification of the good is better than the alternatives – that, for example, the judgment that a specification of "holiness" does not entail refraining from some basic human activities is better than one that requires abstention or renunciation. Such reasoning involves transitions, not merely moving from one good to another, or from one specification to another, but a transition in the basic self-interpretations, the terms in which agents lead their lives.[16] A self-interpretation that is elected in such a transition is rationally preferable if there is an asymmetry in the transition. If one can make the case that it would be better to move from A to B (where both A and B refer to the terms by which one leads one's life), but one cannot make the case that it would be equally good to move from B to A, then the transition from A to B counts as rational. Such transitions involve moves where the original articulation of a way of living (with the goods inherent in it) is self-undermining (perhaps ineluctably riddled with contradictions or fatal tensions that cannot be set aside), such that the move to a nonself-undermining conception of a way of living is rationally required. Or it may be that one of (for example) two possible ways of living being compared is able to resolve difficulties encountered in articulating what is involved in the first, without the opposite being true (such that the later way of living one's life allows us to see what was wrong with the former but not vice versa). Or it may be that the move is an error-reducing transition, so that one sees that the confusion in which one originally found oneself dissolves on making the move.[17] (Taylor's own arguments about how "meaning" is to be cashed out as neither of the two sides of the disjunction, "either mental representation or behavioral propensity," is itself an example of such a transition in the epistemic sphere.)

Such comparative judgments work both inter- and intrasubjectively: They are in play within a single individual deliberating among competing goods and among individuals deliberating with each other. In each case, one moves to a better position but not necessarily to an absolute position. Nothing rules out one's coming to discover a confusion within one's self-understanding – or an understanding of those goods or articulations of those goods intrinsic to such a self-understanding – that had in the past proven to be comparatively better than its competitors, nor of discovering some kind of unforeseen but fatal way in which one's own goods turn out to be self-undermining or to be in irresolvable conflict with each other, nor of anybody articulating a conceptual innovation (such as Hannah Arendt's claim that the Christian conception of forgiveness of one's enemies was a novel political idea). Nothing prevents such practical reasoning from being influenced by completely contingent factors. It can turn out that a given practice in which such goods are embedded can come to be terribly costly, or it may be simply supplanted as the result of war or conquest, or a novel practice may come into view that gives people a new set of alternatives on which to deliberate (one that casts their prior attachments to their goods in a new light).[18] The line in history does not, and need not, run in a straightforwardly progressive direction.

Taylor's point is that explaining historical change entirely from the "outside" misses a crucial element of what is in play in such historical change. Agents are not incidental to history, and history cannot therefore be driven by laws that are completely external to those agents' self-understandings – that is, the way they have come to articulate what matters to them and what kinds of alternatives there are before them. Instead, intrinsic to a historical account is some sense of people acting in light of what matters to them, reasoning practically about their situations in comparative ways, binding themselves to what reason requires in all the usual human ways, and having to orient themselves in situations whose shape cannot be completely chosen or foreseen by them. To understand a historical transition, we must understand it as it was lived on the "inside" by those living through it, and to understand what it was like on the "inside," we must understand the forces and facts that were impinging on agents from the "outside." However, if we cannot understand history without taking into account the ways in which agents orient themselves in the world in which they find themselves, we cannot put aside questions of rationality (or, to speak more loosely, of "value"). We have to ask what was at stake for those agents, what seemed to them to be the better set of choices, and how they might have been blinded by other conceptions they held or by forces external to themselves.

The key question therefore in understanding the sources of the modern conception of the self is threefold: One needs some nuanced account of whether there is such a conception of "the" self in modernity; one needs an interpretive account of what the basic goods are that inform the orientations of such a self; and one needs a judgment as to whether the transition to the modern self can be construed in any way as rational, that is, as marking a transition whose structure is asymmetrical (such that the transition to modernity was rational, but a transition to a premodern understanding could not be taken to be rational).

This sounds very much like Hegel's distinction between empirical history and philosophical history. Philosophical history cannot challenge the facts of empirical history, and it must be consistent with them; its task, though, is different in that it looks at the meaning of history and whether there is any rationality, or reconciliation, to be found in its events. It does not ask if history, or any particular agent or collective was actually aiming at the result in which we find ourselves; it asks instead if there is any way to say that any of the transitions in the understanding of what it means to be human can be counted as more rational than what came before in some nonquestion-begging way that does not presuppose at the outset some conception of rationality that is itself at issue.

Such philosophical history need not recount all the contingencies of history that go to make up the story we now tell about it. The story that it does tell, though, cannot be predetermined; there is nothing in the makeup of things or of agents (on Taylor's view) that determines that all transitions will be rational. People can find that to which they have been unconditionally attached gradually becomes impossible for future generations to sustain because of, for example, conquest. The transition need not be rational in the sense that the change from the old beliefs to the new has always to turn out to be asymmetrical, even if it later proves to be practically impossible to reverse the transition (because of the gradual destruction of the practices, the language, and the culture that sustained the earlier beliefs). The upshot of any such philosophical history, however, has to be some account of what goods are real for us if we are to be in any kind of position to characterize some transitions as rational. It hinges, in Taylor's view, on showing that some kinds of considerations are rational because they are unavoidable in the sense that attempts to do without them fail (either by rendering us incapable of fully being agents or by surreptitiously smuggling back into our lives the very items they were claiming to be excluding). As Taylor puts it, "What is real is what you have to deal with, what won't go away just because it doesn't fit with your prejudices. . . . It means rather that you need these terms to make the best sense of what you're doing."[19] (He calls this, coupled with the notion of the asymmetry of rational transitions, the "best account" principle.)

The kind of story that Taylor tells in *Sources* and elsewhere hinges on his accounts of how certain types of goods came into focus for what reasons at which times – in making a case that there actually were transitions in our views of goods and in laying out the rationale for those transitions. That story has to do in large part with the inward turn that comes about in Western culture, and which is highlighted so clearly in its philosophy, and in the discursive focus so particular to philosophy. (Art and religion also bring these matters into focus, as does politics in a more abstract way; however, they lack the discursive element that makes them ideal for this kind of story.) On Taylor's account, the crucial move comes about when Europeans attempt to come to terms with the new science and their own growing sense of their own interiority as the heritage in large part of Augustinian Christianity. The decisive defeat of the pre-Galilean science by the new science (a transition that conforms perfectly in Taylor's telling with his account of the rationality of transitions) put the issue of our representation of the world on the agenda front and center, as the world began to become more and more disenchanted (in the sense of being devoid of any intrinsic meaning to itself).

If the way we were to lead our lives was not to be determined by nature, then what could orient us? First Descartes and then Locke gave decisive formulations of how this transition was to be made. The "reflexive" turn in modern thought so often associated with their views – the notion that as agents we are fully responsible for whatever normative authority there is for us, and that there is therefore a "gap" between even our strongest desires or our most forceful perceptions and their acquiring any normative authority over us – marked a decisive transition in what counted as authoritative for us. That reflective distance or "normative gap" was taken as a stance of disengagement: For us to be able to responsibly vouch for the claims of the new science against the older pre-Galilean science – and especially when those claims had certain features to them that seemed to call accepted truths (such as those of revealed religion) into question – one had to be able to responsibly and reflectively redeem those claims. Taylor summarizes Locke's achievement in making this transition seem not only rational but also necessary. "What probably made Locke the great teacher of the Enlightenment was that he offered a plausible account of the new science as valid knowledge, intertwined with a theory of rational control of the self; and that he brought the two together under the idea of rational self-responsibility."[20]

What gave that transition its world-historical force was the way in which such a manner of articulating our relation to the world itself brought into view a new set of goods that had previously been obscured by the vocabularies and practices of the premodern world, namely, those bound up with a kind of self-responsibility that helped to establish a new, and in many ways, rationally superior mode of self-relation. We were no longer "called" to lead our lives out in imitation of some hierarchical order in the universe, nor in terms merely of tradition, nor in terms laid down in some sacred texts. Instead, we were called to lead our own lives, and with that a new ideal of self-relation (and therefore new set of moral ideals) also gradually came into view: Each of us, as having a unique calling, was also called to be true to herself, to become an authentic human being.[21]

That new set of goods which was opened up by this new mode of thinking of ourselves (this new "articulation," in Taylor's terminology), was, however, overlain with a deep problem that was at least partially noted by the early modern thinkers but never resolved. A fully disengaged stance toward the world cannot help us to understand the normative force of any of the goods that even that stance itself opens up. It objectifies everything, even ourselves, and thus fully conceals (or at least veils) the goods that are providing the motives that call us to realize this conception of ourselves in practice. Out of that perplexity about itself grows the fully modern ethic in which "the notion of the higher is a form of human life which consists precisely in facing a disenchanted universe with courage and lucidity."[22] A heroism of disengagement calls on us to exercise our reflective powers of reason as the highest and best form of life, while at the same time making it fully unintelligible why anybody would be "called" to do so (as opposed to having simply some very strong, perhaps irrationally instilled desire to do so). Modern life is brought about and partially sustained by bringing the world into view in such a way that the goods such a "view" has revealed and which "call" on us to realize them remain not only concealed in that view, but in most articulations of that view, even seem to be ruled out by the view itself. Modern "naturalism" is the logical outgrowth of the view that calls on us to be heroically disengaged, treat everything as an object in the natural world, and hold ourselves to what disengaged rationality tells us, however unpleasant it may at first seem. But what naturalists cannot grasp is why their own passionate attachment to reason is anything more than just a psychological idiosyncrasy on their part.[23]

That story of the "inward turn" away from the disenchanted natural world that emerged from the new science and its Newtonian aftermath is part and parcel of the account that Kant gave for the necessity of under-standing normative authority as self-legislation, that is, as freedom. As Kant so notably put it in his *Groundwork*,

> We need not now wonder, when we look back upon all the previous efforts that have been made to discover the principle of morality, why they have one and all been bound to fail. Their authors saw man as tied to laws by his duty, but it never occurred to them that he is subject only to laws which are made by himself and yet are universal.[24]

The disenchantment of nature meant that no natural good – even those to be found in our own natural desires and needs – could supply any normative authority on its own. On the Kantian view, if there was to be anything binding in morality at all, then it could not come from some good that was independent of our capacity to legislate for ourselves. Even ordinary "natural" goods, such as self-preservation, have normative authority over us only to the extent that we bestow such authority on them. On the Kantian account, however, this unconditionally binding character of the moral law, although autonomously legislated by us and therefore fully self-legislated, is nevertheless subject to the rules binding all rational agents, since (or such is Kant's overall thesis) without such rules we could not be self-conscious at all; but not even our own "self-consciousness" about our own role in instituting those rules can remove their binding quality on us.

Kant thought that freedom would serve as this kind of good, that only the fully free life – the fully autonomous will – would provide us with a meaningful life. For us to be self-legislating, our wills had to follow laws, since a lawless will would simply be random and contingent, not free in any interesting sense. (It would be pushed around by things and forces external to itself and thus be "heteronomous" in Kant's sense.) Moreover, in the terms Taylor has elected to tell his story, Kant thereby clearly avoided objectifying agency, since the normative force of the moral law cannot be apprehended by regarding ourselves as natural objects; we will simply never get a binding moral law from any naturalistic position.[25] The normative force of the moral law can only be understood from the "inside," not from some neutral, third-person description of us. Kant's own manner of fleshing out what it would take to be able to give an account of the normative force of the moral law, however, required us to think of ourselves as not merely phenomenal but also noumenal agents, and our self-knowledge as noumenal agents could only be practical (something we had to presuppose in deliberation), not theoretical (not anything of which we could give a satisfactory explanation). This conclusion was rejected almost at once by virtually all Kant's successors, and Taylor shares that rejection.

As it became rapidly apparent to Kant's immediate successors, however, his own formulation of the condition of autonomy in a disenchanted world landed him in a kind of paradox. As Kant phrased it in the *Groundwork*: "The will is therefore not merely subject to the law, but is so subject that it must be considered as also *giving the law to itself* and precisely on this account as first of all subject to the law (of which it can regard itself as instituting)."[26] For the will not to be lawless (and therefore to be free), it can only act according to self-imposed reasons (or "laws"). This means that any law imposed on the will without a reason for submitting itself to it results not in a free will and certainly not in a rational will. It also means that the will requires a reason to impose any reason on itself, and therefore the initial reason cannot be self-imposed, since if it were, it would require another reason for its own imposition, and so forth. Kantian autonomy seemed to admit only self-imposed norms and nonetheless to require nonself-imposed norms. We can call this the "Kantian paradox."[27]

Kant himself saw this difficulty and tried to respond to it in a variety of ways. In his second *Critique*, he invoked what he called the "fact of reason": This "fact" is made by ourselves but is such that even in explicating it, we find ourselves bound to it; or, to put it another way, the claims that it makes on us come from our making it claim us. Denying the "fact of reason" would be practically impossible, since the denial would be legislating the "fact" by which it would be denied. Like Kant's noumenal/phenomenal distinction, the appeal to the "fact of reason" found few adherents.

The early Romantic reaction to Kant (and in particular to the "Kantian paradox") in many ways sets the stage for Taylor's own response to that "paradox." (The group of early Romantics includes but is not exhausted by Friedrich Schlegel, Novalis, Schleiermacher, Schelling, and, in some respects, even Hölderlin, who, however, only partially fits that classification.) Faced with the "paradox" (which they heard expounded by Fichte, who attempted an even more daring solution to it), the early Romantics wanted to have both sides of the Kantian coin. The Romantics were dissatisfied with Fichte's solution to the "Kantian paradox," which involved interpreting the distinction between the subjective and objective as itself as a subjectively established distinction. Fichte sought to construct a system whereby the "subject" authorized itself to supply all other forms of normative authority. He thought that the basic tension between spontaneity and receptivity was itself a distinction imposed by our spontaneity on itself. John McDowell's charge of "frictionless spinning in a void"[28] (leveled against modern coherentist theories of justification) nicely captures the dissatisfaction the early Romantics experienced in Fichte's approach.

The early Romantics sought to articulate a way in which we could somehow hold two opposed thoughts together without reducing one to the other: those of spontaneous activity and creativity in the fashioning of vocabularies, and a responsiveness to the way the world really is. Their program for holding those two thoughts together had to do with their shared conviction about how both those oppositions were developments of something deeper and more original, namely, our preconceptual and prereflective orientations in terms of our prior comprehension of a "whole" that contains both nature and human agency. This was their way of reformulating Kant's musing in the *Critique of Judgment* to the effect that aesthetic experience, as oriented by the "indeterminate concept of the supersensible substrate of appearances," yielded the Idea of this indeterminate substrate as "neither nature nor freedom and yet . . . linked with the basis of freedom, the supersensible."[29] Even though we cannot in principle discursively articulate that indeterminate substrate, so they thought, our orientation to it is necessary for achieving the good to be realized in the fulfillment of our "highest vocation," that of being autonomous moral beings. Hölderlin in particular argued that the "Kantian paradox" could be thinkable only if we thought of this orientation as resting on our prereflective comprehension of some deeper unity prior to all judgment and division of subject and object.[30]

The early Romantics wished to avoid the Kantian paradox by adopting Kant's own notion of autonomy but holding that our basic reasons could not all be self-imposed. Instead they involved a "responsiveness" to the world, in particular to a sense of "nature" as a whole, and not just the disenchanted nature of post-Newtonian physics (and, we might anachronistically add, of post-Darwinian biology). This was the "nature," as it were, of Wordsworth, not of Kant. To use Wordsworth's own formulation in his 1805 *Prelude*, "Our destiny, our nature, and our home/Is with infinitude, and only there – ."[31] On the early Romantic view, there are goods in "nature" that supply us with reasons for deliberation, feeling, appreciation, and action that are not self-chosen and which serve to orient us. To be sure, the early Romantic option leaves lots of questions unanswered, and exactly how we are to combine its notions of "spontaneity" and "receptivity" without committing ourselves to some kind of indefensible appeal to immediacy (to directly intuitive knowledge or awareness unmediated by anything else) or to "the myth of the given" was not worked out satisfactorily by the early Romantics. Nonetheless, Taylor clearly opts for holding onto something like the early Romantic option, and his notion of comparative rationality (his "best account" principle), his use of notions such as "horizons of significance" that can never be fully articulated can be interpreted as attempts to supply missing links and steps for the early Romantic case.

Taylor's own post-Romantic response to the "Kantian paradox" is thus modeled on the post-Romantic task he took Hegel to have set for himself and failed to achieve. Hegel, on Taylor's interpretation, tried to "to unite radical autonomy with the fullness of expressive unity with nature" as the means to overcome the "Kantian paradox."[32] Hegel's attempt (on Taylor's reading) to understand nature as the expression of some kind of cosmic, divine development along conceptual lines – understanding nature as the expression of the "Idea" – resolved the "Kantian paradox" by understanding reason to be embedded in and constitutive of the cosmos. On the "expressivist" view, we are responding to reasons that we have not authored ourselves, but of which we can nonetheless regard ourselves as the authors since they express who we are or have come to be. Subsequent developments in science and technology, however, made Hegel's post-Romantic synthesis intellectually unacceptable just as the changing social conditions of industrial society made his political theory more or less obsolete. Although Hegel asked the right question, his answer, brilliant though it was, turned out to be necessarily short-lived, and the failure of his attempt means that the task of producing that kind of unity is still open.[33] What remains is more of a task, a kind of sketching out of what the project of modern philosophy must be once it has become aware of its own social and historical situatedness because of the way its own history has unfolded (interpreted in terms of the "best account" principle).

As Taylor puts it in *Sources of the Self*, "we moderns" now have three frontiers of moral exploration available. First, there is that which lies within the agent's own powers, the result of the turn inward, of which Kantianism is one expression. Second, there are the goods (the moral sources) that lie in the depths of nature as it is reflected in our own nature and desires (and in the growing appreciation for the ecological unities in nature echoed in modern environmental movements). Finally, there is the original theistic foundation of moral life, which needs re-articulation in light of the changes in the other moral sources.[34] Like the early Romantics, Taylor rejects the ways in which all "Fichtean" solutions to the "Kantian paradox" seek to establish some form of "self-grounding," or "self-authorization," because they simply fail to come to terms with the demands of our sheer responsiveness to the world in our lives. Taylor's insistence on "strong evaluations" as making claims on us – and therefore having an authority over us that cannot be rationally explicated in terms of our giving them that authority – is Taylor's way of reformulating that early Romantic insight. The "Kantian paradox" is to be dealt with (if not overcome) by freely acknowledging something that is authoritative for us whose authority is not self-legislated. In this way, Taylor's position, although not "Romantic" in any strict sense, is nonetheless the clear successor theory to the early Romantic response to Kantianism and to Hegel's failed (in Taylor's eyes) attempt to provide a synthesis of modern rationality and Romantic aspirations. It is an attempt to show how, in answering to each other through our social practices, we are also answering to the world in a realist sense.[35]

Like the post-Kantians, Taylor thinks that the rift in our self-understanding and the ensuing alienation from the natural and social worlds around us is by and large not healable in purely secular terms. Although Taylor thinks there is a possibility of wholeness attainable through religion (and that our modern secular worldview simply conceals that possibility and mistakenly thinks that such a concealment is equivalent to having proved its impossibility), any attempt to impose a religious unity on modern, pluralistic societies can only mark a step backward, not forward. (Such a transition could not, in our present stage, count as rational in terms of the best account principle.)[36]

Taken in that way, Taylor's theory of the relation of philosophy to history rests on some admittedly controversial claims about what has failed and what has succeeded in that history. Unlike Hegel, who at least at various times quite confidently thought he had fairly wrapped things up in his own system, Taylor sees this as part of an ongoing struggle for "us moderns." Our now globalized social life is simply too fragmented for there to be anything other than an ongoing contention and controversy over what it means to be human, and, at least for now, that controversy centers around what it means to be free. Taylor's answer is that it cannot be a matter of full self-legislation, since that would never put us in a position of avoiding what I have called the "Kantian paradox."

Yet even Taylor's own arguments about freedom push him in the direction of other post-Kantians, such as Hegel, who (on interpretations other than Taylor's) attempts to resolve the "Kantian paradox" by appeal to a developmental story about social practices and institutions in which agents realize their freedom individually and collectively by virtue of each being both law-giver and subject to the law made by others.[37] In Hegel's own telling of this story (made most effectively in his *Phenomenology of Spirit*), all our past attempts at securing some kind of normative authority independent of our collective wills have broken down because of the "positivity" involved in prior appeals to something other than our own collective efforts to hold ourselves and others to some norms and the inability to redeem those "positivities" by reason. What had looked like norms that would hold our lives together came apart, and the experience of their coming apart meant that we could no longer be those people for whom such norms were authoritative. Ultimately, as Hegel's story goes, the solution to the "Kantian paradox" is not to create a world free of masters and slaves (which would be a world somehow "beyond" our own political and social world, with its irreducible feature of human plurality), but a world in which we are all, as it were, master and slave to each other – each of us at once being both the "author" of the laws and "subject" to them, so that our purchase on these norms is a social and historical achievement reflecting the way in which we become agents through processes of socialization. Such a post-Kantian/Hegelian move cannot (in sharp distinction from Taylor's account) recognize any norm as having authority over us that we have not conferred on it. Seen in that post-Kantian/Hegelian light, the "frontiers" of our own moral culture lie in the realization that as collectively self-legislated, all normative authority is always thereby subject to challenge, and that we ourselves are therefore always subject to challenge in terms of who we have come to be by adopting those norms.[38]

Seen in that light, perhaps Taylor's approach to history and the history of philosophy has revealed that the frontiers of the philosophical future involve a competition between the kind of giddily optimistic naturalist program so popular these days and something like Taylor's own kind of post-Romantic attempt to retrieve what got sedimented and covered over in our recent past. That other Hegelian post-Kantian tradition, seen by Taylor as only one of the steps along the way to our modern malaises, stands at the other edge of that same frontier.[39] How we take our responsiveness not only to history but also to "nature" is crucial, whether we think that appeal to some form of "positivity" or some mode of "disclosure" marks either the last dichotomy to be accepted or marks something yet to be superseded and integrated in a more fully developed self-understanding.

## Notes

I would like to thank Thomas McCarthy, Robert Pippin, and Charles Taylor for helpful comments on an earlier draft of this paper.

1. This is his self-characterization in Charles Taylor, *The Malaise of Modernity*, Concord, Ontario: Anansi Press, 1991.

2. See Terry Pinkard, *Hegel's Phenomenology: The Sociality of Reason*, Cambridge, U.K.: Cambridge University Press, 1994; Terry Pinkard, *Hegel: A Biography*, Cambridge, U.K.: Cambridge University Press, 2000.

3. Charles Taylor, *Sources of the Self: The Making of the Modern Identity*, Cambridge, MA: Harvard University Press, 1989, p. 203. An "interpretive" approach is clearly "explanatory" in a noncausal sense in that it explains how a tension in some kind of meaning for people leads to some other meaning precisely because of the failure of the first.

4. "One has to understand people's self-interpretations and their visions of the good, if one is to explain how they arise; but the second task can't be collapsed into the first, even as the first can't be elided in favor of the second." Charles Taylor, *Sources of the Self: The Making of the Modern Identity*. Cambridge, MA: Harvard University Press, 1989, p. 204.

5. On the idea of its being a "normative matter," see Charles Taylor, "The Importance of Herder" in *Philosophical Arguments*, Cambridge, MA: Harvard University Press, 1995. pp. 79–99. Taylor notes on page 84 that "We can't define the rightness of word by the task without defining the task in terms of the rightness of the words. There is no unidirectional account that can translate our rightness of word in terms of some independently defined form of success. Rightness can't be reductively explained." He clearly does not think that the understanding of what it is like to be an agent is something that is unproblematically grasped. We do not simply "read off" what it is like to be ourselves or "read off" the behavior or expressions of others what it is like to be them. All that involves interpretation at various levels.

6. To say we are self-interpreting animals does not, so Taylor holds, imply that whatever interpretation we make of ourselves is thereby valid, nor does it imply a purely social constructivist view of human agency. There are indeed restrictions on better and worse interpretations of ourselves, even if a naturalistic understanding of the nature we all share as humans does not fully determine which out of a large possible set of interpretations might be given. Taylor's realism about goods, if nothing else, sets limits to self-interpretation, even if it also underwrites the possibility of a wide variety of self-interpretations. There seem to be as many different valid self-interpretations as there are valid concatenations of the various goods that are available to human life.

7. Immanuel Kant, *Critique of Pure Reason*, N. K. Smith (trans.), London: Macmillan, 1964. B 132.

8. Ludwig Wittgenstein, *Philosophical Investigations*. G. E. M. Anscombe (trans.), New York: Macmillan, 1953, ¶¶ 201–2. I have altered Anscombe's translation in order to bring out the affinities of Wittgenstein's text with Taylor's theses; Anscombe translates "*in dem äußert*" as "is exhibited in," which underplays the "expressivist" elements of Wittgenstein's position.

9. Ibid., ¶219.

10. Charles Taylor, "To Follow a Rule" in *Philosophical Arguments*, Cambridge, MA: Harvard University Press, 1995, pp. 165–80.

11. Charles Taylor, *Sources of the Self: The Making of the Modern Identity*, Cambridge, MA: Harvard University Press, 1989, p. 204.

12. Ibid., p. 205.

13. Ibid., p. 160.

14. In *Sources of the Self*, Taylor reserves the term "hypergood" to designate a good that is taken to be determinative of all lesser goods. He also classifies these goods into groups of life-goods, constitutive goods, and so forth. The exact classification is not important for our purposes here. The crucial distinction remains that between "strong" and "weak" evaluations.

15. Charles Taylor, "Explanation and Practical Reason" in *Philosophical Arguments*, Cambridge, MA: Harvard University Press, 1995, pp 34–60.

16. "What we need to *explain* is people living their lives; the terms in which they cannot avoid living them cannot be removed from the explanandum, unless we can propose other terms in which they could live them more clairvoyantly.... Our value terms purport to give us insight into what it is to live in the universe as a human being, and this is a quite different matter from that which physical science claims to reveal and explain." Charles Taylor, *Sources of the Self: The Making of the Modern Identity*, Cambridge, MA: Harvard University Press, 1989, pp. 58–9.

17. This is Taylor's own typology in "Explanation and Practical Reason" in *Philosophical Arguments*, Cambridge, MA: Harvard University Press, 1995. See his summary of his views on p. 54.

18. See *Sources of the Self: The Making of the Modern Identity*, Cambridge, MA: Harvard University Press, 1989, pp. 205–6.

19. Ibid., p. 59. (I have reversed the order in which the sentences occur in the text.)

20. Ibid., p. 174.

21. This is the theme emphasized in Taylor's *The Malaise of Modernity*, Concord, Ontario: Anansi Press, 1991.

22. *Sources of the Self: The Making of the Modern Identity*, Cambridge, MA: Harvard University Press, 1989, pp. 93–4.

23. As Taylor remarks, "disengagement and ... engaged exploration are two very different things." *Sources of the Self: The Making of the Modern Identity*, Cambridge, MA: Harvard University Press, 1989, p. 164.

24. Immanuel Kant. *Groundwork of the Metaphysics of Morals.* H. J. Paton (trans.), New York: Harper and Row, 1964, p. 100 (AA 432).

25. This kind of Kantian (or perhaps post-Kantian) argument has been carried out most prominently by Christine Korsgaard, *The Sources of Normativity*, Cambridge, U.K.: Cambridge University Press, 1996.

26. Immanuel Kant, *Groundwork of the Metaphysics of Morals.* H. J. Paton (trans.), New York: Harper and Row, 1964, p. 98 (AA 431). Emphasis in the original. Translation modified: In particular, I rendered "*davon er sich selbst als Urheber betrachten kann*" as "of which it can regard itself as instituting" instead of translating "*Urheber*" as "author." (More literally, it would be rendered as "instituter" but that seemed more awkward.)

27. I discuss the "Kantian paradox" and its decisive influence on the development of post-Kantian philosophy in Terry Pinkard, *German Philosophy 1760–1860: The Legacy of Idealism*, New York: Cambridge University Press, 2002. This notion of the "Kantian paradox" as basic to post-Kantian idealism was first formulated as far as I know by Robert Pippin; see "Hegel's Practical Philosophy: The Actualization of Freedom" in *Cambridge Companion to German Idealism*. Karl Ameriks (ed.), Cambridge, U.K.: Cambridge University Press, 2000.

28. John McDowell, *Mind and World*, Cambridge, MA: Harvard University Press, 1994, p. 66.

29. Immanuel Kant, *Critique of Judgment.* Werner S. Pluhar (trans.), Indianapolis: Hackett Publishing Company, 1987, §59.

30. See my discussion of Hölderlin's ideas in Terry Pinkard, *German Philosophy 1760–1860: The Legacy of Idealism*, New York: Cambridge University Press, 2002.

31. William Wordsworth, *The Prelude.* Jonathan Wordsworth (ed.), London: Penguin Books, 1995, p. 240 (6: 538–9).

32. Charles Taylor, *Hegel*, Cambridge, U.K.: Cambridge University Press, 1975, p. 570.

33. According to Taylor, Hegel's own faith in the conceptual (that is, philosophical) statement of the "absolute" left no room for the notion of an implicit horizon of understanding that can never be fully articulated (which was the legacy of Herder, as Taylor puts it). Hegel's

> thesis that the Absolute must finally come to complete, explicit clarity in conceptual statement gives the primacy in the end to the descriptive dimension. Our explicit consciousness is no longer surrounded by a horizon of the implicit, of unreflected life and experience, which it is trying to render faithfully but which can never be fully, adequately, definitively brought to light.

Charles Taylor, *Hegel and Modern Society*, Cambridge, U.K.: Cambridge University Press, 1979, p. 165.

34. *Sources of the Self: The Making of the Modern Identity*, Cambridge, MA: Harvard University Press, 1989, pp. 314, 317. The original theistic foundation is not the result of a "better account" movement in history but is rather that which is retained and transformed throughout the historical movement.

35. In this way, Taylor attempts to take a different position from the well-known "pragmatist" stance proposed by Richard Rorty. According to Rorty, we only answer to each other (as expressed in his reliance on the Davidsonian dictum that "beliefs" can only be justified by "other beliefs"). The sense of the "world" involved in saying that our beliefs answer to the world is empty, and hence it is a "world well lost." Rorty makes these claims in many places, but the canonical location for them would be his *Contingency, Irony, Solidarity*, Cambridge, U.K.: Cambridge University Press, 1989.

36. Taylor clearly breaks with Hegel here as elsewhere. Hegel thought that for "we moderns" only philosophy provided us with the full sense of wholeness; both art and religion remained one-sided and their modes of bringing us to unity ultimately could not succeed, since the "absolute" truth about human beings that they were trying to express (ourselves as self-legislating agents) could not be adequately expressed in anything except the conceptual form appropriate to philosophy. Taylor thinks that on the contrary neither art nor philosophy gives us any view of the whole. On the relation of religion, politics, and life, see *A Catholic Modernity?* New York: Oxford University Press, 1999. On page 17, he writes that: "There can never be a total fusion of the faith and any particular society, and the attempt to achieve it is dangerous for the faith." On the next page he claims that

> This kind of freedom, so much the fruit of the gospel, we have only when nobody (that is, no particular outlook) is running the show. So a vote of thanks to Voltaire and others for (not necessarily wittingly) showing us this and for allowing us to live the gospel in a purer way, free of that continual and often bloody forcing of conscience which was the sin and blight of all those 'Christian' centuries.

On page 35, he reflects that "Our being in the image of God is also our standing among others in the stream of love, which is that facet of God's life we try to grasp, very inadequately, in speaking of the Trinity."

37. Hegel reacted to the "Kantian paradox" by understanding the problem developmentally, as occurring between and among agents, rather than resting with Kant's individualist paradigm of willing. Whereas Kant saw the problem as that of an individual agent imposing the law on himself, Hegel saw it as a problem of many agents imposing the law on each other. Hegel worked this out in its introductory fashion in his dialectic of mastery and servitude in the *Phenomenology of Spirit*, in which the "master" turns out to be not really an "author" of the law, since his will remains "natural" – he remains a creature of desire, declaring what he wants to be the law, and he therefore remains a "lawless" will fruitlessly attempting to give the law. The "slave," on the other hand, by internalizing the master's own declarations of the "law" as "right," as the objective point of view itself, through his subordination to and work for the master, actually learns what it means to subject oneself to the law (in subjecting himself to the master) and therefore learns through his own self-subjection to the law what it would mean to be a law-giver. Moreover, as the slave gradually comes to see that the master's laws are in fact not the voice of reason but only the contingent statements of want and preference by a single individual (they are burdened with an intractable "positivity" to them), he comes to understand himself as

not unconditionally bound by those laws, independently of whether he has the power actually to free himself from his real chains.

38. This involves a controversial interpretation of Hegel's texts, particularly of the role of "nature" in his philosophy. This interpretation agrees with Taylor's assessment of Hegel's somewhat Romantic philosophy of nature as failing in the light of the rise of the empirical sciences succeeding it, but differs as to how lethal that objection is to Hegel's attempt to complete a post-Kantian system. In effect, it attempts to keep Kant's overall conception of disenchanted nature intact within a more or less post-Kantian, Hegelian response to these issues. See Terry Pinkard, *German Philosophy 1760–1860: The Legacy of Idealism*, New York: Cambridge University Press, 2002. Robert Pippin's important and influential interpretation of Hegel takes more or less the same lines. See Robert Pippin, *Hegel's Idealism: The Satisfactions of Self-Consciousness*, Cambridge, U.K.: Cambridge University Press, 1989. See also Robert Pippin's *Idealism as Modernism: Hegelian Variations*, Cambridge, U.K.: Cambridge University Press, 1997.

39. It would certainly seem that in a post-Newtonian, Einsteinian, and Darwinian world, any appeal to nature as a moral source is going to suffer from the same kind of dissolution, and that appeals to nature as a "moral frontier" are fated to suffer the same kind of fracturing and splitting that all such previous attempts at "disclosing" a nonself-legislated norm turned out to involve. That is, the same kinds of historical failures of all our other attempts to rely on some kind of "positivity" (something whose authority over us is not traceable to our own collective self-legislation) to give us a vision of a satisfying life (and the motivations that accompany such a vision) are going to surface again.

# BIBLIOGRAPHY

## Books in English by Taylor

*The Explanation of Behaviour* (London: Routledge and Kegan Paul, 1964).

*The Pattern of Politics* (Toronto: McClelland and Stewart, 1970).

*Hegel* (Cambridge, U.K.: Cambridge University Press, 1975).

*Hegel and Modern Society* (Cambridge, U.K.: Cambridge University Press, 1979).

*Social Theory as Practice* (Delhi: Oxford University Press, 1983).

*Human Agency and Language: Philosophical Papers 1* (Cambridge, U.K.: Cambridge University Press, 1985).

*Philosophy and the Human Sciences: Philosophical Papers 2* (Cambridge, U.K.: Cambridge University Press, 1985).

*Sources of the Self: The Making of the Modern Identity* (Cambridge, MA: Harvard University Press, 1989).

*The Malaise of Modernity* (Concord, Ontario: Anansi, 1991). Republished as *The Ethics of Authenticity* (Cambridge, MA: Harvard University Press, 1992).

*Multiculturalism and 'The Politics of Recognition.'* Amy Gutmann, ed. (Princeton: Princeton University Press, 1992). Republished with additional commentaries as *Multiculturalism: Examining the Politics of Recognition*. Amy Gutmann, ed. (Princeton: Princeton University Press, 1994).

*Reconciling the Solitudes: Essays in Canadian Federalism and Nationalism*. Guy Laforest, ed. (Montreal and Kingston: McGill-Queen's University Press, 1993).

*Philosophical Arguments* (Cambridge, MA: Harvard University Press, 1995).

*A Catholic Modernity? Charles Taylor's Marianist Award Lecture, with Responses by William M. Shea, Rosemary Luling Haughton, George Marsden, and Jean Bethke Elshtain*. James L. Heft, ed. (New York: Oxford University Press, 1999).

*Varieties of Religion Today: William James Revisited* (Cambridge, MA: Harvard University Press, 2002).

## Books in English about Taylor

Abbey, Ruth. *Charles Taylor* (Princeton: Princeton University Press; Teddington, U.K.: Acumen Publishing, 2000).

215

Redhead, Mark. *Charles Taylor: Thinking and Living Deep Diversity* (Lanham, MD: Rowman and Littlefield, 2002).

Smith, Nicholas H. *Charles Taylor: Meaning, Morals and Modernity* (Cambridge, U.K.: Polity, 2002).

Tully, James, ed. *Philosophy in an Age of Pluralism: The Philosophy of Charles Taylor in Question* (Cambridge, U.K.: Cambridge University Press, 1994).

# Index